Introduction to 64 Bit Windows Assembly Programming

Ray Seyfarth

Ray Seyfarth
Hattiesburg, MS
USA

Seyfarth, Ray
Introduction to 64 Bit Windows Assembly Programming
Includes index
ISBN-13: 978-1543138849
ISBN-10: 1543138845

© 2017 Ray Seyfarth   All rights reserved.

This work may not be translated or copied in whole or in part without the written permission of the copyright holder, except for brief excerpts in connection with reviews or scholarly analyses.

Preface

The Intel CPU architecture has evolved over 3 decades from a 16 bit CPU with no memory protection, through a period with 32 bit processors with sophisticated architectures into the current series of processors which support all the old modes of operation in addition to a greatly expanded 64 bit mode of operation. Assembly textbooks tend to focus on the history and generally conclude with a discussion of the 32 bit mode. Students are introduced to the concepts of 16 bit CPUs with segment registers allowing access to 1 megabyte of internal memory. This is an unnecessary focus on the past.

With the x86-64 architecture there is almost a complete departure from the past. Segment registers are essentially obsolete and more register usage is completely general purpose, with the glaring exception of the repeat-string loops which use specific registers and have no operands. Both these changes contribute to simpler assembly language programming.

There are now 16 general purpose integer registers with a few specialized instructions. The archaic register stack of the 8087 has been superseded by a well-organized model providing 16 floating point registers with floating point instructions along with the SSE and AVX extensions. In fact the AVX extensions even allow a three operand syntax which can simplify coding even more.

Overall the x86-64 assembly language programming is simpler than its predecessors. Today most personal computers ship with 64 bit operating systems. In fact the latest versions of the Apple OS X operating system are only available in 64 bits, though Linux and Microsoft Windows still have 32 and 64 bit versions. The era of 32 bit CPUs and operating systems is nearly over. Together these trends indicate that it is time to teach 64 bit assembly language.

The focus in this textbook is on early hands-on use of 64 bit assembly programming. There is no 16 or 32 bit programming and the discussion of the history is focused on explaining the origin of the old register names and the few non-orthogonal features of the instruction set.

The first version of this book discussed using the yasm assembler and the gdb debugger directly. Now the author provides a free integrated development environment named "ebe", which automates the process of using nasm[1]. The ebe environment is a GUI program written in C++ using the Qt system and supports C and C++ in addition to assembly language, though its purpose is to support assembly programming. There was a previous version of ebe written in Python, but the newer version offers many more features. The Qt version of ebe is available at http://qtebe.sourceforge.net.

This version of the book discusses assembly programming for the Windows operating system. There is a companion book discussing assembly programming for Linux and OS X which use a different function call interface. There is a discussion of the function call protocol differences for Linux, OS X and Windows, so having one of the two books should be sufficient for someone interested in programming on multiple operating systems.

The Linux/OS X book contains examples using gdb for debugging. Alas this seems to be impractical under Windows and, in fact, under OS X. The nasm assembler does not generate sufficient information under Windows or OS X to determine source code line numbers from memory addresses. Ebe uses the nasm listing file along with the addresses of global symbols like **main** to build translations internally while using memory addresses for breakpoints and to determine line numbers with gdb. The ebe user perceives a simple interface, but using gdb manually would require the user to compute addresses for break points and observe source code in a separate window. For this reason this book has abandoned the use of debugging with gdb,

Another issue with Windows is the prevalence of assembly code examples built around structured exception handling (SEH). The idea there is to augment the code with data which describes the stack frame and register usage in such a manner that SEH can "unwind" the stack to determine which exception handler is the first to be found to handle a particular exception. Exception handling is arguably a critical feature in C++, but it is possibly too cumbersome for beginning assembly programmers. The model used in the book is compatible with C and far simpler than the code one finds which addresses SEH. Most likely any assembly code used in C++ will be used for high efficiency and will not generate any exceptions, so I feel the decision to write simpler assembly code is useful in practice in addition to being far easier to understand.

---

[1] A switch was made in 2017 from yasm to nasm due to a .bss memory reservation problem with yasm.

Due to costs this book is printed in black and white. The pictures captured from ebe would have been prettier and perhaps more useful in color, but the cost of the book would have been roughly double the cost of a black and white version. The added utility of color is certainly not worth the extra cost. Generally the highlighted text in ebe is shown with a colored background while the printed version presents this text with a light gray background.

Most of the sample code execution in the first edition was illustrated using gdb. This function has been superseded with screen captures from ebe.

There are assignments using the computer from the very first chapter. Not every statement will be fully understood at the start, but the assignments are still possible.

The primary target for this book is beginning assembly language programmers and for a gentle introduction to assembly programming, students should study chapters 1, 2, 3, 5, 6, 7, 8, 9, 10 and 11. Chapter 4 on memory mapping is not critical to the rest of the book and can be skipped if desired.

Chapters 12 through 15 are significantly more in depth. Chapter 15 is about data structures in assembly and is an excellent adjunct to studying data structures in C/C++. The subject will be much clearer after exposure to assembly language.

The final four chapters focus on high performance programming, including discussion of SSE and AVX programming.

The author provides slides for classroom instruction along with sample code and errata at **http://rayseyfarth.com/asm**.

If you find errors in the book or have suggestions for improvement, please email the author as **ray.seyfarth@gmail.com**. Your suggestions will help improve the book and are greatly appreciated.

You may also email me with questions or suggestions about ebe. Your email will assist me with providing better on-line support and will help improve the quality of the software.

Thank you for buying the book and I hope you find something interesting and worthwhile inside.

Acknowledgements

No book is created in isolation. This book is certainly no exception. I am indebted to numerous sources for information and assistance with this book.

Dr. Paul Carter's PC assembly language book was used by this author to study 32 bit assembly language programming. His book is a free PDF file downloadable from his web site. This is a 195 page book which covers the basics of assembly language and is a great start at 32 bit assembly language.

While working on this book, I discovered a treatise by Drs. Bryant and O'Hallaron of Carnegie Mellon about how gcc takes advantage of the features of the x86-64 architecture to produce efficient code. Some of their observations have helped me understand the CPU better which assists with writing better assembly code. Programmers interested in efficiency should study their work.

I found the Intel manuals to be an invaluable resource. They provide details on all the instructions of the CPU. Unfortunately the documents cover 32 bit and 64 bit instructions together which, along with the huge number of instructions, makes it difficult to learn assembly programming from these manuals. I hope that reading this book will make a good starting point, but a short book cannot cover many instructions. I have selected what I consider the most important instructions for general use, but an assembly programmer will need to study the Intel manuals (or equivalent manuals from AMD).

I thank my friends Maggie and Tim Hampton for their editing contributions to the book.

I am indebted to my CSC 203 - Assembly Language class at the University of Southern Mississippi for their contributions to this book. Teaching 64 bit assembly language has uncovered a few mistakes and errors in the original Create Space book from July 2011. In particular I wish to thank Isaac Askew, Evan Stuart, Brandon Wolfe and Zachary Dillon for locating errors in the book.

Thanks to Ken O'Brien for helping locate mistakes in the book. Thanks go to Christian Korn and Markus Bohm of Germany who have assisted with "debugging" this book. Thanks also to Francisco Perdomo of the Canary Islands for assistance. Carsten Hansen of Denmark has also assisted with debugging the book. David Langer has contributed some code comment repairs.

Thanks to Quentin Gouchet for locating several typos which had persisted for several years.

Thanks for Keiji Omori for pointing out that the stack size limits for Linux processes are now quite generous. At some point there was a hard kernel limit which could be changed by recompiling the kernel. Now it can be changed in `/etc/security/limits.conf`.

Thanks to Wendell Xe for offering suggestions for improving the book and also suggestions for ebe.

Last I thank my wife, Phyllis, and my sons, David and Adam, for their encouragement and assistance. Phyllis and Adam are responsible for the cover design for both this and the Create Space book.

Contents

Preface iii
Acknowledgements vi
Chapter 1 Introduction 1
   1.1 Why study assembly language? 2
       So what is good about assembly language? 2
   1.2 What is a computer? 3
       Bytes 4
       Program execution 4
   1.3 Machine language 5
   1.4 Assembly language 6
   1.5 Assembling and linking 8
   1.6 Using ebe to run the program 8
Chapter 2 Numbers 12
   2.1 Binary numbers 12
   2.2 Hexadecimal numbers 14
   2.3 Integers 16
       Binary addition 18
       Binary multiplication 19
   2.4 Floating point numbers 19
       Converting decimal numbers to floats 22
       Converting floats to decimal 23
       Floating point addition 23
       Floating point multiplication 24
   2.5 Exploring with the bit bucket 25
Chapter 3 Computer memory 28
   3.1 Memory mapping 28
   3.2 Process memory model in Windows 29
   3.3 Memory example 30
   3.4 Examining memory with ebe 32
       Setting a breakpoint 33

Running a program and viewing a variable 33

Chapter 4 Memory mapping in 64 bit mode 38

    4.1 The memory mapping register 38

    4.2 Page Map Level 4 39

    4.3 Page Directory Pointer Table 40

    4.4 Page Directory Table 40

    4.5 Page Table 41

    4.6 Large pages 41

    4.7 CPU Support for Fast Lookups 41

Chapter 5 Registers 44

    5.1 Observing registers in ebe 46

    5.2 Moving a constant into a register 47

    5.3 Moving values from memory to registers 49

    5.4 Moving values from a register to memory 51

    5.5 Moving data from one register to another 52

Chapter 6 A little bit of math 55

    6.1 Negation 55

    6.2 Addition 56

    6.3 Subtraction 58

    6.4 Multiplication 60

        One operand `imul` 60

        Two and three operand `imul` 62

        Testing for a Pythagorean triple 62

    6.5 Division 65

    6.6 Conditional move instructions 67

    6.7 Why move to a register? 67

Chapter 7 Bit operations 70

    7.1 Not operation 70

    7.2 And operation 71

    7.3 Or operation 72

    7.4 Exclusive or operation 73

    7.5 Shift operations 74

7.6 Bit testing and setting 80

7.7 Extracting and filling a bit field 84

Chapter 8 Branching and looping 88

8.1 Unconditional jump 88

8.2 Conditional jump 90

Simple if statement 91

If/else statement 91

If/else-if/else statement 92

8.3 Looping with conditional jumps 93

While loops 93

Counting 1 bits in a memory quad-word 94

Do-while loops 96

Counting loops 98

8.4 Loop instructions 99

8.5 Repeat string (array) instructions 99

String instructions 100

Chapter 9 Functions 105

9.1 The stack 105

9.2 Call instruction 106

9.3 Linux Function calls 110

9.4 Return instruction 110

9.5 Function parameters and return value 112

9.6 Stack frames 115

Function to print the maximum of 2 integers 119

9.7 Recursion 122

Chapter 10 Arrays 126

10.1 Array address computation 126

10.2 General pattern for memory references 127

10.3 Allocating arrays 130

10.4 Processing arrays 131

Creating the array 132

Filling the array with random numbers 132

Printing the array 133

Finding the minimum value 134

Main program for the array minimum 134

10.5 Command line parameter array 136

Chapter 11 Floating point instructions 141

11.1 Floating point registers 141

11.2 Moving floating point data 143

Moving scalars 143

Moving packed data 143

11.3 Addition 144

11.4 Subtraction 144

11.5 Multiplication and division 145

11.6 Conversion 146

Converting to a different length floating point 146

Converting floating point to/from integer 147

11.7 Floating point comparison 147

11.8 Mathematical functions 148

Minimum and maximum 149

Rounding 149

Square roots 150

11.9 Sample code 150

Distance in 3D 150

Dot product of 3D vectors 150

Polynomial evaluation 151

Chapter 12 Accessing Files 155

12.1 File access with the Windows API 156

Creating a file 156

Writing to a file 157

Complete program to create a file 158

Reading from a file 160

Program to copy a file 160

12.2 Portable C file access functions 164

    open 165

    read and write 167

    lseek 167

    close 168

Chapter 13 Structs 170

    13.1 Symbolic names for offsets 171

    13.2 Allocating and using an array of structs 174

Chapter 14 Using the C stream I/O functions 177

    14.1 Opening a file 178

    14.2 fscanf and fprintf 179

    14.3 fgetc and fputc 179

    14.4 fgets and fputs 180

    14.5 fread 181

    14.5 fseek and ftell 182

    14.6 fclose 183

Chapter 15 Data structures 185

    15.1 Linked lists 185

        List node structure 186

        Creating an empty list 186

        Inserting a number into a list 186

        Traversing the list 187

    15.2 Doubly-linked lists 189

        Doubly-linked list node structure 190

        Creating a new list 190

        Inserting at the front of the list 190

        List traversal 191

    15.3 Hash tables 192

        A good hash function for integers 193

        A good hash function for strings 194

        Hash table node structure and array 194

        Function to find a value in the hash table 194

        Insertion code 195

Printing the hash table 196
Testing the hash table 198
15.4 Binary trees 199
Binary tree node and tree structures 199
Creating an empty tree 200
Finding a key in a tree 200
Inserting a key into the tree 201
Printing the keys in order 202

Chapter 16 High performance assembly 205
16.1 Efficient use of cache 205
16.2 Common subexpression elimination 207
16.3 Strength reduction 207
16.4 Use registers efficiently 207
16.5 Use fewer branches 207
16.6 Convert loops to branch at the bottom 208
16.7 Unroll loops 208
16.8 Merge loops 210
16.9 Split loops 210
16.10 Interchange loops 210
16.11 Move loop invariant code outside loops 211
16.12 Remove recursion 211
16.13 Eliminate stack frames 212
16.14 Inline functions 212
16.15 Reduce dependencies to allow super-scalar execution 212
16.16 Use specialized instructions 212

Chapter 17 Counting bits in an array 215
17.1 C function 215
17.2 Counting 1 bits in assembly 216
17.3 Precomputing the number of bits in each byte 218
17.4 Using the popcnt instruction 219

Chapter 18 Sobel filter 222
18.1 Sobel in C 222

18.2 Sobel computed using SSE instructions	223
Chapter 19 Computing Correlation	230
19.1 C implementation	230
19.2 Implementation using SSE instructions	231
19.3 Implementation using AVX instructions	233
Appendix A Installing ebe	238
Installing from binary packages	238
Installing from source on Windows	238
Installing Cygwin	239
Installing Qt	239
Downloading the source code	239
Compiling ebe and installing	240
Appendix B Using ebe	241
Major features	241
Tooltips	241
Help	241
Menu	242
Movable toolbars	242
Movable subwindows	242
Editing	244
Navigation	245
Cut, copy and paste	245
Undo/redo	246
Find and replace	246
Deleting text	246
Using tabs	246
Auto-indent	246
Prettify	247
Indent/unindent	247
Comment/uncomment	247
Word/number completion	247
Editing multiple files	247

Debugging 248

    Breakpoints 248

    Running a program 248

    Terminal window 249

    Next and step 250

    Continue 250

    Assembly Data window..250

    Register window 250

    Floating point register window 251

Projects 251

    Viewing the project window 252

    Creating a new project..252

    Opening a project 253

    Adding files to a project 253

    Closing a project 253

Toy box..253

Bit bucket 254

Backtrace window 255

Console 255

Ebe settings..256

Ebe Register Alias Macros 256

    alias..257

    fpalias..257

Appendix C Using **scanf** and **printf**...258

    scanf..258

    printf...259

Appendix D Using macros in nasm 261

    Single line macros..261

    Multi-line macros...262

    Preprocessor variables...263

Appendix E Sources for more information..264

    nasm user manual 264

Stephen Morse's 8086/8088 primer 264

Dr. Paul Carter's free assembly book 264

64 bit machine level programming 264

GDB manual 265

Intel documentation 265

Index 266

Chapter 1
Introduction

This book is an introduction to assembly language programming for the x86-64 architecture of CPUs like the Intel Core processors and the AMD Athlon, Zen and Opteron processors. While assembly language is no longer widely used in general purpose programming, it is still used to produce maximum efficiency in core functions in scientific computing and in other applications where maximum efficiency is needed. It is also used to perform some functions which cannot be handled in a high-level language.

The goal of this book is to teach general principles of assembly language programming. It targets people with some experience in programming in a high level language (ideally C or C++), but with no prior exposure to assembly language.

Assembly language is inherently non-portable and this text focuses on writing code for the Windows operating system, taking advantage of the free availability of excellent compilers, assemblers and debuggers. There is a companion book for Linux and OS X which both use the same function call ABI (application binary interface) which differs substantially from the Windows function call ABI. Differences between assembly programming for Linux and OS X systems will be detailed as the work unfolds

The primary goal of this text is to learn how to write functions callable from C or C++ programs. This focus should give the reader an increased understanding of how a compiler implements a high level language. This understanding will be of lasting benefit in using high level languages.

A secondary goal of this text is to introduce the reader to using SSE and AVX instructions. The coming trend is for the size of SIMD (Single Instruction Multiple Data) registers to increase and it generally requires assembly language to take maximum advantage of the SIMD capabilities.

1.1 Why study assembly language?

In a time when the latest fads in programming tend to be object-oriented high-level languages implemented using byte-code interpreters, the trend is clearly to learn to write portable programs with high reliability in record time. It seems that worrying about memory usage and CPU cycles is a relic from a by-gone era. So why would anyone want to learn assembly language programming?

Assembly language programming has some of the worst "features" known in computing. First, assembly language is the poster child for non-portable code. Certainly every CPU has its own assembly language and many of them have more than one. The most common example is the Intel CPU family along with the quite similar AMD CPU collection. The latest versions of these chips can operate in 16 bit, 32 bit and 64 bit modes. In each of these modes there are differences in the assembly language. In addition the operating system imposes additional differences. Further the function call interface (ABI – application binary interface) employed in x86-64 Linux and OS X systems differs from that used in Microsoft Windows systems. Portability is difficult if not impossible in assembly language.

An even worse issue with assembly language programming is reliability. In modern languages like Java the programmer is protected from many possible problems like pointer errors. Pointers exist in Java, but the programmer can be blissfully unaware of them. Contrast this to assembly language where every variable access is essentially a pointer access. Furthermore high level language syntax resembles mathematical syntax, while assembly language is a sequence of individual machine instructions which bears no syntactic resemblance to the problem being solved.

Assembly language is generally accepted to be much slower to write than higher level languages. While experience can increase one's speed, it is probably twice as slow even for experts. This makes it more expensive to write assembly code and adds to the cost of maintenance.

So what is good about assembly language?

The typical claim is that assembly language is more efficient than high level languages. A skilled assembly language coder can write code which uses less CPU time and less memory than that produced by a compiler. However modern C and C++ compilers do excellent optimization and beginning assembly programmers are no match for a good compiler. The compiler writers understand the CPU architecture quite well. On the other hand an assembly programmer with similar skills can achieve remarkable results. A good example is the Atlas (Automatically Tuned Linear Algebra Software) library which can achieve over 95% of the possible CPU performance. The Atlas matrix multiplication function is probably at least 4 times as efficient as similar code written well in C. So, while it is true that assembly language can offer performance benefits, it is unlikely to outperform C/C++ for most general purpose tasks. Furthermore it takes intimate knowledge of the CPU to achieve these gains. In this book we will point out some general strategies for writing efficient assembly programs.

One advantage of assembly language is that it can do things not possible in high level languages. Examples of this include handling hardware interrupts and managing memory mapping features of a CPU. These features are essential in an operating system, though not required for application programming.

So far we have seen that assembly language is much more difficult to use than higher level languages and only offers benefits in special cases to well-trained programmers. What benefit is there for most people?

The primary reason to study assembly language is to learn how a CPU works. This helps when programming in high level languages. Understanding how the compiler implements the features of a high level language can aid in selecting features for efficiency. More importantly understanding the translation from high level language to machine language is fundamental in understanding why bugs behave the way they do. Without studying assembly language, a programming language is primarily a mathematical concept obeying mathematical laws. Underneath this mathematical exterior the computer executes machine instructions which have limits and can have unexpected behavior. Assembly language skills can help in understanding this unexpected behavior and improve one's debugging skills.

1.2 What is a computer?

A computer is a machine for processing bits. A bit is an individual unit of computer storage which can take on either of 2 values: 0 and 1. We use computers to process information, but all the information is represented as bits. Collections of bits can represent characters, numbers, or any other information. Humans interpret these bits as information, while computers simply manipulate the bits.

The memory of a computer (ignoring cache) consists mainly of a relatively large amount of "main memory" which holds programs and data while programs are executing. There is also a relatively small collection of memory within the CPU chip called the "register set" of the computer. The registers primarily function as a place to store intermediate values during calculations based on values from main memory.

Bytes

Modern computers access memory in 8 bit chunks. Each 8 bit quantity is called a "byte". The main memory of a computer is effectively an array of bytes with each byte having a separate memory address. The first byte address is 0 and the last address depends on the hardware and software in use.

A byte can be interpreted as a binary number. The binary number `01010101` equals the decimal number 85 (64+16+4+1). If this number is interpreted as a machine instruction the computer will push the value of the `rbp` register onto the run-time stack. The number 85 can also be interpreted as the upper case letter "U". The number 85 could be part of a larger number in the computer. The letter "U" could be part of a string in memory. It's all a matter of interpretation.

Program execution

A program in execution occupies a range of addresses for the instructions of the program. The following 18 bytes constitute a very simple program which simply exits (with status 5):

Address	Value
401740	85
401741	72
401742	137
401743	229
401744	72
401745	131
401746	236
401747	32
401748	185
401749	5
40174a	0
40174b	0
40174c	0
40174d	232
40174e	102
40174f	93
401750	0
401751	0

The addresses are listed in hexadecimal though they could have started with the equivalent decimal number 4200256. Hexadecimal values are more informative as memory addresses since the computer memory is mapped into pages of 4096 bytes each. This means that the rightmost 3 hexadecimal digits (also called "nibbles") contain an offset within a page of memory. We can see that the address of the first instruction of the program is at offset `0x740` of a page.

1.3 Machine language

Each type of computer has a collection of instructions it can execute. These instructions are stored in memory and fetched, interpreted and executed during the execution of a program. The sequence of bytes (like the previous 18 byte program) is called a "machine language" program. It would be quite painful to use machine language. You would have to enter the correct bytes for each instruction of your program and you would need to know the addresses of all data used in your program. A more realistic program would have branching instructions. The address to branch to depends on where the computer loads your program into memory when it is executed. Furthermore the address to branch to can change when you add, delete or change instructions in your program.

The very first computers were programmed in machine language, but people soon figured out ways to make the task easier. The first improvement was to use words like **mov** to indicate the selection of a particular instruction. In addition people started using symbolic names to represent addresses of instructions and data in a program. Using symbolic names prevents the need to calculate addresses and insulates the programmer from changes in the source code.

1.4 Assembly language

Very early in the history of computing (1950s), programmers developed symbolic assembly languages. This rapidly replaced the use of machine language, eliminating a lot of tedious work. Machine languages are considered "first-generation" programming languages, while assembly languages are considered "second-generation".

Many programs continued to be written in assembly language after the invention of FORTRAN and COBOL ("third-generation" languages) in the late 1950s. In particular operating systems were typically nearly 100% assembly until the creation of C as the primary language for the UNIX operating system

The source code for the 18 byte program from earlier is listed below:

```
;       Program: exit
;
;       Executes the exit system call
;
;       No input
;
;       Output: only the exit status
;               %errorlevel%
;               $? In the Cygwin shell
;
        segment   .text
        global    main
        extern    exit
main:
        push      rbp
        mov       rbp, rsp
        sub       rsp, 32    ; shadow parameter space
        mov       ecx, 5     ; parameter for exit function
        call      exit
```

You will observe the use of ";" to signal the start of comments in this program. Some of the comments are stand-alone comments and others are end-of-line comments. It is fairly common to place end-of-line comments on each assembly instruction.

Lines of assembly code consist of labels and instructions. A label is a string of letters, digits and underscore with the first character either a letter or an underscore. A label usually starts in column 1, but this is not required. A label establishes a symbolic name for the current point in the assembly. A label on a line by itself must have a colon after it, while the colon is optional if there is more to the line. It is safer to always use a colon after a label definition to avoid confusion.

Instructions can be machine instructions, macros or instructions to the assembler. Instructions usually are placed further right than column 1. Many people establish a pattern of starting all instructions in the same column. I suggest using indentation to represent the high level structure of code, though spacing constraints limit the indentation in the examples.

The statement "**segment .text**" is an instruction to the assembler itself rather than a machine instruction. This statement indicates that the data or instructions following it are to be placed in the **.text** segment or section. This is where the instructions of a program are located.

The statement "**global main**" is another instruction to the assembler called an assembler directive or a pseudo opcode (pseudo-op). This pseudo-op informs the assembler that the label **main** is to be made known to the linker when the program is linked. When the system runs a program it transfers control to the main function. A typical C program has a **main** function which is called indirectly via a start function in the C library. Some operating system use "_" as a prefix or suffix for functions. The OS X gcc prefixes each function name with an underscore, but gcc under Linux leaves the names alone. So "**main**" in an OS X C program is automatically converted to "_main". Windows leaves the names alone.

The line beginning with **main** is a label. Since no code has been generated up to this point, the label refers to location 0 of the **main**'s text segment. Later when the program is linked and executed this first location of main will be relocated to an address like **0x401740**.

The remaining lines use symbolic opcodes representing the 5 executable instructions in the program. The first two instructions prepare a stack frame for main. The third instruction subtracts 32 from the stack pointer, **rsp**. This is done to leave space for a called function to store register parameters on the stack if needed. The fourth instruction places 5 in register **rcx** which is the first and only parameter for the **exit** call made in the last instruction.

1.5 Assembling and linking

This book introduces the use of the ebe program as an integrated development environment for assembly and C programming. Internally ebe uses the nasm assembler to produce an object file from an assembly source code file. This is adequate for debugging but some people will want to prepare makefiles or scripts to build their programs. For this purpose we list the commands required to assemble and link assembly programs. Here is the nasm command:

```
nasm -f win64 -P ebe.inc -l exit.lst exit.asm
```

The `-f win64` option selects a 64 bit output format which is compatible with Windows and gcc. The `-P ebe.inc` option tells nasm to prefix `exit.asm` with `ebe.inc` which handles naming differences between Linux and OS X. Ebe will prepare a copy of `ebe.inc` in the same directory as the assembly file for each assembly. The `-l exit.lst` option asks for a listing file which shows the generated code in hexadecimal.

The nasm command produces an object file named `exit.o`, which contains the generated instructions and data in a form ready to link with other code from other object files or libraries. Linking is done with the gcc command:

```
gcc -o exit exit.o
```

The `-o exit` option gives a name to the executable file produced by gcc. The actual name will be "`exit.exe`" following Windows naming conventions. Without that option, gcc produces a file named `a.exe`.

You can execute the program using:

```
exit.exe
```

Normally you don't have to specify ".`exe`" when running a program, but "`exit`" is a command which is interpreted by the command shell.

1.6 Using ebe to run the program

To use ebe to assemble, link and run the program is quite simple. First start ebe by entering "`ebe`" from a command shell or click on the ebe icon, a green alien. This will create a window with several subwindows including a source code subwindow as shown in the figure below. The various subwindows can be rearranged by dragging them by their title bars. They can be dropped on top of each other to create tabbed subwindows, they can be resized, they can be hidden and they can be dragged out of the main window to become stand-alone windows.

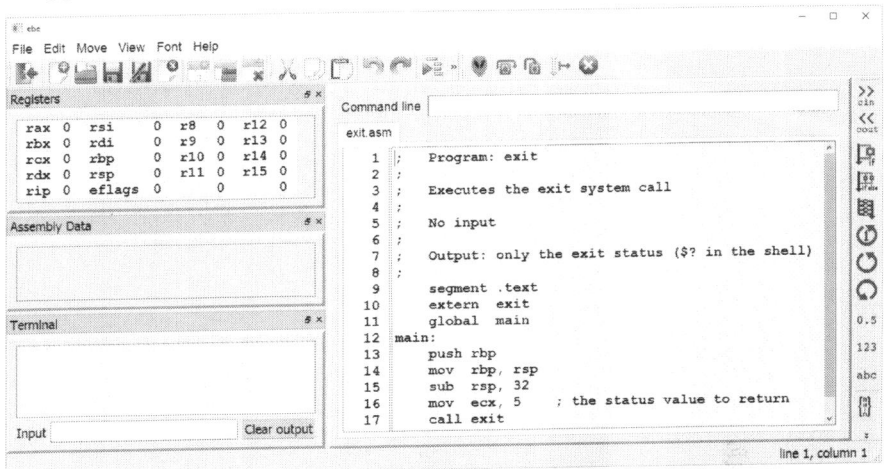

For better visibility the next figure shows ebe without the register, assembly data and terminal windows. Using the source code window you can enter the text shown and use the File menu to save the file as "`exit.asm`". To run the program simply click on the "Run" button, the icon which looks like a green alien (or gray). There is an arrow pointing to the "Run" button. If there were any output from the program, it would be displayed in the terminal subwindow. After saving the file once, you can start ebe using "`ebe exit.asm`".

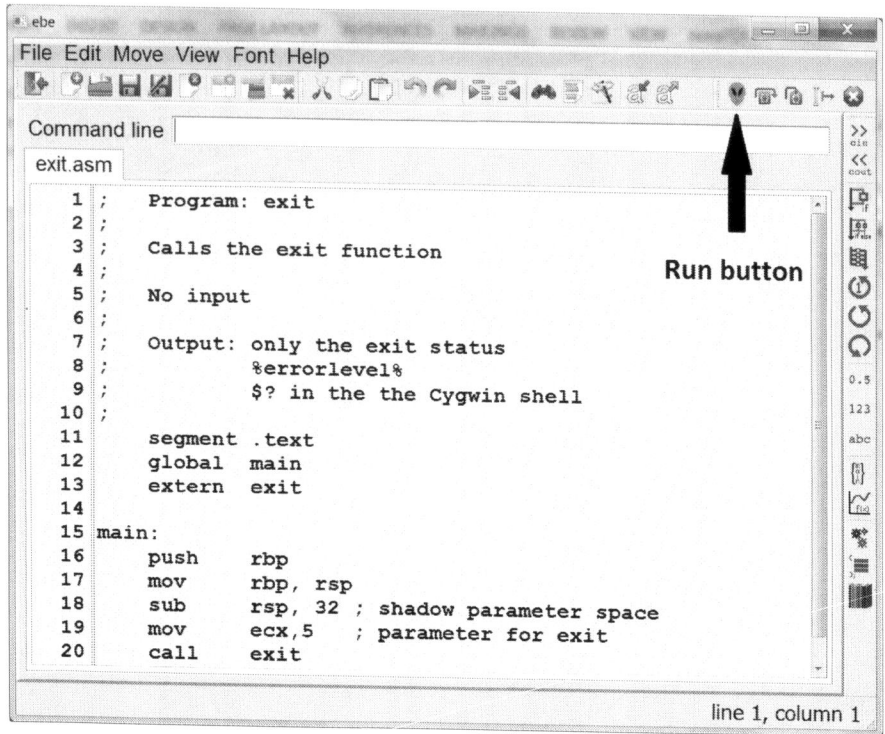

More details on using ebe will be illustrated later and a chapter on ebe is included in the appendix. This is sufficient for the first chapter.

Exercises

1. Enter the assembly language program from this chapter and assemble and link it. Then execute the program from the command line and enter "`echo %errorlevel%`". By convention in UNIX systems, a non-zero status from a program indicates an error. Change the program to yield a 0 status.

2. Use the "dir" command to determine the sizes of exit.asm, exit.o and exit.exe. Which file is the largest? Why?

3. In C and many other languages, 0 means false and 1 (or non-zero) means true. In the shell 0 for the status of a process means success and non-zero means an error. Shell if statements essentially use 0 for true. Why did the writer of the first UNIX shell decide to use 0 for true?

4. In the sample program we see that main begins at offset 0x740 within a page of memory. What might be placed in the bytes of the page before main?

Chapter 2
Numbers

All information in a computer is stored as collections of bits. These bits can be interpreted in a variety of ways as numbers. In this chapter we will discuss binary numbers, hexadecimal numbers, integers and floating point numbers.

2.1 Binary numbers

We are used to representing numbers in the decimal place-value system. In this representation, a number like 1234 means $10^3 + 2*10^2 + 3*10 + 4$. Similarly binary numbers are represented in a place-value system using 0 and 1 as the "digits" and powers of 2 rather than powers of 10.

Let's consider the binary number 10101111. This is an 8 bit number so the highest power of 2 is 2^7. So this number is

$$\begin{aligned} 10101111 &= 2^7 + 2^5 + 2^3 + 2^2 + 2 + 1 \\ &= 128 + 32 + 8 + 4 + 2 + 1 \\ &= 175 \end{aligned}$$

The bits of an 8 bit number are numbered from 0 to 7 with 0 being the least significant bit and 7 being the most significant bit.

The number 175 has its bits defined below.

bit value	1	0	1	0	1	1	1	1
bit position	7	6	5	4	3	2	1	0

The conversion from binary to decimal is straightforward. It takes a little more ingenuity to convert from decimal to binary. Let's examine the number 741. The highest power of 2 less than or equal to 741 is $2^9 = 512$. So we have

$$\begin{aligned} 741 &= 512 + 229 \\ &= 2^9 + 229 \end{aligned}$$

Now we need to work on 229. The highest power of 2 less than 229 is $2^7 = 128$. So we now have
$$741 = 512 + 128 + 101$$
$$= 2^9 + 2^7 + 101$$

The process continues with 101. The highest power of 2 less than 101 is $2^6 = 64$. So we get
$$741 = 512 + 128 + 64 + 37$$
$$= 2^9 + 2^7 + 2^6 + 37$$

Next we can find that 37 is greater than $2^5 = 32$, so
$$741 = 512 + 128 + 64 + 32 + 5$$
$$= 2^9 + 2^7 + 2^6 + 2^5 + 5$$

Working on the 5 we see that
$$741 = 512 + 128 + 64 + 32 + 4 + 1$$
$$= 2^9 + 2^7 + 2^6 + 2^5 + 2^2 + 1$$

Below is 741 expressed as a 16 bit integer.

bit value	1	0	1	1	1	0	0	1	0	1
bit position	9	8	7	6	5	4	3	2	1	0

A binary constant can be represented in the nasm assembler by appending "b" to the end of a string of 0's and 1's. So we could represent 741 as **1011100101b**.

An alternative method for converting a decimal number to binary is by repeated division by 2. At each step, the remainder yields the next higher bit.

Let's convert 741 again.

division		quotient	remainder	binary number
741/2	=	370	1	1
370/2	=	185	0	01
185/2	=	92	1	101
92/2	=	46	0	0101
46/2	=	23	0	00101
23/2	=	11	1	100101
11/2	=	5	1	1100101
5/2	=	2	1	11100101
2/2	=	1	0	011100101
1/2	=	0	1	1011100101

The repeated division algorithm is easier since you don't have to identify (guess?) powers of 2 less than or equal to the number under question. It is also easy to program.

2.2 Hexadecimal numbers

Binary numbers are a fairly effective way of representing a string of bits, but they can get pretty tedious if the string is long. In a 64 bit computer it is fairly common to work with 64 bit integers. Entering a number as 64 bits followed by a "b" would be tough. Decimal numbers are a much more compact representation, but it is not immediately apparent which bits are 0's and 1's in a decimal number. Enter hexadecimal...

A hexadecimal number is a number in base 16. So we need "digits" from 0 to 15. The digits from 0-9 are just like in decimal. The digits from 10-15 are represented by the letters 'A' through 'F'. We can also use lower case letters. Fortunately both nasm and C/C++ represent hexadecimal numbers using the prefix 0x. You could probably use 0X but the lower case x tends to make the numbers more visually obvious.

Let's consider the value of 0xa1a. This number uses a which means 10, so we have

$$\begin{aligned} 0xa1a &= 10 * 16^2 + 1 * 16 + 10 \\ &= 10 * 256 + 16 + 10 \\ &= 2586 \end{aligned}$$

Converting a decimal number to hexadecimal follows a pattern like the one used before for binary numbers except that we have to find the highest power of 16 and divide by that number to get the correct "digit". Let's convert 40007 to hexadecimal. The first power of 16 to use is $16^3 = 4096$. $40007/4096 = 9$ with a remainder of 3143, so we have

$$40007 = 9 * 16^3 + 3143.$$

$3143/16^2 = 3143/256 = 12$ with a remainder of 71, so we get

$$40007 = 9 * 16^3 + 12 * 16^2 + 71.$$

$71/16 = 4$ with a remainder of 7, so the final result is

$$40007 = 9 * 16^3 + 12 * 16^2 + 4 * 16 + 7 = 0x9C47.$$

As with conversion to binary we can perform repeated division and build the number by keeping the remainders.

division		quotient	remainder	hexadecimal
40007/16	=	2500	7	0x7
2500/16	=	156	4	0x47
156/16	=	9	12	0xc47
12/16	=	0	12	0x9c47

Converting back and forth between decimal and binary or decimal and hexadecimal is a bit painful. Computers can do that quite handily, but why would you want to convert from decimal to hexadecimal? If you are entering a value in the assembler, simply enter it in the form which matches your interpretation. If you're looking at the number 1027 and need to use it in your program to perform arithmetic, enter it as a decimal number. If you want to represent some pattern of bits in the computer, then your choices are binary and hexadecimal. Binary is pretty obvious to use, but only for fairly short binary strings. Hexadecimal is more practical for longer binary strings.

The bottom line is conversion between binary and hexadecimal is all that one normally needs to do. This task is made easier since each hexadecimal "digit" represents exactly 4 bits (frequently referred to as a "nibble"). Consult the table below to convert between binary and hexadecimal.

Hex	Binary
0	0000
1	0001
2	0010
3	0011
4	0100
5	0101
6	0110
7	0111
8	1000
9	1001
a	1010
b	1011
c	1100
d	1101
e	1110
f	1111

Let's now consider converting `0x1a5b` to binary. 1 = 0001, a = 1010, 5 = 0101 and b = 1011, so we get

`0x1a5b` = 0001 1010 0101 1011 = 0001101001011011b

Below `0x1a5b` is shown with each bit position labeled:

Bit value	0	0	0	1	1	0	1	0	0	1	0	1	1	0	1	1
Bit position	15	14	13	12	11	10	9	8	7	6	5	4	3	2	1	0

The value of each bit position is 2 raised to that power. In the number above the leftmost 1 bit is in position 12, so it represents $2^{12} = 4096$. So the number is

$$2^{12} + 2^{11} + 2^9 + 2^6 + 2^4 + 2^3 + 2^1 + 2^0$$
$$4096 + 2048 + 512 + 64 + 16 + 8 + 2 + 1$$
$$6737$$

2.3 Integers

On the x86-64 architecture integers can be 1 byte, 2 bytes, 4 bytes, or 8 bytes in length. Furthermore for each length the numbers can be either signed or unsigned. Below is a table listing minimum and maximum values for each type of integer.

Variety	Bits	Bytes	Minimum	Maximum
unsigned	8	1	0	255
signed	8	1	-128	127
unsigned	16	2	0	65535
signed	16	2	-32768	32767
unsigned	32	4	0	4294967295
signed	32	4	-2147483648	2147483647
unsigned	64	8	0	18446744073709551615
signed	64	8	-9223372036854775808	9223372036854775807

Let's consider the maximum unsigned 16 bit integer. This maximum number is 16 bits all equal to 1 or 1111111111111111. The leftmost bit is bit 15 so its value is 2^{15}. Now suppose we add 1 to 1111111111111111. It's pretty clear that we will get a carry in every position and the result is 10000000000000000. This new number has 17 bits and the first bit position is 16, so we get

$$1111111111111111 + 1 = 2^{16}$$

Phrasing this more conveniently

$$1111111111111111 = 2^{16} - 1 = 65536 - 1 = 65535$$

Similarly the maximum unsigned 64 bit integer is $2^{64} - 1$ and the maximum signed 64 bit integer is $2^{63} - 1$. The range of 64 bit integers is large enough for most needs. Of course there are exceptions, like 20! = 51090942171709440000.

Unsigned integers are precisely the binary numbers discussed earlier. Signed integers are stored in a useful format called "two's complement". The first bit of a signed integer is the sign bit. If the sign bit is 0, the number is positive. If the sign bit is 1, the number is negative. The most obvious way to store negative numbers would be to use the remaining bits to store the absolute value of the number.

sign bit   value

31   0

Let's consider 8 bit signed integers and what we would get if we used the existing circuitry to add 2 such integers. Let's add -1 and 1. Well, if we store -1 with a sign bit and then the value we would get

$$\begin{array}{rcl} -1 & = & 10000001 \\ 1 & = & 00000001 \\ \hline -1+1 & = & 10000010 \end{array}$$

Oops! We end up with -2 rather than 0.

Let's try storing 8 bit numbers as a sign bit and invert the bits for the absolute value part of the number:

$$\begin{array}{rcl} -1 & = & 11111110 \\ 1 & = & 00000001 \\ \hline -1+1 & = & 11111111 \end{array}$$

Now this is interesting: the result is actually -0, rather than 0. This sounds somewhat hopeful. Let's try a different pair of numbers:

$$\begin{array}{rcl} -1 & = & 11111110 \\ 4 & = & 00000100 \\ \hline -1+4 & = & 00000010 = 2 \end{array}$$

Too bad! It was close. What we need is to add one to the complemented absolute value for the number. This is referred to as "two's complement" arithmetic. It works out well using the same circuitry as for unsigned numbers and is mainly a matter of interpretation.

So let's convert -1 to its two's complement format.

```
       00000001 for the absolute value
       11111110 for the complement
       11111111 after adding 1
-1 =   11111111
```

Using two's complement numbers the largest negative 8 bit integer is 10000000. To convert this back, complement the number and add 1. This gives 01111111 + 1 = 10000000 = 128, so 10000000 = -128. You may have noticed in the table of minimums and maximums that the minimum values were all 1 larger in absolute value than the maximums. This is due to complementing and adding 1. The complement yields a string of 1's and adding 1 to that yields a single 1 with a bunch of 0's. The result is that the largest value for an n-bit signed integer is $2^{n-1} - 1$ and the smallest value is -2^{n-1}.

Now let's convert the number -750 to a signed binary number.

$$750 = 512 + 128 + 64 + 32 + 8 + 4 + 2 = 1011101110b$$

Now expressing this as a 16 bit binary number (with spaces to help keep track of the bits) we get 0000 0010 1110 1110. Next we invert the bits to get **1111 1101 0001 0001**. Finally we add 1 to get -750 = **1111 1101 0001 0010** = **0xFD12**.

Next let's convert the hexadecimal value **0xFA13** from a 16 bit signed integer to a decimal value. Start by converting to binary: **1111 1010 0001 0011**. Then invert the bits: **0000 0101 1110 1100**. Add 1 to get the 2's complement: **0000 0101 1110 1101**. Convert this to decimal: $1024 + 256 + 128 + 64 + 32 + 8 + 4 + 1 = 1517$, so **0xFA13** = -1517.

Let's add -750 and -1517 in binary:

```
  1111 1101 0001 0010
+ 1111 1010 0001 0011
  ───────────────────
1 1111 0111 0010 0101
```

We can ignore the leading 1 bit (a result of a carry). The 16 bit sum is **1111 0111 0010 0101**, which is negative. Inverting: **0000 1000 1101 1010**. Next adding 1 to get the two's complement: **0000 1000 1101 1011**. So the number is $2048 + 128 + 64 + 16 + 8 + 2 + 1 = 2267$. So we have -750 + -1517 = -2267.

Binary addition

Performing binary addition is a lot like decimal addition. Let's add 2 binary numbers

```
  10001111
+ 01011010
  ────────
         1
```

The first pair of bits was easy. Adding the second pair of bits gives a value of 2, but 2 = **10b**, so we place a 0 on the bottom and carry a 1

```
         1
  10001111
+ 01011010
  ────────
        01
```

We continue in the same way:

```
         1
  10001111
+ 01011010
  ────────
       001
```

```
         1
  10001111
+ 01011010
  ────────
      1001
```

```
        1
  10001111
+ 01011010
     01001

    . . .

  10001111
+ 01011010
  11101001
```

Binary multiplication

Binary multiplication is also much like decimal multiplication. You multiply one bit at a time of the second number by the top number and write these products down staggered to the left. Of course these "products" are trivial. You are multiplying by either 0 or 1. In the case of 0, you just skip it. For 1 bits, you simply copy the top number in the correct columns.

After copying the top number enough times, you add all the partial products. Here is an example:

```
        1010101
  x       10101
        1010101
       1010101
      1010101
    11011111001
```

2.4 Floating point numbers

The x86-64 architecture supports 3 different varieties of floating point numbers: 32 bit, 64 bit and 80 bit numbers. These numbers are stored in IEEE 754 format

Below are the pertinent characteristics of these types:

Variety	Bits	Exponent	Exponent Bias	Fraction	Precision
float	32	8	127	23	7 digits
double	64	11	1023	52	16 digits
long double	80	15	16383	64	19 digits

The IEEE format treats these different length numbers in the same way, but with different lengths for the fields. In each format the highest order bit is the sign bit. A negative number has its sign bit set to 1 and the remaining bits are just like the corresponding positive number. Each number has a binary exponent and a fraction. We will focus on the `float` type to reduce the number of bits involved.

```
31 30      23 22                                                      0
```

The exponent for a float is an 8 bit field. To allow large numbers or small numbers to be stored, the exponent is interpreted as positive or negative. The actual exponent is the value of the 8 bit field minus 127. 127 is the "exponent bias" for 32 bit floating point numbers.

The fraction field of a `float` holds a small surprise. Since 0.0 is defined as all bits set to 0, there is no need to worry about representing 0.0 as an exponent field equal to 127 and fraction field set to all 0's. All other numbers have at least one 1 bit, so the IEEE 754 format uses an implicit 1 bit to save space. So if the fraction field is 10000000000000000000000, it is interpreted as 1.10000000000000000000000. This allows the fraction field to be effectively 24 bits. This is a clever trick made possible by making exponent fields of `0x00` and `0xFF` special.

A number with exponent field equal to `0x00` is defined to be 0. Interestingly, it is possible to store a negative 0. An exponent of `0xFF` is used to mean either negative or positive infinity. There are more details required for a complete description of IEEE 754, but this is sufficient for our needs.

To illustrate floating point data, consider the following assembly file, "`fp.asm`"

```
        segment .data
zero    dd      0.0
one     dd      1.0
neg1    dd      -1.0
a       dd      1.75
b       dd      122.5
d       dd      1.1
e       dd      10000000000.
```

This is not a program, it is simply a definition of 7 `float` values in the data segment. The `dd` command specifies a double word data item. Other options include `db` (data byte), `dw` (data word) and `dq` (data quad-word). A word is 2 bytes, a double word is 4 bytes and a quad-word is 8 bytes.

Now consider the listing file, "fp.lst", produced by executing the following command to assemble the file and produce a listing

```
nasm -f win64 -l fp.lst fp.asm
```

Here are the contents of the listing:[2]

```
1                              segment .data
2 00000000 00000000    zero   dd    0.0
3 00000004 0000803F    one    dd    1.0
4 00000008 000080BF    neg1   dd    -1.0
5 0000000C 0000E03F    a      dd    1.75
6 00000010 0000F542    b      dd    122.5
7 00000014 CDCC8C3F    d      dd    1.1
8 00000018 F9021550    e      dd    10000000000.0
```

The listing has line numbers in the first column. If not blank characters 3-10 (8-15 in the original) are relative addresses in hexadecimal. Characters 12-19 (again, if not blank) are the assembled bytes of data. So we see that **zero** occupies bytes 0-3, **one** occupies bytes 4-7, etc. We can also examine the data produced from each variable definition.

The **zero** variable is stored as expected - all 0 bits. The other numbers might be a little surprising. Look at **one** - the bytes are backwards! Reverse them and you get **3F800000**. The most significant byte is **3F**. The sign bit is 0. The exponent field consists of the other 7 bits of the most significant byte and the first bit of the next byte. This means that the exponent field is 127 and the actual binary exponent is 0. The remaining bits are the binary fraction field all 0's. Thus the value is $1.0 * 2^0 = 1.0$.

There is only 1 negative value shown: -1.0. It differs in only the sign bit from 1.0.

You will notice that 1.75 and 122.5 have a significant number of 0's in the fraction field. This is because .75 and .5 are both expressible as sums of negative powers of 2.

$$0.75 = 0.5 + 0.25 = 2^{-1} + 2^{-2}$$

On the other hand 1.1 is a repeating sequence of bits when expressed in binary. This is somewhat similar to expressing 1/11 in decimal:

$$1/11 = 0.09\overline{09}$$

Looking at **1.1** in the proper order **1.1 = 0x3F8CCCCD**. The exponent is 0 and the fraction field in binary is **00011001100110011001101**. It looks like the last bit has been rounded up and that the repeated pattern is **1100**.

---

[2] There are numerous spaces removed to make this fit the page.

$$1.1_{10} = 1.0001100110011001\overline{1100}_2$$

Having seen that floating point numbers are backwards, then you might suspect that integers are backwards also. This is indeed true. Consider the following code which defines some 32 bit integers:

```
         segment data
zero     dd       0
one      dd       1
neg1     dd       -1
a        dd       175
b        dd       4097
d        dd       65536
e        dd       100000000
```

The associated listing file shows the bits generated for each number. The bytes are backwards. Notice that 4097 is represented as `0x01100000` in memory. The first byte is the least significant byte. We would prefer to consider this as `0x00001001`, but the CPU stores the least significant byte first.

```
1                             segment .data
2 00000000 00000000   zero    dd       0
3 00000004 01000000   one     dd       1
4 00000008 FFFFFFFF   neg1    dd       -1
5 0000000C AF000000   a       dd       175
6 00000010 01100000   b       dd       4097
7 00000014 00000100   d       dd       65536
8 00000018 00E1F505   e       dd       100000000
```

Converting decimal numbers to floats

Let's work on an example to see how to do the conversion. Let's convert -121.6875 to its binary representation.

First let's note that the sign bit is 1. Now we will work on 121.6875.

It's fairly easy to convert the integer portion of the number: 121 = 1111001b. Now we need to work on the fraction.

Let's suppose we have a binary fraction x = 0.abcdefgh, where the letters indicate either a 0 or a 1. Then 2*x= a.bcdefgh. This indicates that multiplying a fraction by 2 will expose a bit.

We have 2 * 0.6875 = 1.375 so the first bit to the right of the binary point is 1. So far our number is 1111001.1b.

Next multiply the next fraction: 2 * 0.375 = 0.75, so the next bit is 0. We have 1111001.10b.

Multiplying again: 2 * .75 = 1.5, so the next bit is 1. We now have `1111001.101b`.

Multiplying again: 2 * 0.5 = 1, so the last bit is 1 leaving the final `1111001.1011b`.

So our number -121.6875 = `-1111001.1011b`. We need to get this into exponential notation with a power of 2.

$$121.6875 = -1111001.1011$$
$$= -1.1110011011 * 2^6$$

We now have all the pieces. The sign bit is 1, the fraction (without the implied 1) is `11100110110000000000000` and the exponent field is 127+6 = 133 = `10000101`. So our number is

`1 10000101 11100110110000000000000`

Organized into nibbles, this is `1100 0010 1111 0011 0110 0000 0000 0000` or `0xc2f36000`. Of course if you see this in a listing it will be reversed: `0060f3c2`.

Converting floats to decimal

An example will illustrate how to convert a float to a decimal number. Let's work on the float value `0x43263000`.

The sign bit is 0, so the number is positive. The exponent field is `010000110` which is 134, so the binary exponent is 7. The fraction field is `010 0110 0011 0000 0000 0000 0000`, so the fraction with implied 1 is `1.01001100011`.

$$
\begin{aligned}
1.01001100011_2 * 2^7 &= 10100110.0011_2 \\
&= 166 + 2^{-3} + 2^{-4} \\
&= 166 + 0.125 + 0.0625 \\
&= 166.1875
\end{aligned}
$$

Floating point addition

In order to add two floating point numbers, we must first convert the numbers to binary real numbers. Then we need to align the binary points and add the numbers. Finally we need to convert back to floating point.

Let's add the numbers 41.275 and 0.315. In hexadecimal these numbers are `0x4225199a` and `0x3ea147ae`. Now let's convert `0x4225199a` to a binary number with a binary exponent. The exponent field is composed of the first two nibbles and a 0 bit from the next nibble.

This is $10000100_2 = 132$, so the exponent is 132-127=5. The fractional part with the understood 1 bit is

$$1.01001010001100110011010_2$$

So we have

$$\texttt{0x4225199a} = 1.01001010001100110011010_2 * 2^5$$
$$= 101001.010001100110011010_2$$

Similarly `0x3ea147ae` has an exponent field of the first 2 nibbles and a 1 from the third nibble. So the exponent field is $01111101_2 = 125$ yielding an exponent of -2. The fractional part with the understood 1 bit is

$$1.01000101000111101011110_2$$

So we have

$$\texttt{0x3ea147ae} = 1.01000101000111101011110_2 * 2^{-2}$$
$$= 0.0101000101000111101011110_2$$

Now we can align the numbers and add

```
  101001.010001100110011010
+      0.0101000101000111101011110
  ─────────────────────────────────
  101001.1001011100001010010101110
```

Now we have too many bits to store in a 32 bit float. The rightmost 7 bits will be rounded (dropped in this case) to get

$$101001.100101110000101001_2 = 1.01001100101110000101001_2 * 2^5$$

So the exponent is 5 and the exponent field is again 132. Next we combine the sign bit, the exponent field and the fraction field (dropping the implied 1) bit and convert to hexadecimal

```
0     10000100    01001100101110000101001
sign  exponent    fraction
0100 0010 0010 0110 0101 1100 0010 1001  as nibbles
  4    2    2    6    5    c    2    9  hexadecimal
```

So we determine that the sum is `0x42265c29` which is 41.59 (approximately).

You should be able to see that we lost some bits of precision on the smaller number. In an extreme case we could try to add 1.0 to a number like 10^{38} and have no effect.

Floating point multiplication

Floating point multiplication can be performed in binary much like decimal multiplication. Let's skip the floating point to/from binary conversion and just focus on the multiplication of 7.5 and 4.375. First observe that $7.5 = 111.1_2$ and $4.375 = 100.011_2$. Then we multiply binary numbers and place the binary point in the correct place in the product.

```
   111.1              1111
   100.011          * 100011
                      1111
                     1111
                    1111
                    1000001101
```

$\qquad$ 100000.1101 placing binary point in product

So we have the product 32.8125 as expected.

2.5 Exploring with the bit bucket

One of the subwindows of the ebe program is called the "bit bucket". The purpose of the bit bucket is to explore fundamental bit operations. Figure 2.1 shows the bit bucket at the start of a decimal to binary conversion.

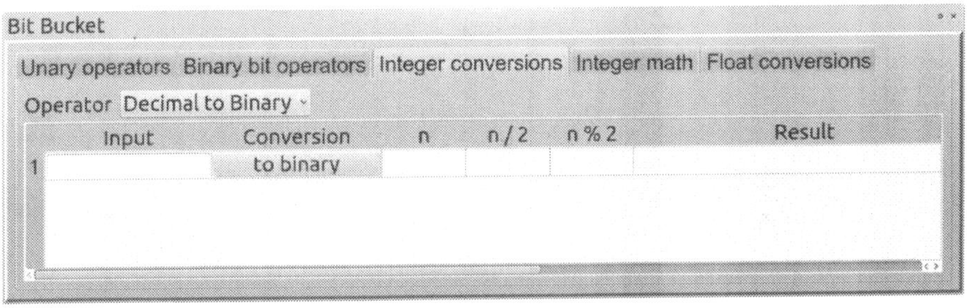

Figure 2.1 Bit bucket before decimal to binary conversion

There are 5 tabs which can be selected at the top of the bit bucket window, allowing you to explore unary operators, binary operators, integer conversions, integer math and float conversions. I have selected the integer conversions tab. Using the pull down list to the right of "Operator" I have chosen "Decimal to Binary". After selecting the conversion the table is cleared as you see it. There is a field for entering a number. In these fields in the bit bucket you can enter a hexadecimal number by using the prefix "0x" and you can also enter a binary number using the prefix "0b". After entering a number, you would step through the conversion by clicking on the "to binary" button. This button will move down the table through each step of the conversion.

Figure 2.2 shows the results from entering the number 131 and stepping through its conversion into binary.

Bit Bucket						
Unary operators	Binary bit operators	Integer conversions	Integer math	Float conversions		
Operator	Decimal to Binary					
Input	Conversion	n	n/2	n % 2	Result	
1 131		131	65	1	1	divide by 2
2		65	32	1	1 1	divide by 2
3		32	16	0	0 1 1	divide by 2
4		16	8	0	0 0 1 1	divide by 2
5		8	4	0	0 0 0 1 1	divide by 2
6		4	2	0	0 0 0 0 1 1	divide by 2
7		2	1	0	0 0 0 0 0 1 1	divide by 2
8		1	0	1	1 0 0 0 0 0 1 1	divide by 2

Figure 2.2 Bit bucket after converting 131 to binary

The bit bucket will help you explore the way that the computer represents and performs operations with numbers. There are conversions from decimal, binary and hexadecimal to the alternative forms. There are conversions for 32 bit floating point numbers in addition to integer conversions. All the arithmetic and bit operations on integers are also available for exploration.

Exercises

1. Convert the following integers to binary.
   a.   37   b.   65   c.   350   d.   427

2. Convert the following 16 bit signed integers to decimal.
   a.   0000001010101010b   c.   0x0101
   b.   1111111111101101b   d.   0xffcc

3. Convert the following 16 bit unsigned integers to binary.
   a.   0x015a   c.   0x0101
   b.   0xfedc   d.   0xacdc

4. Convert the following numbers to 32 bit floating point.
   a.   1.375   c.   -571.3125
   b.   0.041015625   d.   4091.125

5. Convert the following numbers from 32 bit floating point to decimal.
   a.   0x3F82000   c.   0x4F84000
   b.   0xBF82000   d.   0x3C86000

6. Perform the binary addition of the 2 unsigned integers below. Show each carry as a 1 above the proper position.

   ```
     0001001011001011
   + 1110110111101011
   ```

7. Perform the binary multiplication of the following unsigned binary numbers. Show each row where a 1 is multiplied times the top number. You may omit rows where a 0 is multiplied times the top

   ```
        1011001011
   x       1101101
   ```

8. Write an assembly "program" (data only) defining data values using **dw** and **dd** for all the numbers in exercises 1-4.

9. Write a C or C++ program to start with 0.0 in a float and add 1.0 in a loop to the float until it stops changing. What is this minimum value?

Chapter 3
Computer memory

In this chapter we will discuss how a modern computer performs memory mapping to give each process a protected address space and how Windows manages the memory for a process. A practical benefit of this chapter is a discussion of how to examine memory using ebe.

3.1 Memory mapping

The memory of a computer can be considered an array of bytes. Each byte of memory has an address. The first byte is at address 0, the second byte at address 1, and so on until the last byte of the computer's memory.

In modern CPUs there are hardware mapping registers which are used to give each process a protected address space. This means that multiple people can each run a program which starts at address `0x4004c8` at the same time. These processes perceive the same "logical" addresses, while they are using memory at different "physical" addresses.

The hardware mapping registers on an x86-64 CPU can map pages of 2 different sizes - 4096 bytes and 2 megabytes. Windows, Linux and OS X all use 2 MB pages for the kernel and 4 KB pages for most other uses. All three operating systems allow user processes to use 2 MB pages. In some of the more recent CPUs there is also support for 1 GB pages.

The operation of the memory system is to translate the upper bits of the address from a process's logical address to a physical address. Let's consider only 4 KB pages. Then an address is translated based on the page number and the address within the page. Suppose a reference is made to logical address `0x4000002220`. Since $4096 = 2^{12}$, the offset within the page is the right-most 12 bits (`0x220`). The page number is the rest of the bits (`0x4000002`). A hardware register (or multiple registers) translates this page number to a physical page address, let's say `0x780000`. Then the two addresses are combined to get the physical address `0x780220`.

Amazingly the CPU generally performs the translations without slowing down and this benefits the users in several ways. The most obvious benefit is memory protection. User processes are limited to reading and writing only their own pages. This means that the operating system is protected from malicious or poorly coded user programs. Also each user process is protected from other user processes. In addition to protection from writing, users can't read other users' data.

There are instructions used by the operating system to manage the hardware mapping registers. These instructions are not discussed in this book. Our focus is on programming user processes.

So why bother to discuss paging, if we are not discussing the instructions to manage paging? Primarily this improves one's understanding of the computer. It's useful to understand how several processes can use the same logical addresses. It's also useful when debugging. When you write software which accesses data beyond the end of an array, you sometimes get a segmentation fault. However you only get a segmentation fault when your logical address reaches far enough past the end of the array to cause the CPU to reference a page table entry which is not mapped into your process.

3.2 Process memory model in Windows

In Windows memory for a process is divided into 4 logical regions: text, data, heap and stack. The stack by default is 1 MB and is typically located at an address below `0x400000`. Immediately above the stack is the text segment (for instructions), followed by the data segment. The heap occupies memory from the end of the data segment to the highest address for a user process – `0x7fffffffff`. The total number of bits in the highest user process address is 43 which amounts to 8 TB of virtual address space.

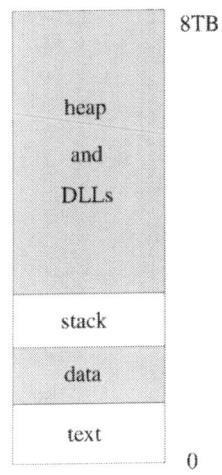

To the right we see the arrangement of the various memory segments. At the lowest address we have the text segment. This segment is shown starting at 0, though the actual location is at a higher address – typically about 0x400000 for `main`. Above the text and data is the stack. The stack is limited in size and can be as large as 1 GB which might possibly alter the layout. Above these two segments is the heap segment which will contain allocated data and dynamic-link libraries. The data and text segments are limited to the first 2 GB of address space, so the relative sizes are quite distorted in the diagram.

The data segment starts with the `.data` segment which contains initialized data. Above that is the `.bss` segment which stands for "block started by symbol". The `.bss` segment contains data which is statically allocated in a process, but is not stored in the executable file. Instead this data is allocated when the process is loaded into memory. The initial contents of the `.bss` segment are all 0 bits.

The heap is not really a heap in the sense discussed in a data structures course. Instead it is a dynamically resizable region of memory which is used to allocate memory to a process through functions like `malloc` in C and the `new` operator in C++. In 64 bit Windows this region can grow to very large sizes. The limit is imposed by the sum of physical memory and swap space.

The default stack size of 1 MB sounds pretty small, but the stack is used to make function calls. For each call the return address and the function parameters (well, more or less) are pushed on the stack. Also the called function places local variables on the stack. Assuming each call uses about 6 parameters and has 4 local variables this would end up requiring about 100 bytes per call. This means that 1 MB of stack space would support a call depth of 10000. Problems requiring much depth of recursion or arrays as local variables might require stack size modification when the program is linked.

This simple memory layout is greatly simplified. There are dynamic-link libraries (DLLs) which can be mapped into a process at load time and after the program is loaded which will result in regions in the heap range being used to store instructions and data. This region is also used for mapping shared memory regions into a process. Also to improve security Windows uses somewhat random stack, text, data, and heap start addresses. This means that the top of the stack would differ each time a program is executed. Likewise the address of `main` might vary each time a program is executed.

If you wish to examine the memory used by one of your programs, you can download the VMMap program from Microsoft by searching for vmmap at `http://technet.microsoft.com`.

3.3 Memory example

Here is a sample assembly program, "`memory.asm`" with several memory items defined:

```
        segment .data
a       dd      4
b       dd      4.4
c       times   10 dd 0
d       dw      1, 2
e       db      0xfb
f       db      "hello world", 0

        segment .bss
g       resd    1
h       resd    10
i       resb    100

        segment .text
        global  main    ; tell linker about main
main:
    push    rbp         ; set up a stack frame
    mov     rbp, rsp    ; rbp points to stack frame
    sub     rsp, 32     ; leave room for shadow parameters
                        ; rsp on a 16 byte boundary
    xor     eax, eax    ; rax = 0 for return value
    leave               ; undo stack frame changes
    ret
```

After assembling the program we get the following listing file:

```
 1                              %line 1+1 memory.asm
 2                              [section .data]
 3 00000000 04000000             a dd 4
 4 00000004 CDCC8C40             b dd 4.4
 5 00000008 00000000<rept>       c times 10 dd 0
 6 00000030 01000200             d dw 1, 2
 7 00000034 FB                   e db 0xfb
 8 00000035 68656C6C6F20776F72-  f db "hello world", 0
 9 00000035 6C6400
10
11                              [section .bss]
12 00000000 <gap>                g resd 1
13 00000004 <gap>                h resd 10
14 0000002C <gap>                i resb 100
15
16                              [section .text]
17                              [global main]
18                              main:
19 00000000 55                   push rbp
20 00000001 4889E5               mov rbp, rsp
21 00000004 4883EC10             sub rsp, 16
22 00000008 31C0                 xor eax, eax
```

```
23 0000000A C9              leave
24 0000000B C3              ret
```

You can see from the listing the relative addresses of the defined data elements. In the data segment we have a double word (4 bytes) named **a** at location 0. Notice that the bytes of **a** are reversed compared to what you might prefer.

Following **a** is a double word defined as a floating point value named **b** at relative address 4. The bytes for **b** are also reversed. Ordered logically it is `0x408ccccd`. Then the sign bit is 0, the exponent field is the rightmost 7 bits of the "first" byte, `0x40`, with the leftmost bit of the next byte, `0x8c`. So the exponent field is `0x81` = 129, which is a binary exponent of 2. The fraction field (with the implied initial 1 bit) is `0x8ccccd`. So b = $1.00011001100110011001101 * 2^2 = 4.4$.

The next data item is the array **c** defined with the `times` pseudo-op which has 10 double word locations. The relative location for **c** is 8 and **c** consists of 40 bytes, so the next item after **c** is at relative address 48 or `0x30`.

Following **c** is the length 2 array **d** with values 1 and 2. Array **d** is of type `word` so each value is 2 bytes. Again you can see that the bytes are reversed for each word of **d**.

The next data item is the byte variable **e** with initial value `0xfb`. After **e** is the byte array **f** which is initialized with a string. Notice that I have added a terminal null byte explicitly to **f**. Strings in nasm do not end in null bytes.

After the data segment I have included a `.bss` segment with 3 variables. These are listed with their relative addresses as part of the bss segment. After linking the bss data items will be loaded into memory beginning with **g** defined by the `resd` op-code which means "reserve" double word. With `resd` the number 1 means 1 double word. The next bss item is **h** which has 10 reserved double words. The last bss item is **i** which has 100 reserved bytes. All these data items are shown in the listing with addresses relative to the start of the bss segment. They will all have value 0 when the program starts.

3.4 Examining memory with ebe

In this section we will give a brief introduction to examining memory with ebe. We will show how to start the memory program with a breakpoint so that we can examine the variables defined in the program.

Setting a breakpoint

A breakpoint is a marker for an instruction which is used by a debugger to stop the execution of a program when that instruction is reached. The general pattern for debugging is to set a breakpoint and then run the program. The program will run until the breakpoint is reached and stop just before executing that instruction.

Ebe uses the line number column to the left of the source code to indicate breakpoints. Left clicking on one of the line numbers will set (or clear if already set) a breakpoint on that line of code. Ebe indicates the existence of a breakpoint by coloring that line number with a red background.

The picture below shows the ebe source window with the memory program with a breakpoint set on line 17. The breakpoint is shown with a gray background in the printed book. Also this picture has been updated with an arrow pointing to the ebe "Run" button.

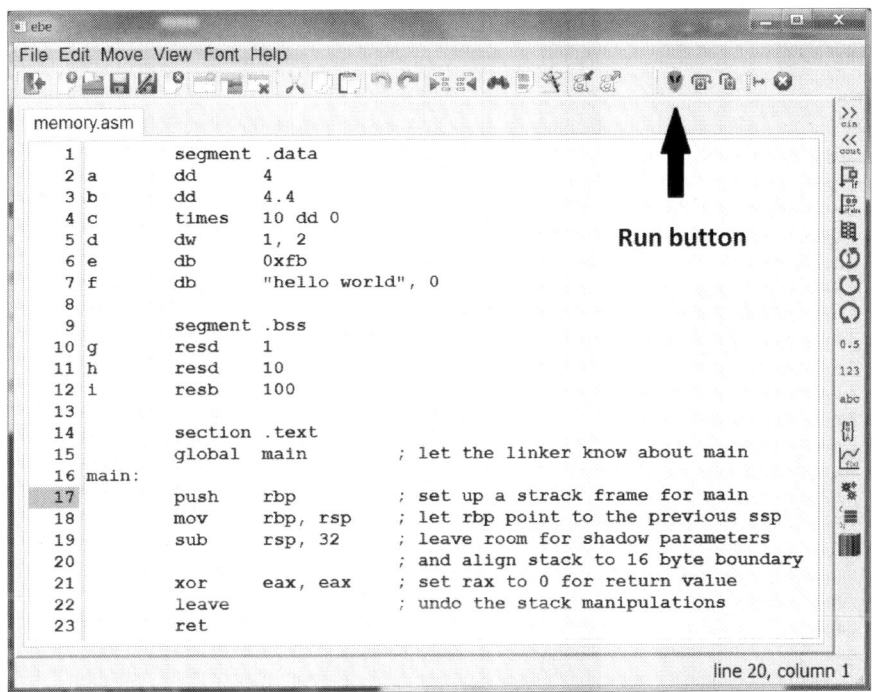

Running a program and viewing a variable

Having set the breakpoint on line 17, if we now click on the "Run" button (the alien icon pointed to by the arrow) the program will be assembled, linked and executed. It will stop execution with the "push rbp" instruction as the next instruction to execute. The source window will indicate the next line to execute by giving that line a blue-green background (gray in the illustration).

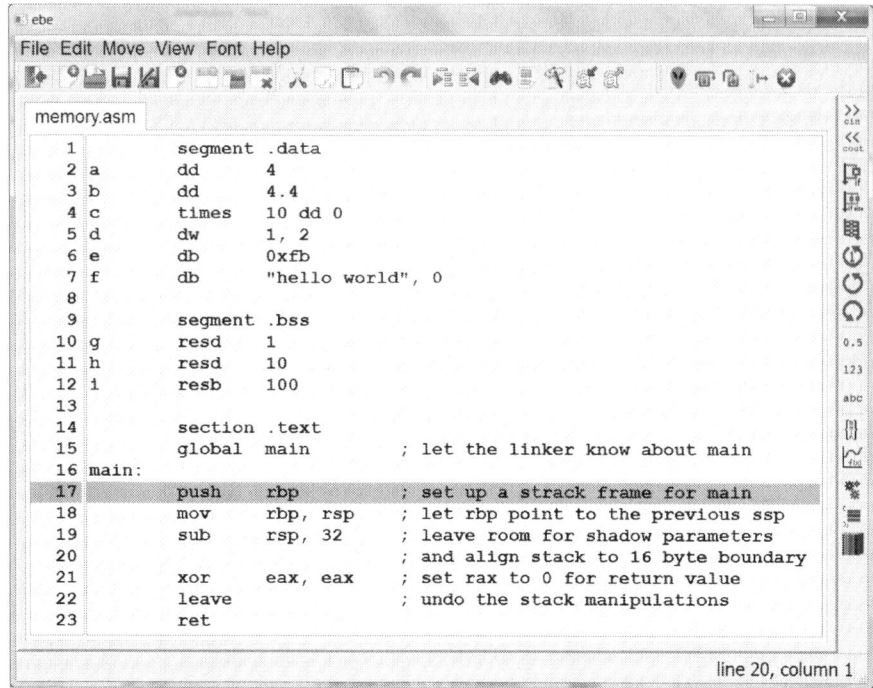

Ebe will discover the assembly variables and display them in a subwindow call the "assembly data window". You may need to use the "View" menu to select the assembly data window. If it is visible you can drag it by its title bar and make it a stand-alone window. This is shown below:

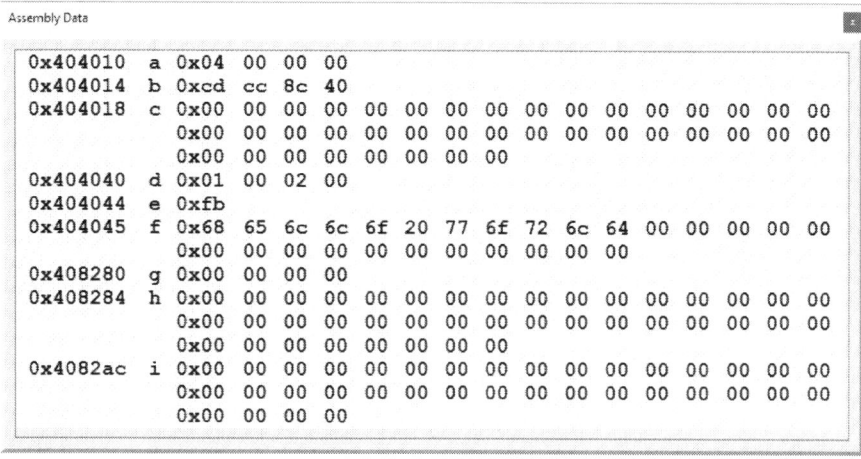

Ebe will attempt to run the "ebedecl" program to determine sizes and types of variables. If it succeeds it may know that b should be displayed as a float variable. If not, it will display it as 4 bytes in hexadecimal. Also some size determinations may be a little large without ebedecl.

You may prefer to change the format for a variable displayed in the assembly data window. To do so, right-click on the line with the desired variable and it will popup a window. Here I have right-clicked on b and then slid right to select the "Float" choice under "Float format". This will present the number as 4.4.

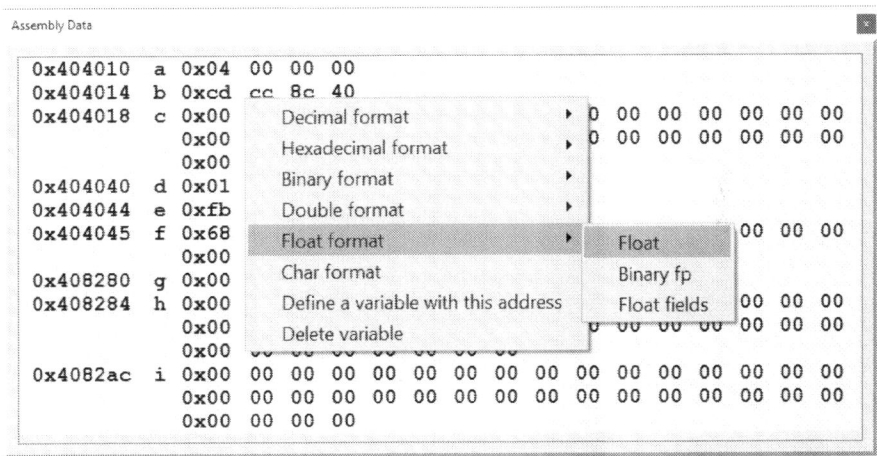

Below is the assembly data window after changing the formats to more appropriate values:

```
Assembly Data
0x404010   a  4
0x404014   b  4.4
0x404018   c  0           0            0            0
              0           0            0            0
              0           0
0x404040   d  1           2
0x404044   e  -5
0x404045   f  h     e  l  l  o     w  o  r  l  d  00 00 00 00 00
              00    00 00 00 00 00 00 00 00 00 00
0x408280   g  0x00        00
0x408284   h  0x00        00        00        00        00        00
              0x00        00        00        00        00        00
              0x00        00        00        00
0x4082ac   i  0x00  00 00 00 00 00 00 00 00 00 00 00 00 00 00 00
              0x00  00 00 00 00 00 00 00 00 00 00 00 00 00 00 00
              0x00  00 00 00
```

35

For the decimal formats the choices are different sizes. I chose 4 for **a** and **c** and I chose 2 for **d** to match their definitions. I chose "Char format" for **f** which displays characters, C notations like "\n" or hexadecimal values. The other format choices for float were binary float or float fields. These would be quite useful in Chapter 2.

Below is the assembly data window with **b** displayed as a binary float.

```
Assembly Data
0x404010   a  4
0x404014   b  1.0001100110011001101 * 2**2
0x404018   c  0                    0                    0              0
              0                    0                    0              0
              0                    0
0x404040   d  1           2
0x404044   e  -5
0x404045   f  h     e     1     1     o           w     o     r     1     d     00  00
              00    00    00    00    00    00    00    00    00    00    00
0x408280   g  0x00        00
0x408284   h  0x00        00          00          00          00          00          00
              0x00        00          00          00          00          00          00
              0x00        00          00          00
0x4082ac   i  0x00  00    00    00    00    00    00    00    00  00  00  00  00
              0x00  00    00    00    00    00    00    00    00  00  00  00  00
              0x00  00    00    00
```

36

Exercises

1. Write a data-only program like the one in this chapter to define an array of 10 8 byte integers in the data segment, an array of five 2 byte integers in the bss segment, and a string terminated by 0 in the data segment. Use ebe's data command to print the 8 byte integers in hexadecimal, the 2 byte integers as unsigned values, and the string as a string.

2. Assuming that the stack size limit is 1MB, about how large can you declare an array of **double**s inside a C++ function. Do not use the keyword **static**.

3. Use the command line and compile a C program with an array of 1 million doubles. You will probably need to use -Wl,--stack,8000000 option on the gcc command. Note that this option has a lowercase 'L' after the 'W' not a '1'. Test the program by writing a loop and placing 0.0 throughout the array. Determine the smallest number which works to the nearest 1000.

4. Print the value of **rsp** in ebe. How many bits are required to store this value?

Chapter 4
Memory mapping in 64 bit mode

In this chapter we discuss the details of how virtual addresses are translated to physical addresses in the x86-64 architecture. Some of the data for translation is stored in the CPU and some of it is stored in memory.

4.1 The memory mapping register

The CPU designers named this register "Control Register 3" or just CR3. A simplified view of CR3 is that it is a pointer to the top level of a hierarchical collection of tables in memory which define the translation from virtual addresses (the addresses your program sees) to physical addresses. The CPU retains quite a few page translations internally, but let's consider first how the CPU starts all this translation process.

Somewhere in the kernel of the operating system, an initial hierarchy of the translation tables is prepared and CR3 is filled with the address of the top level table in the hierarchy. This table is given the illustrious name "Page Map Level 4" or PML4. When the CPU is switched to using memory mapping on the next memory reference it uses CR3 to fetch entries from PML4.

4.2 Page Map Level 4

A virtual address can be broken into fields like this:

63 48	47 39	38 30	29 21	20 12	11 0
unused	PML4 index	page directory pointer index	page directory index	page table index	page offset

Here we see that a virtual or logical address is broken into 6 fields. The top-most 16 bits are ignored. They are supposed to be a sign extension of bit 47, but they are not part of the address translation. Windows uses 44 bits of address space for memory, with bit 43 set to 1 for the kernel. It also uses addresses with bits 48-63 set to 1 for special purposes like device addresses. Bit 47 is left as 0 in user processes in Linux and OS X so bits 47-63 are all 0's. In both operating systems bits 47-63 are all 1 for kernel addresses. We will focus on user process memory management. Following the unused bits are four 9 bit fields which undergo translation and finally a 12 bit page offset. The result of the translation process will be a physical address like `0x7f88008000` which is combined with the offset (let's say it was `0x1f0`) to yield a physical address of `0x7f880081f0`.

Pages of memory are $2^{12} = 4096$ bytes, so the 12 bit offset makes sense. What about those 9 bit fields? Well, addresses are 8 bytes so you can store 512 addresses in a page and $512 = 2^9$, so 9 bit fields allow storing each of the 4 types of mapping tables in a page of memory.

Bits 47-39 of a virtual address are used as an index into the PML4 table. The PML4 table is essentially an array of 512 pointers (32 would be enough for Windows since bits 44-47 are all 0). These pointers point to pages of memory, so the rightmost 12 bits of each pointer can be used for other purposes like indicating whether an entry is valid or not. Generally not all entries in the PML4 will be valid.

Let's suppose that CR3 has the physical address `0x4ffff000`. Then let's suppose that bits 47-39 of our sample address are `0x001`, then we would have an array in memory at `0x4ffff000` and we would access the second entry (index 1) to get the address of a page directory pointer table: `0x3467000`.

	PML4 at 0x4ffff000
0	0x3466000
1	0x3467000
2	0x3468000

	...
511	unused

4.3 Page Directory Pointer Table

The next level in the memory translation hierarchy is the collection of page directory pointer tables. Each of these tables is also an array of 512 pointers. These pointers are to page directory tables. Let's assume that our sample address has the value **0x002** for bits 38-30. Then the computer will fetch the third entry of the page directory pointer table to lead next to a page directory table at address **0x3588000**.

Page Directory Pointer Table at **0x3467000**

0	0x3587000
1	unused
2	0x3588000
...	...
511	unused

4.4 Page Directory Table

The third level in the memory translation hierarchy is the collection of page directory tables. Each of these tables is an array of 512 pointers, which point to page tables. Let's assume that our sample address has the value **0x000** for bits 29-21. Then the computer will fetch the first entry of the page directory table to lead next to a page table at address **0x3678000**.

Page Directory Table at **0x3588000**

0	0x3678000
1	0x3679000
2	unused
...	...
511	unused

4.5 Page Table

The fourth and last level in the memory translation hierarchy is the collection of page tables. Again each of these tables is an array of 512 pointers to pages. Let's assume that our sample address has the value `0x1ff` for bits 20-12. Then the computer will fetch the last entry of the page table to lead next to a page at address `0x5799000`.

	Page Table at 0x3678000
0	0x5788000
1	0x5789000
2	0x578a000
...	. . .
511	0x5799000

After using 4 tables we reach the address of the page of memory which was originally referenced. Then we can or in the page offset (bits 11-0) of the original - say `0xfa8`. This yields a final physical address of `0x5799fa8`.

4.6 Large pages

The normal size page is 4096 bytes. The CPU designers have added support for large pages using three levels of the existing translation tables. By using 3 levels of tables, there are $9 + 12 = 21$ bits left for the within page offset field. This makes large pages $2^{21} = 2097152$ bytes.

Some of the latest CPUs support pages using 2 levels of page tables which results in having pages of size 2^{30} which is 1 GB. These huge pages will be popular for applications requiring large amounts of RAM like database management systems and virtual machine emulators.

4.7 CPU Support for Fast Lookups

This process would be entirely too slow if done every time by traversing through all these tables. Instead whenever a page translation has been performed, the CPU adds this translation into a cache called a "Translation Lookaside Buffer" or TLB. Then hopefully this page will be used many times without going back through the table lookup process.

A TLB operates much like a hash table. It is presented with a virtual page address and produces a physical page address or failure within roughly 1/2 of a clock cycle. In the case of a failure the memory search takes from 10 to 100 cycles. Typical miss rates are from 0.01% to 1%.

Clearly there is a limit to the number of entries in the TLB for a CPU. The Intel Core 2 series has a total of 16 entries in a level 1 TLB and 256 entries in a level 2 TLB. The Core i7 has 64 level 1 TLB entries and 512 level 2 entries. The AMD Athlon II CPU has 1024 TLB entries, while the Ryzen has 3 levels of TLBs with more than 2000 total TLB entries.

Given the relatively small number of TLB entries in a CPU it seems like it would be a good idea to migrate to allocating 2 MB pages for programs. Windows, Linux and OS X all support 2 MB pages for user processes though the default is 4 KB. Linux also supports 1 GB pages which might be quite useful for a dedicated database server with lots of RAM.

Exercises

1. Suppose you were given the opportunity to redesign the memory mapping hierarchy for a new CPU. We have seen that 4 KB pages seem a little small. Suppose you made the pages $2^{17} = 131072$ bytes. How many 64 bit pointers would fit in such a page?

2. How many bits would be required for the addressing of a page table?

3. How would you break up the bit fields of virtual addresses?

4. Having much larger pages seems desirable. Let's design a memory mapping system with pages of $2^{20} = 1048576$ bytes but use partial pages for memory mapping tables. Design a system with 3 levels of page mapping tables with at least 48 bits of usable virtual address space.

5. Suppose a virtual memory address is `0x123456789012`. Divide this address into the 4 different page table parts and the within page offset.

6. Suppose a virtual memory address is `0x123456789012`. Suppose this happens to be an address within a 2MB page. What is the within page offset for this address?

7. Write an assembly language program to compute the cost of electricity for a home. The cost per kilowatt hour will be an integer number of pennies stored in a memory location. The kilowatt hours used will also be an integer stored in memory. The bill amount will be $5.00 plus the cost per kilowatt hour times the number of kilowatt hours over 1000. You can use a conditional move to set the number of hours over 1000 to 0 if the number of hours over 1000 is negative. Move the number of dollars into one memory location and the number of pennies into another.

Chapter 5
Registers

Computer memory is essentially an array of bytes which software uses for instructions and data. While the memory is relatively fast, there is a need for a small amount of faster data to permit the CPU to execute instructions faster. A typical computer executes at 3 GHz and many instructions can execute in 1 cycle. However for an instruction to execute the instruction and any data required must be fetched from memory. One fairly common form of memory has a latency of 6 nanoseconds, meaning the time lag between requesting the memory and getting the data. This 6 nanoseconds would equal 18 CPU cycles. If the instructions and data were all fetched from and stored in memory there would probably be about 18 nanoseconds required for common instructions. 18 nanoseconds is time enough for 54 instructions at 1 instruction per cycle. There is clearly a huge need to avoid using the relatively slow main memory.

One type of faster memory is cache memory, which is perhaps 10 times as fast as main memory. Cache operates by storing memory contents along with their addresses in a faster memory system which is later used to fetch memory more quickly than from RAM. The cache memory typically performs a hash of a memory address to determine its possible location in cache. Then the cache cell's memory address is compared with the desired address and it it matches the cache cell's data is returned shot-circuiting the original memory fetch. The use of cache memory can help address the speed problem, but it is not enough to reach the target of 1 instruction per CPU cycle. A second type of faster memory is the CPU's register set. Cache might be several megabytes, but the CPU has only a few registers. However the registers are accessible in roughly one half of a CPU cycle or less. The use of registers is essential to achieving high performance. The combination of cache and registers provides roughly half of a modern CPU's performance. The rest is achieved with pipelining and multiple execution units. Pipelining means dividing instructions into multiple steps and executing several instructions simultaneously though each at different steps. Pipelining and multiple execution units are quite important to CPU design but these features are not part of general assembly language programming, while registers are a central feature.

The x86-64 CPUs have 16 general purpose 64 bit registers and 16 modern floating point registers. These floating point registers are either 128 or 256 bits depending on the CPU model and can operate on multiple integer or floating point values. There is also a floating point register stack which we will not use in this book. The CPU has a 64 bit instruction pointer register (**rip**) which contains the address of the next instruction to execute. There is also a 64 bit flags register (**rflags**). There are additional registers which we probably won't use. Having 16 registers means that a register's "address" is only 4 bits. This makes instructions using registers much smaller than instructions using memory addresses.

The 16 general purpose registers are 64 bit values stored within the CPU. Software can access the registers as 64 bit values, 32 bit values, 16 bit values and 8 bit values. Since the CPU evolved from the 8086 CPU, the registers have evolved from 16 bit registers to 32 bit registers and finally to 64 bit registers.

On the 8086 registers were more special purpose than general purpose:

ax - accumulator for numeric operations

bx - base register (array access)

cx - count register (string operations)

dx - data register

si - source index

di - destination index

bp - base pointer (for function stack frames)

sp - stack pointer

In addition the 2 halves of the first 4 registers can be accessed using **al** for the low byte of **ax**, **ah** for the high byte of **ax**, and **bl**, **bh**, **cl**, **ch**, **dl** and **dh** for the halves of **bx**, **cx** and **dx**.

When the 80386 CPU was designed the registers were expanded to 32 bits and renamed as **eax**, **ebx**, **ecx**, **edx**, **esi**, **edi**, **ebp**, and **esp**. Software could also use the original names to access the lower 16 bits of each of the registers. The 8 bit registers were also retained without allowing direct access to the upper halves of the registers.

For the x86-64 architecture the registers were expanded to 64 bits and 8 additional general purpose registers were added. The names used to access the 64 bit registers are **rax**, **rbx**, **rcx**, **rdx**, **rsi**, **rdi**, **rbp**, and **rsp** for the compatible collection and **r8-r15** for the 8 new registers. As you might expect you can still use **ax** to access the lowest word of the **rax** register along with **eax** to access the lower half of the register. Likewise the other 32 bit and 16 bit register names still work in 64 bit more. You can also access registers **r8-r15** as byte, word, or double word registers by appending **b**, **w** or **d** to the register name.

The **rflags** register is a 64 bit register, but currently only the lower 32 bits are used, so it is generally sufficient to refer to **eflags**. In addition the flags register is usually not referred to directly. Instead conditional instructions are used which internally access 1 or more bits of the flags register to determine what action to take.

Moving data seems to be a fundamental task in assembly language. In the case of moving values to/from the integer registers, the basic command is **mov**. It can move constants, addresses and memory contents into registers, move data from 1 register to another and move the contents of a register into memory.

5.1 Observing registers in ebe

One of the windows managed by ebe is the register window. After each step of program execution ebe obtains the current values of the general purpose registers and displays them in the register window. Similarly ebe displays the floating point registers in the floating point register window. Below is a sample of the register window.

You can select a different format for the registers by right clicking on the name of a register. This will popup a list of choices. You can choose either decimal or hexadecimal format for that register or for all the general purpose registers. Another choice is to define a variable using a register's value as an address. This would be useful for allocated data.

You can see below the general purpose registers, the instruction pointer register (**rip**) and the flags register (**eflags**). For simplicity the set bits of **eflags** are displayed by their acronyms. Here the parity flag (**PF**), the zero flag (**ZF**) and the interrupt enable flag (**IF**) are all set.

Registers							
rax	0x0	rsi	0x29	r8	0x2f34c0	r12	0x2f5f30
rbx	0x1	rdi	0x2f5f70	r9	0x8	r13	0x0
rcx	0x1	rbp	0x8	r10	0x0	r14	0x0
rdx	0x2f5f30	rsp	0x22fe68	r11	0x286	r15	0x0
rip	0x40174c	eflags	PF ZF IF				

5.2 Moving a constant into a register

The first type of move is to move a constant into a register. A constant is usually referred to as an immediate value. It consists of some bytes stored as part of the instruction. Immediate operands can be 1, 2 or 4 bytes for most instructions. The `mov` instruction also allows 8 byte immediate values.

```
mov     rax, 100
mov     eax, 100
```

Surprisingly, these two instructions have the same effect - moving the value 100 into `rax`. Arithmetic operations and moves with 4 byte register references are zero-extended to 8 bytes. The program shown below in ebe illustrates the `mov` instruction moving constants into register `rax`.

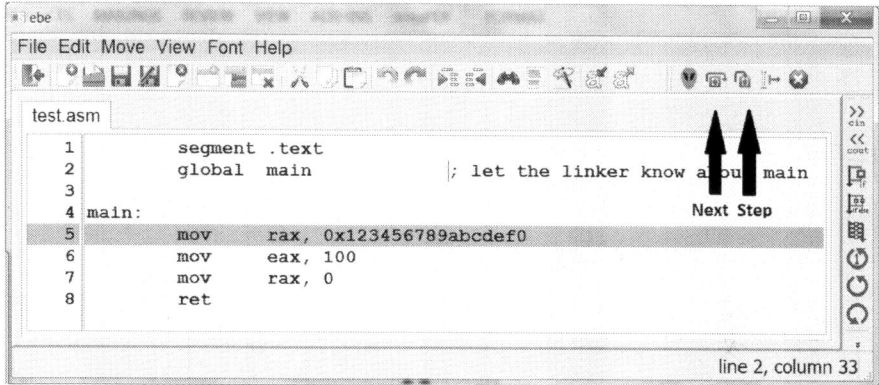

There has been a breakpoint set on line 5 and the program has been run by clicking the "Run" button. At this point the first `mov` has not been executed. You can advance the program by clicking on either "Next" or "Step" (highlighted with arrows in the picture). The difference is that "Step" will step into a function if a function call is made, while "Next" will execute the highlighted statement and advance to the next statement in the same function. The effect is the same in this code and here is the source window and the register window after executing the first `mov`:

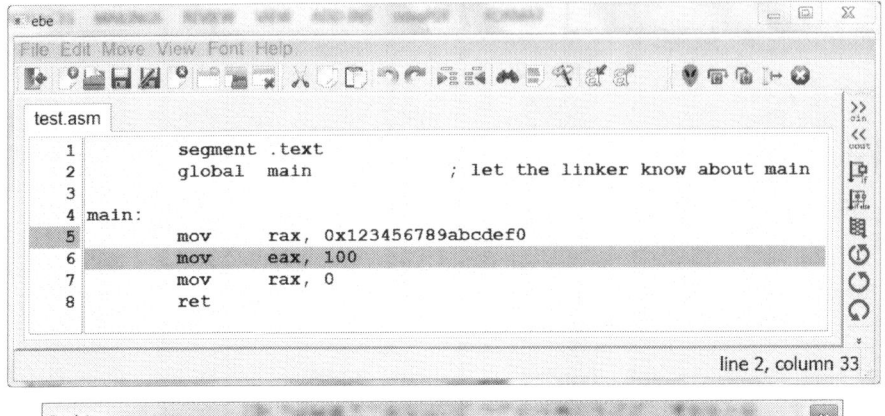

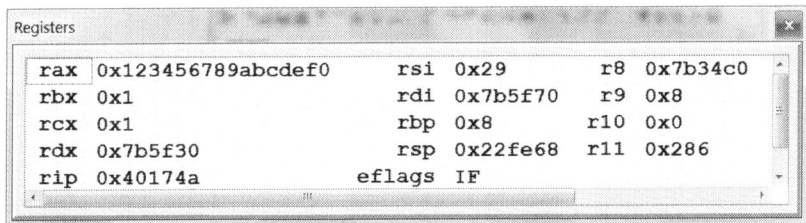

You can observe that the value 0x123456789abcdef0 has been placed into rax and that clearly the next mov has not been executed. There is little value in repeatedly displaying the source window but here is the register window after executing the mov at line 6:

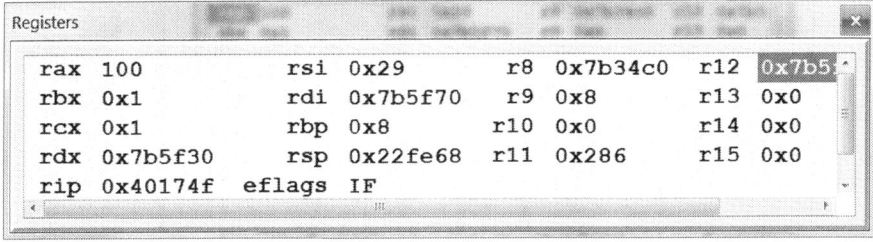

For convenience the display format for rax has been switched to decimal and you can observe that "mov eax, 100" results in moving 100 into the lower half of rax and 0 into the upper half.

You can follow the sequence of statements and observe that moving 100 into eax will clear out the top half of rax. It turns out that a 32 bit constant is stored in the instruction stream for the mov which moves 100. Also the instruction to move into eax is 1 byte long and the move into rax is 3 bytes long. The shorter instruction is preferable. You might be tempted to move 100 into al, but this instruction does not clear out the rest of the register.

5.3 Moving values from memory to registers

In order to move a value from memory into a register, you must use the address of the value. Consider the program shown below

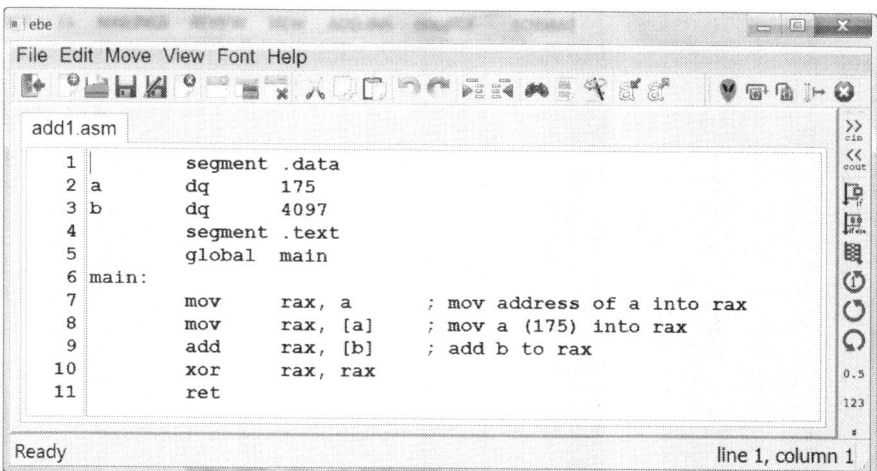

The label **a** is will be replaced by the address of **a** if included in an instruction under Windows or Linux. Windows and Linux place the data and bss segments within the first 4 GB of a program's virtual address space so the addresses fit into 32 bits. OS X uses relative addressing and **a** will be replaced by its address relative to register **rip**. The reason is that OS X addresses are too big to fit in 32 bits. In fact nasm will not allow moving an address under OS X. The alternative is to use the **lea** (load effective address) instruction which will be discussed later. Consider the following statement in the .**text** segment.

```
        mov     rax, a
```

The instruction has a 32 bit constant field which is replaced with the address of **a** when the program is executed on Windows. When tested, the **rax** register receives the value **0x408010** as shown below:

Registers							
rax	0x408010	rsi	0x29	r8	0x373490	r12	0x375ed0
rbx	0x1	rdi	0x375f10	r9	0x8	r13	0x0
rcx	0x1	rbp	0x8	r10	0x0	r14	0x0
rdx	0x375ed0	rsp	0x22fe68	r11	0x286	r15	0x0
rip	0x401747	eflags	IF				

The proper syntax to get the value of **a**, 175, is from line 8 of the program and also below:

```
        mov     rax, [a]
```

The meaning of an expression in square brackets is to use that expression as a memory address and to load or store from that address. In this case it loads the value from the address represented by a. This is basically a different instruction from the other **mov**. The other is "load constant" and the latest one is "load from memory".

After executing line 8 we see that **rax** has the value 175. In the register display below I have used a decimal format to make the effect more obvious.

```
Registers
rax  175           rsi  0x29        r8   0x373490   r12  0x375ed0
rbx  0x1           rdi  0x375f10    r9   0x8        r13  0x0
rcx  0x1           rbp  0x8         r10  0x0        r14  0x0
rdx  0x375ed0      rsp  0x22fe68    r11  0x286      r15  0x0
rip  0x40174f      eflags  IF
```

In line 9 of the program I have introduced the **add** instruction to make things a bit more interesting. The effect of line 9 is to add the contents of b, 4097, to **rax**. The result of the **add** instruction is shown below:

```
Registers
rax  4272          rsi  0x29        r8   0x373490   r12  0x375ed0
rbx  0x1           rdi  0x375f10    r9   0x8        r13  0x0
rcx  0x1           rbp  0x8         r10  0x0        r14  0x0
rdx  0x375ed0      rsp  0x22fe68    r11  0x286      r15  0x0
rip  0x401757      eflags  AF IF
```

You will notice that my main routine calls no other function. Therefore there is no need to establish a stack frame and no need to force the stack pointer to be a multiple of 16. Real programs tend to be longer and call many functions, so generally I tend to prepare a stack frame in **main**.

There are other ways to move data from memory into a register, but this is sufficient for simpler programs. The other methods involve storing addresses in registers and using registers to hold indexes or offsets in arrays.

You can also move integer values less than 8 bytes in size into a register. If you specify an 8 bit register such as **al** or a 16 bit register such as **ax**, the remaining bits of the register are unaffected. However it you specify a 32 bit register such as **eax**, the remaining bits are set to 0. This may or may not be what you wish.

Alternatively you can use move and sign extend (**movsx**) or move and zero extend (**movzx**) to control the process. In these cases you would use the 64 bit register as a destination and add a length qualifier to the instruction. There is one surprise - a separate instruction to move and sign extend a double word: movsxd. Here are some examples:

```
movsx   rax, byte [data]   ; move byte, sign extend
movzx   rbx, word [sum]    ; move word, zero extend
movsxd  rcx, dword [count] ; move dword, sign extend
```

5.4 Moving values from a register to memory

Moving data from a register to memory is very similar to moving from memory to a register - you simply swap the operands so that the memory address is on the left (destination).

```
mov    [sum], rax
```

Below is a program which adds 2 numbers from memory and stores the sum into a memory location named sum:

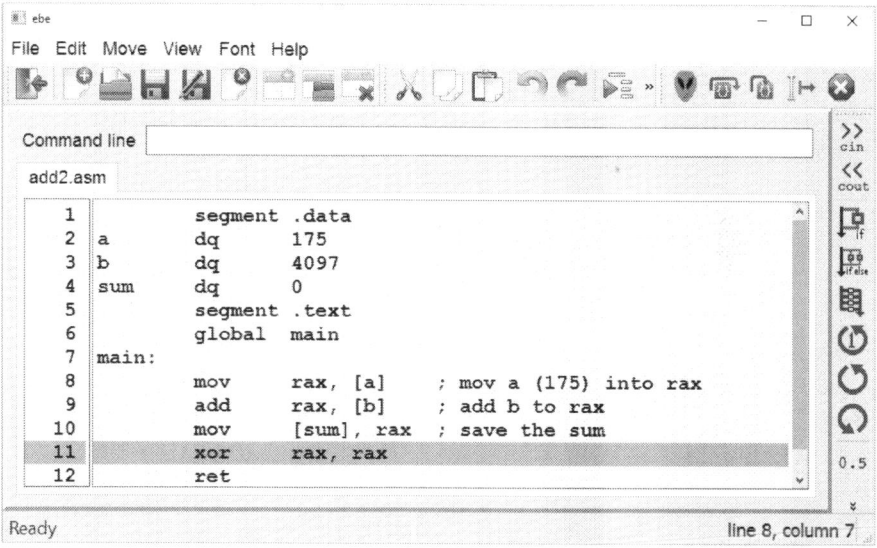

The source window shows line 11 highlighted which means that the mov instruction saving the sum has been executed. You can see that there is a breakpoint on line 8 and clearly the "Run" button was used to start the program and "Next" was clicked 3 times. Below is the data for the program after storing the run of a and b into sum.

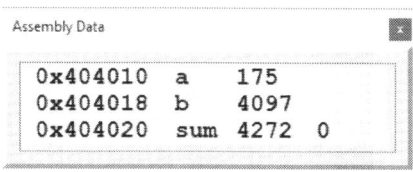

5.5 Moving data from one register to another

Moving data from one register to another is done as you might expect - simply place 2 register names as operands to the `mov` instruction.

```
mov     rbx, rax    ; move value in rax to rbx
```

Below is a program which moves the value of **a** into **rax** and then moves the value into **rbx** so that the value can be used to compute **a+b** and also **a-b**.

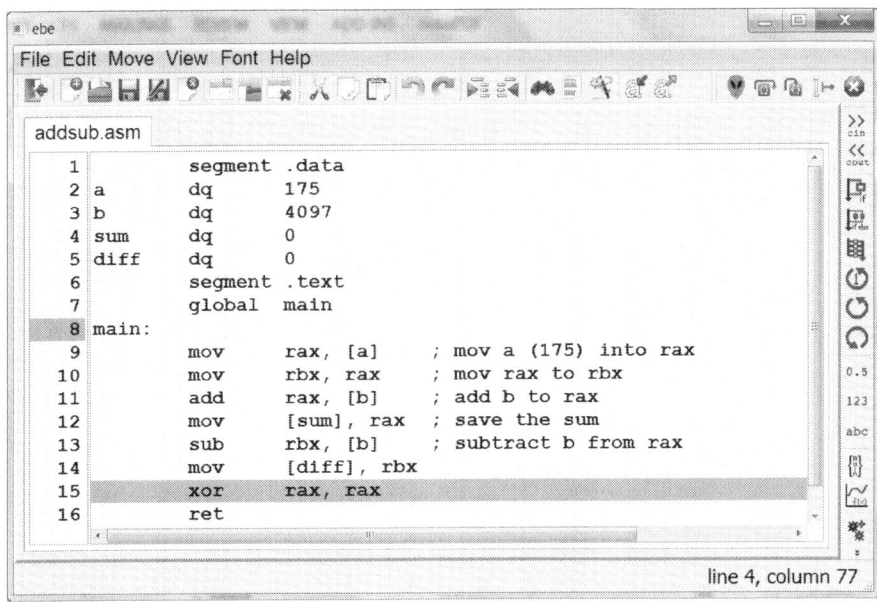

You can see that there is a breakpoint on line 8 and that line 15 is the next to be executed. This program introduces the **sub** instruction which subtracts one value from another. In this case it subtracts the value from memory location **b** from **rbx** with the difference being placed in **rbx**.

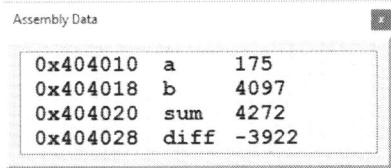

It might be a little interesting to note the value of **eflags** shown in the registers for the addition and subtraction program. You will see **SF** in the flag values which stands for "sign flag" and indicates that the last instruction which modified the flags, **sub**, resulted in a negative value.

rax	4272	rsi	0x2b	r8	0x9e3490	r12	
rbx	0xffffffffffff0ae	rdi	0x9e5f10	r9	0x8	r13	
rcx	0x1	rbp	0x8	r10	0x0	r14	
rdx	0x9e5ed0	rsp	0x22fe68	r11	0x286	r15	
rip	0x40176b	eflags	CF SF IF				

Exercises

1. Write an assembly program to define 4 integers in the .data segment. Give two of these integers positive values and 2 negative values. Define one of your positive numbers using hexadecimal notation. Write instructions to load the 4 integers into 4 different registers and add them with the sum being left in a register. Use ebe to single-step through your program and inspect each register as it is modified.

2. Write an assembly program to define 4 integers - one each of length 1, 2, 4 and 8 bytes. Load the 4 integers into 4 registers using sign extension for the shorter values. Add the values and store the sum in a memory location.

3. Write an assembly program to define 3 integers of 2 bytes each. Name these a, b and c. Compute and save into 4 memory locations a+b, a-b, a+c and a-c.

Chapter 6
A little bit of math

So far the only mathematical operations we have discussed are integer addition and subtraction. With negation, addition, subtraction, multiplication and division it is possible to write some interesting programs. For now we will stick with integer arithmetic.

6.1 Negation

The **neg** instruction performs the two's complement of its operand, which can be either a general purpose register or a memory reference. You can precede a memory reference with a size specifier from the following table:

Specifier	Size in bytes
byte	1
word	2
dword	4
qword	8

The **neg** instruction sets the sign flag (**SF**) if the result is negative and the zero flag (**ZF**) if the result is 0, so it is possible to do conditional operations afterwards.

The following code snippet illustrates a few variations of **neg**:

```
neg     rax          ; negate the value in rax
neg     dword [x]    ; negate 4 byte int at x
neg     byte [x]     ; negate byte at x
```

6.2 Addition

Integer addition is performed using the **add** instruction. This instruction has 2 operands: a destination and a source. As is typical for the x86-64 instructions, the destination operand is first and the source operand is second. It adds the contents of the source and the destination and stores the result in the destination.

The source operand can be an immediate value (constant) of 32 bits, a memory reference or a register. The destination can be either a memory reference or a register. Only one of the operands may be a memory reference. This restriction to at most one memory operand is another typical pattern for the x86-64 instruction set.

The **add** instruction sets or clears several flags in the **rflags** register based on the results of the operation. These flags can be used in conditional statements following the **add**. The overflow flag (**OF**) is set if the addition overflows. The sign flag (**SF**) is set to the sign bit of the result. The zero flag (**ZF**) is set if the result is 0. Some other flags are set related to performing binary-coded-decimal arithmetic.

There is no special **add** for signed numbers versus unsigned numbers since the operations are the same. The same is true for subtraction, though there are special signed and unsigned instructions for division and multiplication.

There is a special increment instruction (**inc**), which can be used to add 1 to either a register or a memory location.

Below is a sample program with some **add** instructions. You can see that there is a breakpoint on line 7. After clicking the run button the program is stopped before it executes line 8. The two instructions on lines 8 and 9 are commonly used to create a "stack frame". Line 10 subtracks 32 from to leave space on the stack for 4 possible register parameters to be stored on the stack if a function needs to save its register parameters in memory. These 3 instructions are so common that there is a **leave** instruction which can undo the effect of them to prepare for returning from a function.

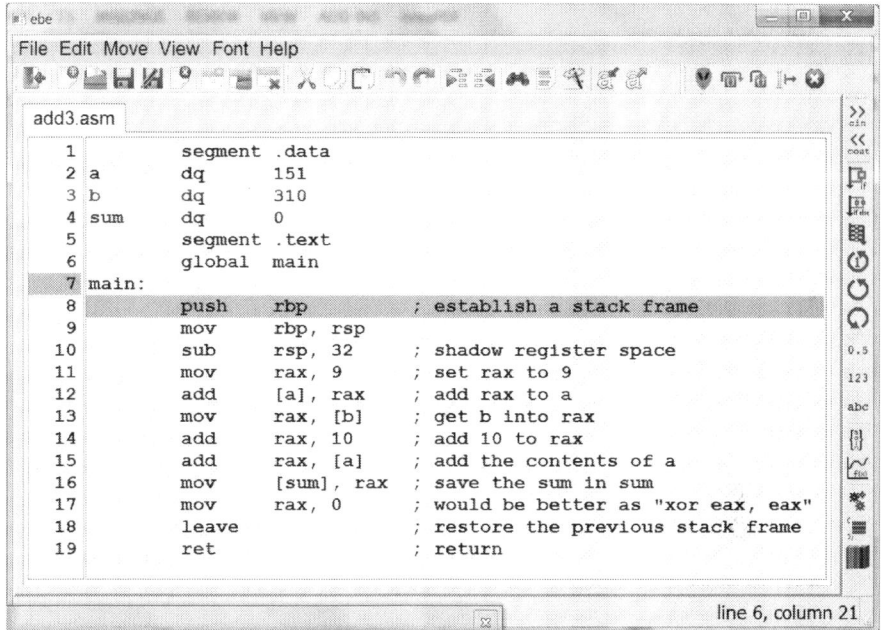

Next we see the registers and data for the program after executing lines 10 through 12.

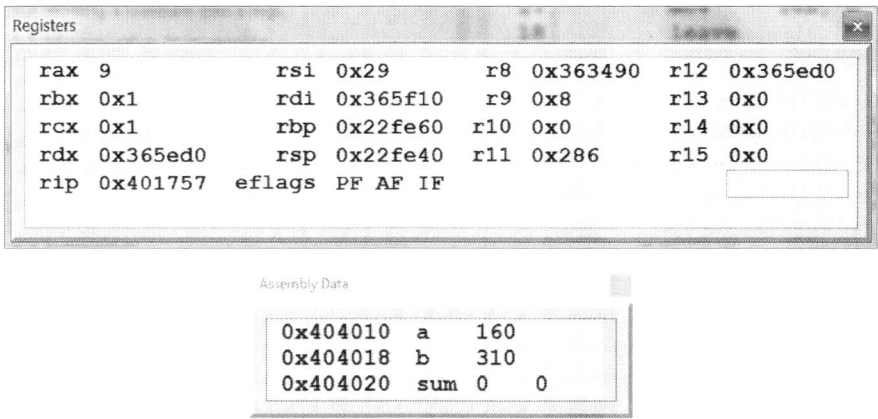

You can see that the sum computed on line 12 has been stored in memory in location **a**.

Below we see the registers and data after executing lines 13 through 16. This starts by moving **b** (310) into **rax**. Then it adds 10 to **rax** to get 320. After adding **a** (160) we get 480 which is stored in **sum**.

```
Registers
rax  480           rsi 0x29         r8  0x7d3490   r12 0x7d5ed0
rbx  0x1           rdi 0x7d5f10     r9  0x8        r13 0x0
rcx  0x1           rbp 0x22fe60     r10 0x0        r14 0x0
rdx  0x7d5ed0      rsp 0x22fe40     r11 0x286      r15 0x0
rip  0x401773      eflags IF
```

```
Assembly Data
0x404010   a    160
0x404018   b    310
0x404020   sum  480  0
```

6.3 Subtraction

Integer subtraction is performed using the **sub** instruction. This instruction has 2 operands: a destination and a source. It subtracts the contents of the source from the destination and stores the result in the destination.

The operand choices follow the same pattern as **add**. The source operand can be an immediate value (constant) of 32 bits, a memory reference or a register. The destination can be either a memory reference or a register. Only one of the operands can be a memory reference.

The **sub** instruction sets or clears the overflow flag (**OF**), the sign flag (**SF**), and the zero flag (**ZF**) like **add**. Some other flags are set related to performing binary-coded-decimal arithmetic.

As with addition there is no special subtract for signed numbers versus unsigned numbers.

There is a decrement instruction (**dec**) which can be used to decrement either a register or a value in memory.

Below is a program with some **sub** instructions. You can see that the program has a breakpoint on line 8 and that gdb has stopped execution just after establishing the stack frame. Near the end this program uses "**xor rax, rax**" as an alternative method for setting **rax** (the return value for the function) to 0. This instruction is a 3 byte instruction. The same result can be obtained using "**xor eax, eax**" using 2 bytes which can reduce memory usage. Both alternatives will execute in 1 cycle, but using fewer bytes may be faster due to using fewer bytes of instruction cache.

```
sub.asm
 1              segment .data
 2    a         dq      100
 3    b         dq      200
 4    diff      dq      0
 5              segment .text
 6              global  main
 7    main:
 8              push    rbp
 9              mov     rbp, rsp
10              sub     rsp, 32
11              mov     rax, 10
12              sub     [a], rax      ; subtract 10 from a
13              sub     [b], rax      ; subtract 10 from b
14              mov     rax, [b]      ; move b into rax
15              sub     rax, [a]      ; set rax to b-a
16              mov     [diff], rax   ; move the difference to diff
17              xor     rax, rax      ; was "mov    rax, 0"
18              leave
19              ret
```

line 3, column 20

The next two figures show the registers and data for the program after executing lines 11 through 13 which subtract 10 from memory locations **a** and **b**.

```
Registers
rax  10            rsi  0x28        r8   0x2e3490    r12  0x2e5ed0
rbx  0x1           rdi  0x2e5f10    r9   0x8         r13  0x0
rcx  0x1           rbp  0x22fe60    r10  0x0         r14  0x0
rdx  0x2e5ed0      rsp  0x22fe40    r11  0x286       r15  0x0
rip  0x40175f      eflags  PF AF IF
```

```
Assembly Data
0x404010   a      90
0x404018   b      190
0x404020   diff   0       0
```

Next we see the results of executing lines 14 through 16, which stores **b-a** in **diff**.

```
Registers
rax  100           rsi  0x28        r8   0x2e3490    r12  0x2e5ed0
rbx  0x1           rdi  0x2e5f10    r9   0x8         r13  0x0
rcx  0x1           rbp  0x22fe60    r10  0x0         r14  0x0
rdx  0x2e5ed0      rsp  0x22fe40    r11  0x286       r15  0x0
rip  0x401777      eflags  IF
```

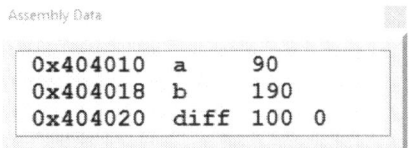

6.4 Multiplication

Multiplication of unsigned integers is performed using the `mul` instruction, while multiplication of signed integers is done using `imul`. The `mul` instruction is fairly simple, but we will skip it in favor of `imul`.

The `imul` instruction, unlike `add` and `sub`, has 3 different forms. One form has 1 operand (the source operand), a second has 2 operands (source and destination) and the third form has 3 operands (destination and 2 source operands).

One operand `imul`

The 1 operand version multiples the value in rax by the source operand and stores the result in **rdx:rax**. The source could be a register or a memory reference. The reason for using 2 registers is that multiplying two 64 bit integers yields a 128 bit result. Perhaps you are using large 64 bit integers and need all 128 bits of the product. Then you need this instruction. The low order bits of the answer are in **rax** and the high order bits are in **rdx**.

```
imul    qword [data] ; multiply rax by data
mov     [high], rdx  ; store top of product
mov     [low], rax   ; store bottom of product
```

Note that nasm requires the quad-word attribute for the source for the single operand version which uses memory. It issued a warning during testing, but did the correct operation.

Here is a sample program which uses the single operand version of `imul` to illustrate a product which requires both **rax** and **rdx**.

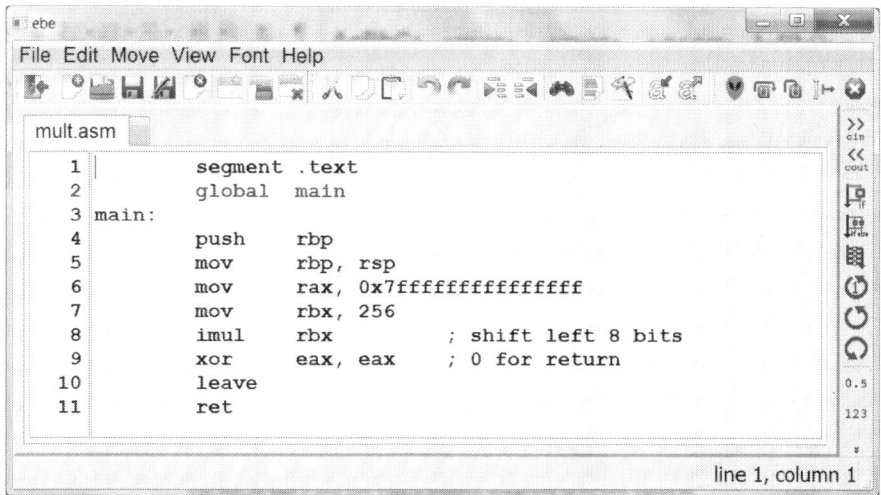

The `mov` in line 6 fills rax with a number composed of 63 bits equal to 1 and a 0 for the sign bit. This is the largest 64 bit signed integer, $2^{63} - 1$. The `imul` instruction in line 8 will multiply this large number by 256. Note that multiplying by a power of 2 is the same as shifting the bits to the left, in this case by 8 bits. This will cause the top 8 bits of `rax` to be placed in `rdx` and 8 zero bits will be introduced in the right of `rax`.

Here are the registers before `imul`:

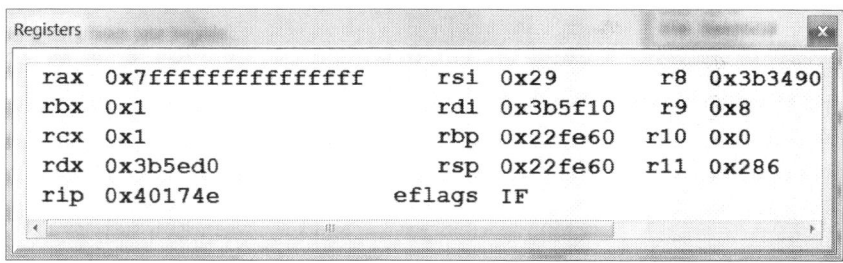

and then after `imul`:

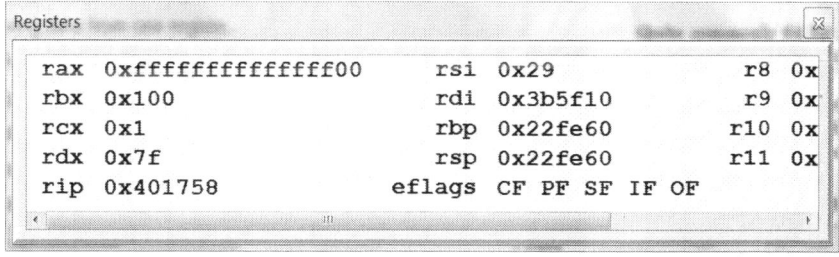

61

Two and three operand `imul`

Quite commonly 64 bit products are sufficient and either of the other forms will allow selecting any of the general purpose registers as the destination register.

The two-operand form allows specifying the source operand as a register, a memory reference or an immediate value. The source is multiplied times the destination register and the result is placed in the destination.

```
imul    rax, 100    ; multiply rax by 100
imul    r8, [x]     ; multiply r8 by x
imul    r9, r10     ; multiply r9 by r10
```

The three-operand form is the only form where the destination register is not one of the factors in the product. Instead the second operand, which is either a register or a memory reference, is multiplied by the third operand which must be an immediate value.

```
imul    rbx, [x], 100 ; store 100*x in rbx
imul    rdx, rbx, 50  ; store 50*rbx in rdx
```

The carry flag (CF) and the overflow flag (OF) are set when the product exceeds 64 bits (unless you explicitly request a smaller multiply). The zero flag and sign flags are undefined, so testing for a zero, positive or negative result requires an additional operation.

Testing for a Pythagorean triple

Below is shown a program which uses `imul`, `add` and `sub` to test whether 3 integers, a, b, and c, form a Pythagorean triple. If so, then $a^2 + b^2 = c^2$.

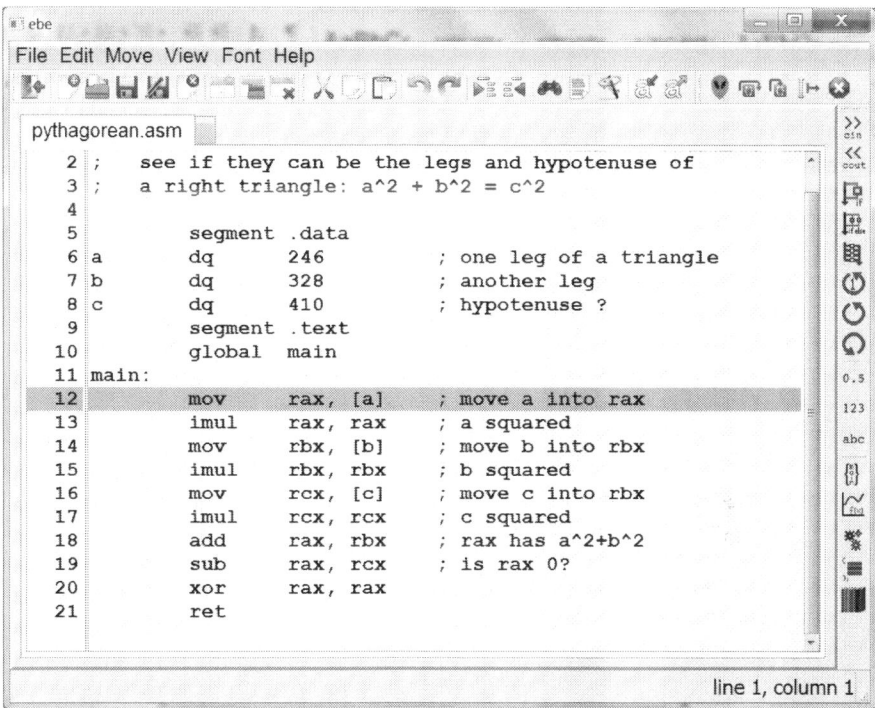

You can see that there is a breakpoint on line 12 and the next line to execute is 12. After clicking on "Next" line 12 will be executed and you can see that the value of `a` is placed in `rax`.

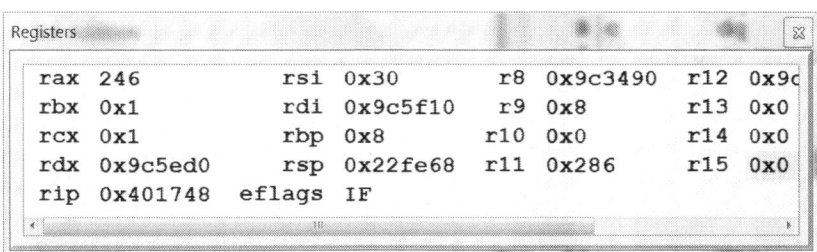

Next `rax` is multiplied by itself to get a^2 in `rax`.

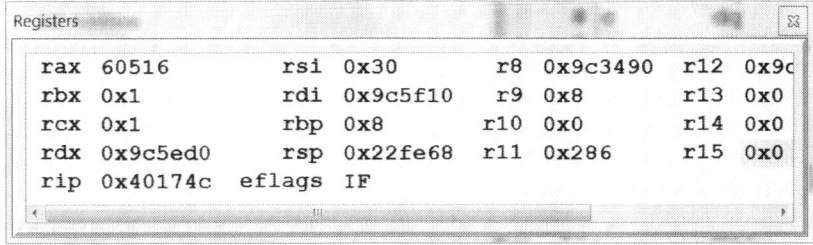

Line 14 moves the value of `b` into `rbx`.

```
Registers
rax  60516         rsi  0x30        r8  0x9c3490   r12 0x9c
rbx  328           rdi  0x9c5f10    r9  0x8        r13 0x0
rcx  0x1           rbp  0x8         r10 0x0        r14 0x0
rdx  0x9c5ed0      rsp  0x22fe68    r11 0x286      r15 0x0
rip  0x401754      eflags  IF
```

Then **rbx** is multiplied by itself to get b^2 in **rbx**.

```
Registers
rax  60516         rsi  0x30        r8  0x9c3490   r12 0x9c
rbx  107584        rdi  0x9c5f10    r9  0x8        r13 0x0
rcx  0x1           rbp  0x8         r10 0x0        r14 0x0
rdx  0x9c5ed0      rsp  0x22fe68    r11 0x286      r15 0x0
rip  0x401758      eflags  IF
```

Line 16 moves the value of **c** into **rcx**.

```
Registers
rax  60516         rsi  0x30        r8  0x9c3490   r12 0x9c
rbx  107584        rdi  0x9c5f10    r9  0x8        r13 0x0
rcx  410           rbp  0x8         r10 0x0        r14 0x0
rdx  0x9c5ed0      rsp  0x22fe68    r11 0x286      r15 0x0
rip  0x401760      eflags  IF
```

Then **rcx** is multiplied by itself to get c^2 in **rcx**.

```
Registers
rax  60516         rsi  0x30        r8  0x9c3490   r12 0x9c
rbx  107584        rdi  0x9c5f10    r9  0x8        r13 0x0
rcx  168100        rbp  0x8         r10 0x0        r14 0x0
rdx  0x9c5ed0      rsp  0x22fe68    r11 0x286      r15 0x0
rip  0x401764      eflags  IF
```

Line 18 adds **rbx** to **rax** so **rax** holds $a^2 + b^2$.

```
Registers
rax  168100        rsi  0x30        r8  0x9c3490   r12 0x9c
rbx  107584        rdi  0x9c5f10    r9  0x8        r13 0x0
rcx  168100        rbp  0x8         r10 0x0        r14 0x0
rdx  0x9c5ed0      rsp  0x22fe68    r11 0x286      r15 0x0
rip  0x401767      eflags  IF
```

Finally line 19 subtracts **rcx** from **rax**. After this **rax** holds $a^2 + b^2 - c^2$. If the 3 numbers form a Pythagorean triple then **rax** must be 0. You can see that **rax** is 0 and also that the zero flag (ZF) is set in **eflags**.

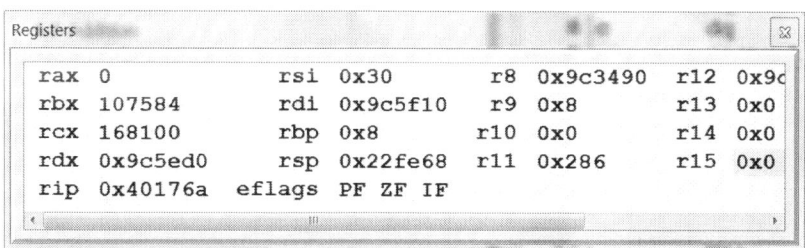

If we used a few more instructions we could test to see if **ZF** were set and print a success message.

6.5 Division

Division is different from the other mathematics operations in that it returns 2 results: a quotient and a remainder. The **idiv** instruction behaves a little like the inverse of the single operand **imul** instruction in that it uses **rdx:rax** for the 128 bit dividend.

The **idiv** instruction uses a single source operand which can be either a register or a memory reference. The unsigned division instruction **div** operates similarly on unsigned numbers. The dividend is the two registers **rdx** and **rax** with **rdx** holding the most significant bits. The quotient is stored in **rax** and the remainder is stored in **rdx**.

The **idiv** instruction does not set any status flags, so testing the results must be done separately.

Below is a program which illustrates the **idiv** instruction. You can see that a breakpoint was placed on line 8 and the program was started using the "Run" button.

```
  idiv.asm
   1              segment .data
   2  x           dq       325        ; dividend
   3  y           dq       16         ; divisor
   4  quot        dq       0          ; quotient
   5  rem         dq       0          ; remainder
   6              segment .text
   7              global  main
   8  main:
   9              mov      rax, [x]   ; move a into rax
  10              mov      rdx, 0     ; rdx:rax is dividend
  11              idiv     qword [y]  ; divide x by y
  12              mov      [quot], rax ; save the quotient
  13              mov      [rem], rdx  ; save the remainder
  14              xor      rax, rax
  15              ret
```

line 8, column 6

Next we see the registers after loading **x** into **rax** and zeroing out **rdx**.

```
Registers
  rax  325            rsi  0x29         r8  0x3c3490    r12  0x3c
  rbx  1              rdi  0x3c5f10     r9  0x8         r13  0x0
  rcx  1              rbp  0x8          r10 0x0         r14  0x0
  rdx  0              rsp  0x22fe68     r11 0x286       r15  0x0
  rip  0x40174f       eflags IF
```

The next display shows the changes to **rax** and **rdx** from executing the **idiv** instruction. The quotient is 20 and the remainder is 5 since $325 = 20 * 16 + 5$.

```
Registers
  rax  20             rsi  0x29         r8  0x3c3490    r12  0x3c
  rbx  1              rdi  0x3c5f10     r9  0x8         r13  0x0
  rcx  1              rbp  0x8          r10 0x0         r14  0x0
  rdx  5              rsp  0x22fe68     r11 0x286       r15  0x0
  rip  0x401757       eflags IF
```

The final display shows the variables after executing lines 12 and 13.

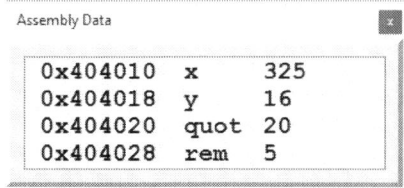

```
Assembly Data
  0x404010   x      325
  0x404018   y      16
  0x404020   quot   20
  0x404028   rem    5
```

66

6.6 Conditional move instructions

There are a collection of conditional move instructions which can be used profitably rather than using branching. Branching causes the CPU to perform branch prediction which will be correct sometimes and incorrect other times. Incorrect predictions slow down the CPU dramatically by interrupting the instruction pipeline, so it is worthwhile to learn to use conditional move instructions to avoid branching in simple cases.

The conditional move instructions have operands much like the `mov` instruction. There are a variety of them which all have the same 2 operands as `mov`, except that there is no provision for immediate operands.

instruction	effect
cmovz	move if result was zero
cmovnz	move if result was not zero
cmovl	move if result was negative
cmovle	move if result was negative or zero
cmovg	move if result was positive
cmovge	move if result was positive or zero

There are lot more symbolic patterns which have essentially the same meaning, but these are an adequate collection. These all operate by testing for combinations of the sign flag (`SF`) and the zero flag (`ZF`).

The following code snippet converts the value in rax to its absolute value:

```
mov     rbx, rax    ; save original value
neg     rax         ; negate rax
cmovl   rax, rbx    ; replace rax if negative
```

The code below loads a number from memory, subtracts 100 and replaces the difference with 0 if the difference is negative:

```
mov     rbx, 0      ; set rbx to 0
mov     rax, [x]    ; get x from memory
sub     rax, 100    ; subtract 100 from x
cmovl   rax, rbx    ; set rax to 0 if x-100 < 0
```

6.7 Why move to a register?

Both the `add` and `sub` instructions can operate on values stored in memory. Alternatively you could explicitly move the value into a register, perform the operation and then move the result back to the memory location. In this case it is 1 instruction versus 3. It seems obvious that 1 instruction is better.

Now if the value from memory is used in more than 1 operation, it might be faster to move it into a register first. This is a simple optimization which is fairly natural. It has the disadvantage of requiring the programmer to keep track of which variables are in which registers. If this code is not going to be executed billions of times, then the time required will probably not matter. In that case don't overwhelm yourself with optimization tricks. Also if the 2 uses are more than a few instructions apart, then keep it simple.

Exercises

1. Write an assembly language program to compute the distance squared between 2 points in the plane identified as 2 integer coordinates each, stored in memory.

   Remember the Pythagorean Theorem!

2. If we could do floating point division, this exercise would have you compute the slope of the line segment connecting 2 points. Instead you are to store the difference in x coordinates in 1 memory location and the difference in y coordinates in another. The input points are integers stored in memory. Leave register **rax** with the value 1 if the line segment is vertical (infinite or undefined slope) and 0 if it is not. You should use a conditional move to set the value of **rax**.

3. Write an assembly language program to compute the average of 4 grades. Use memory locations for the 4 grades. Make the grades all different numbers from 0 to 100. Store the average of the 4 grades in memory and also store the remainder from the division in memory.

Chapter 7
Bit operations

A computer is a machine to process bits. So far we have discussed using bits to represent numbers. In this chapter we will learn about a handful of computer instructions which operate on bits without any implied meaning for the bits like signed or unsigned integers.

Individual bits have the values 0 and 1 and are frequently interpreted as false for 0 and true for 1. Individual bits could have other interpretations. A bit might mean male or female or any assignment of an entity to one of 2 mutually exclusive sets. A bit could represent an individual cell in Conway's game of Life.

Sometimes data occurs as numbers with limited range. Suppose you need to process billions of numbers in the range of 0 to 15. Then each number could be stored in 4 bits. Is it worth the trouble to store your numbers in 4 bits when 8 bit bytes are readily available in a language like C++? Perhaps not if you have access to a machine with sufficient memory. Still it might be nice to store the numbers on disk in half the space. So you might need to operate on bit fields.

7.1 Not operation

The not operation is a unary operation, meaning that it has only 1 operand. The everyday interpretation of not is the opposite of a logical statement. In assembly language we apply not to all the bits of a word. C has two versions of not, "!" and "~". "!" is used for the opposite of a true or false value, while "~" applies to all the bits of a word. It is common to distinguish the two nots by referring to "!" as the "logical" not and "~" as the "bit-wise" not. We will use "~" since the assembly language `not` instruction inverts each bit of a word. Here are some examples, illustrating the meaning of not (pretending the length of each value is as shown).

```
~00001111b == 11110000b
~10101010b == 01010101b
~0xff00    == 0x00ff
```

The not instruction has a single operand which serves as both the source and the destination. It can be applied to bytes, words, double words and quad-words in registers or in memory. Here is a code snippet illustrating its use.

```
mov     rax, 0
not     rax             ; rax == 0xffffffffffffffff
mov     rdx, 0          ; preparing for divide
mov     rbx, 15         ; will divide by 15 (0xf)
div     rbx             ; unsigned divide
                        ; rax == 0x1111111111111111
not     rax             ; rax == 0xeeeeeeeeeeeeeeee
```

Let's assume that you need to manage a set of 64 items. You can associate each possible member of the set with 1 bit of a quad-word. Using not will give you the complement of the set.

7.2 And operation

The and operation is also applied in programming in 2 contexts. First it is common to test for both of 2 conditions being true - && in C. Secondly you can do an and operation of each pair of bits in 2 variables - & in C. We will stick with the single & notation, since the assembly language and instruction matches the C bit-wise and operation.

Here is a truth table for the and operation:

&	0	1
0	0	0
1	0	1

Applied to some bit fields we get:

```
11001100b & 00001111b == 00001100b
11001100b & 11110000b == 11000000b
0xabcdefab & 0xff == 0xab
0x0123456789 & 0xff00ff00ff == 0x0100450089
```

You might notice that the examples illustrate using & as a bit field selector. Wherever the right operand has a 1 bit, the operation selected that bit from the left operand. You could say the same thing about the left operand, but in these examples the right operand has more obvious "masks" used to select bits.

Below is a code snippet illustrating the use of the **and** instruction:

```
mov     rax, 0x12345678
mov     rbx, rax
and     rbx, 0xf        ; rbx has nibble 0x8
mov     rdx, 0          ; prepare to divide
mov     rcx, 16         ; by 16
idiv    rcx             ; rax has 0x1234567
and     rax, 0xf        ; rax has nibble 0x7
```

It is a little sad to use a divide just to shift the number 4 bits to the right, but shift operations have not been discussed yet.

Using sets of 64 items you can use **and** to form the intersection of 2 sets. Also you can use **and** and **not** to form the difference of 2 sets, since $A - B = A \cap \bar{B}$.

7.3 Or operation

The or operation is the final bit operation with logical and bit-wise meanings. First it is common to test for either (or both) of 2 conditions being true - || in C. Secondly you can do an **or** operation of each pair of bits in 2 variables - | in C. We will stick with the single | notation, since the assembly language **or** instruction matches the bit-wise or operation.

You need to be aware that the "or" of everyday speech is commonly used to mean 1 or the other but not both. When someone asks you if you want of cup of "decaf" or "regular", you probably should not answer "Yes". The "or" of programming means one or the other or both.

Here is a truth table for the or operation:

|	0	1
0	0	1
1	1	1

Applied to some bit fields we get:

```
11001100b  | 00001111b  == 11001111b
11001100b  | 11110000b  == 11111100b
0xabcdefab | 0xff       == 0xabcdefff
0x0123456789 | 0xff00ff00ff == 0xff23ff67ff
```

You might notice that the examples illustrate using | as a bit setter. Wherever the right operand has a 1 bit, the operation sets the corresponding bit of the left operand. Again, since or is commutative, we could say the same thing about the left operand, but the right operands have more obvious masks.

Here is a code snippet using the `or` instruction to set some bits:

```
mov     rax, 0x1000
or      rax, 1          ; make the number odd
or      rax, 0xff00     ; set bits 15-8 to 1
```

Using sets of 64 items you can use `or` to form the union of 2 sets.

7.4 Exclusive or operation

The final bit-wise operation is exclusive-or. This operation matches the everyday concept of one or the other but not both. The C exclusive-or operator is "^".

Here is a truth table for the exclusive-or operation:

^	0	1
0	0	1
1	1	0

From examining the truth table you can see that exclusive-or could also be called "not equals". In my terminology exclusive-or is a "bit-flipper". Consider the right operand as a mask which selects which bits to flip in the left operand. Consider these examples:

```
00010001b ^ 00000001b == 00010000b
01010101b ^ 11111111b == 10101010b
01110111b ^ 00001111b == 01111000b
0xaaaaaaaa ^ 0xffffffff == 0x55555555
0x12345678 ^ 0x12345678 == 0x00000000
```

The x86-64 exclusive-or instruction is named `xor`. The most common use of `xor` is as an idiom for setting a register to 0. This is done because moving 0 into a register requires 7 bytes for a 64 bit register, while `xor` requires 3 bytes. You can get the same result using the 32 bit version of the intended register which requires only 2 bytes for the instruction.

Observe some uses of `xor`:

```
mov     rax, 0x1234567812345678
xor     eax, eax            ; set to 0
mov     rax, 0x1234
xor     rax, 0xf            ; change to 0x123b
```

You can use `xor` to form the symmetric difference of 2 sets. The symmetric difference of 2 sets are the elements which are in one of the 2 sets but not both. If you don't like exclusive-or, another way to compute this would be using $A \Delta B = (A \cup B) \cap \overline{A \cap B}$. Surely you like exclusive-or.

7.5 Shift operations

In the code example for the **and** instruction I divided by 16 to achieve the effect of converting `0x12345678` into `0x1234567`. This effect could have been obtained more simply by shifting the register's contents to the right 4 bits. Shifting is an excellent tool for extracting bit fields and for building values with bit fields.

In the x86-64 architecture there are 4 varieties of shift instructions: shift left (`shl`), shift arithmetic left (`sal`), shift right (`shr`), and shift arithmetic right (`sar`). The `shl` and `sal` shift left instructions are actually the same instruction. The `sar` instruction propagates the sign bit into the newly vacated positions on the left which preserves the sign of the number, while `shr` introduces 0 bits from the left.

Here we see the effect of shifting right 3 bits. Note that 0 is being placed into position 15, so this matches `shr` rather than `sar`.

15															0
1	0	1	0	1	1	0	0	1	0	1	1	0	1	1	0
0	1	0	1	0	1	1	0	0	1	0	1	1	0	1	1
0	0	1	0	1	0	1	1	0	0	1	0	1	1	0	1
0	0	0	1	0	1	0	1	1	0	0	1	0	1	1	0

There are 2 operands for a shift instruction. The first operand is the register or memory location to shift and the second is the number of bits to shift. The number to shift can be 8, 16, 32 or 64 bits in length. The number of bits can be an immediate value or the `cl` register. There are no other choices for the number of bits to shift.

C contains a shift left operator (<<) and a shift right operator (>>). The decision of logical or arithmetic shift right in C depends on the data type being shifted. Shifting a signed integer right uses an arithmetic shift.

Here are some examples of shifting:

```
10101010b >> 2 == 00101010b
10011001b << 4 == 100110010000b
0x12345678 >> 4 == 0x01234567
0x1234567 << 4 == 0x12345670
0xabcd >> 8 == 0x00ab
```

To extract a bit field from a word, you first shift the word right until the right most bit of the field is in the least significant bit position (bit 0) and then "and" the word with a value having a string of 1 bits in bit 0 through n-1 where n is the number of bits in the field to extract. For example to extract bits 4-7, shift right four bits, and then and with `0xf`.

To place some bits into position, you first need to clear the bits and then "or" the new field into the value. The first step is to build the mask with the proper number of 1's for the field width starting at bit 0. Then shift the mask left to align the mask with the value to hold the new field. Negate the mask to form an inverted mask. And the value with the inverted mask to clear out the bits. Then shift the new value left the proper number of bits and or this with the value.

Now consider the following program which extracts a bit field and then replaces a bit field.

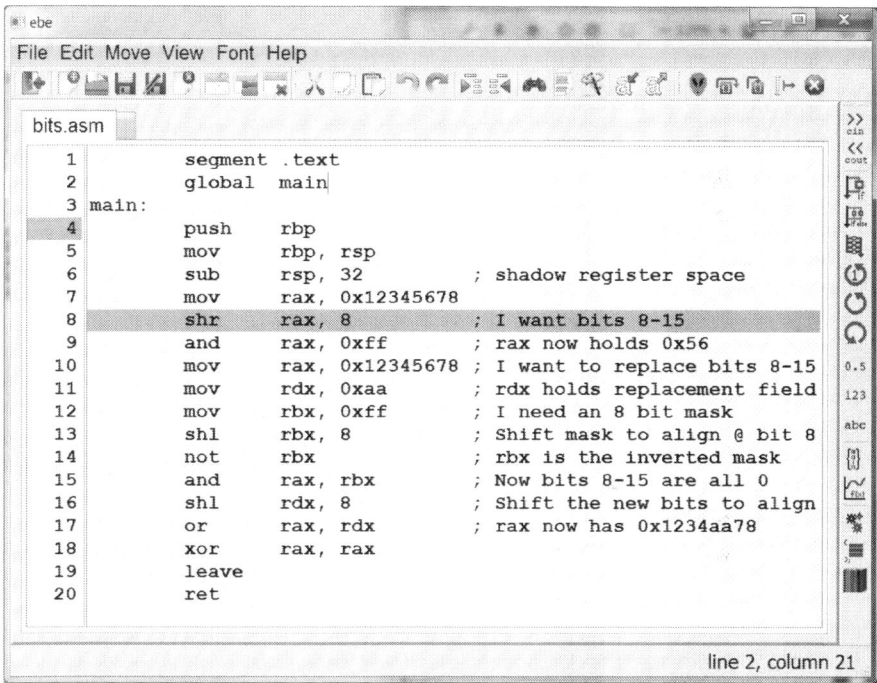

The program was started with a breakpoint on line 4 and I used "Next" until line 7 was executed which placed 0x12345678 into rax.

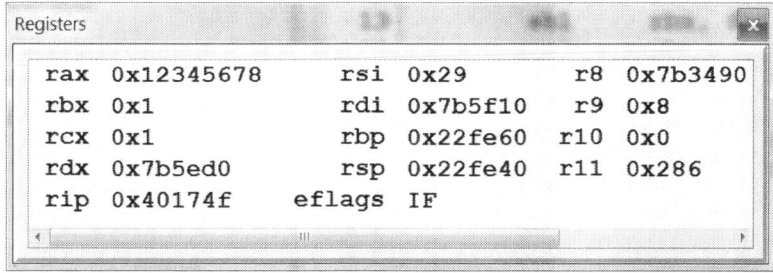

The first goal is to extract bits 8-15. We start by shifting right 8 bits. This leave the target bits in bits 0-7 of rax.

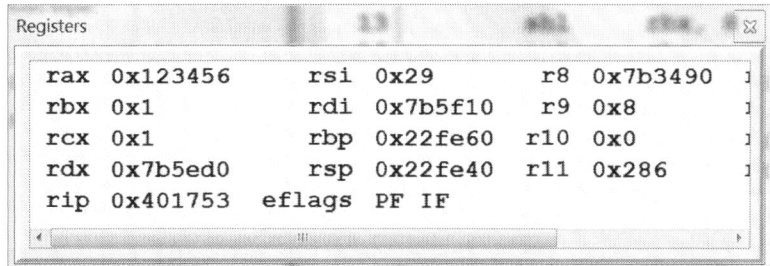

Next we must get rid of bits 8-63. The easiest way to do this is to **and** with `0xff`.

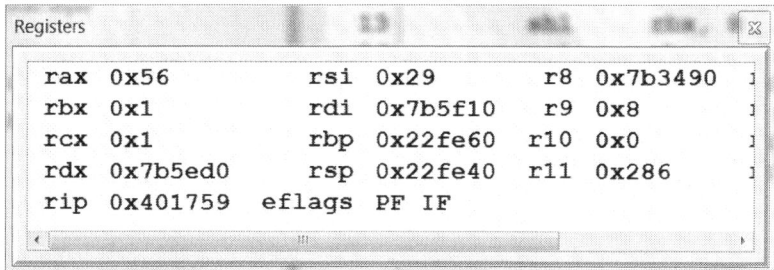

The next goal is to replace bits 8-15 of `0x12345678` with `0xaa` yielding `0x1234aa78`. We start by moving `0x12345678` into `rax`.

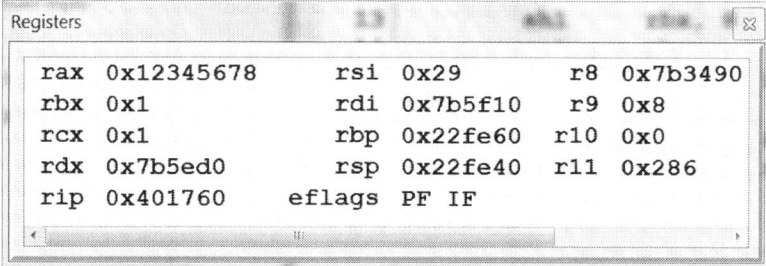

The second step is to get the value `0xaa` into `rdx`.

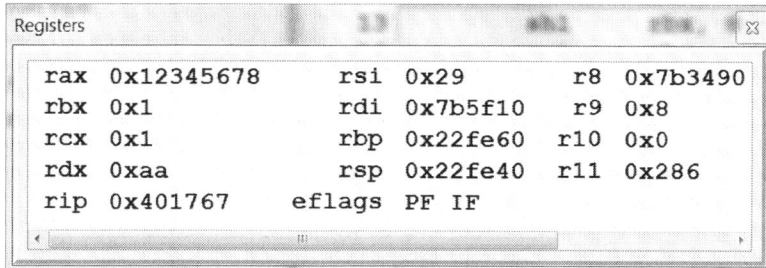

We need a mask to clear out bits 8-15. We start building the mask by placing `0xff` into `rbx`.

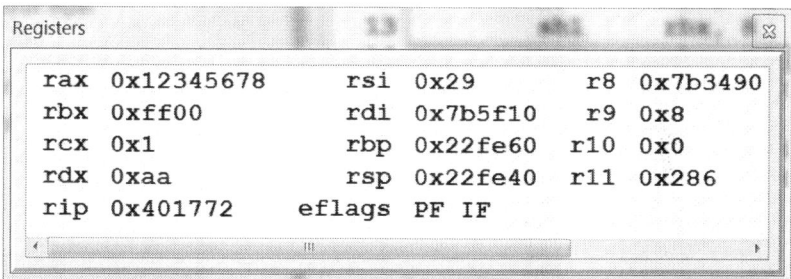

Then we shift **rbx** left 8 positions to align the mask with bits 8-15. We could have started with `0xff00`.

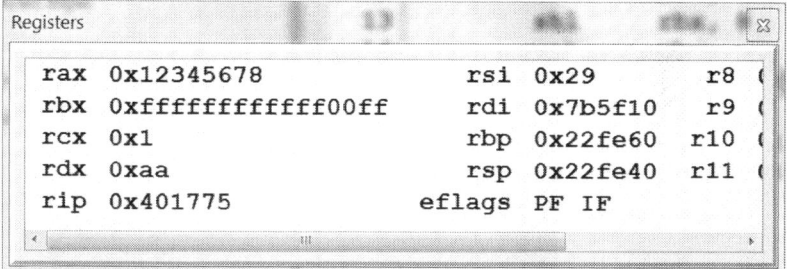

The final preparation of the mask is to complement all the bits with **not**. We could have started with `0xffffffffffff00ff`, but that would require some counting and is not as generally useful.

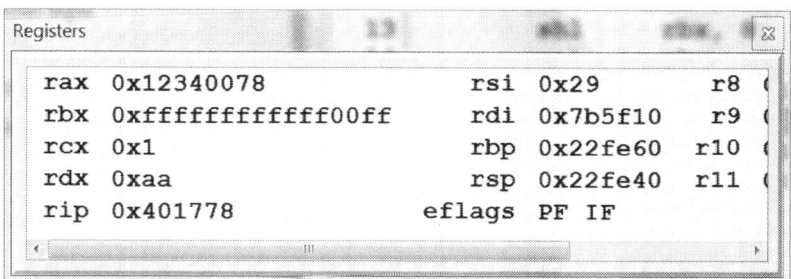

Using **and** as a bit selector we select each bit of **rax** which has a corresponding 1 bit in **rbx**.

Now we can shift `0xaa` left 8 positions to align with bits 8-15.

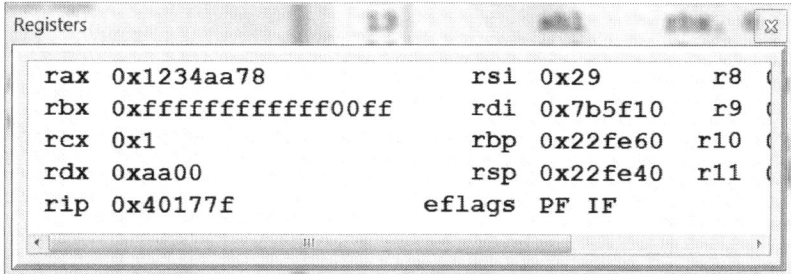

Having cleared out bits 8-15 of `rax`, we now complete the task by or'ing `rax` and `rdx`.

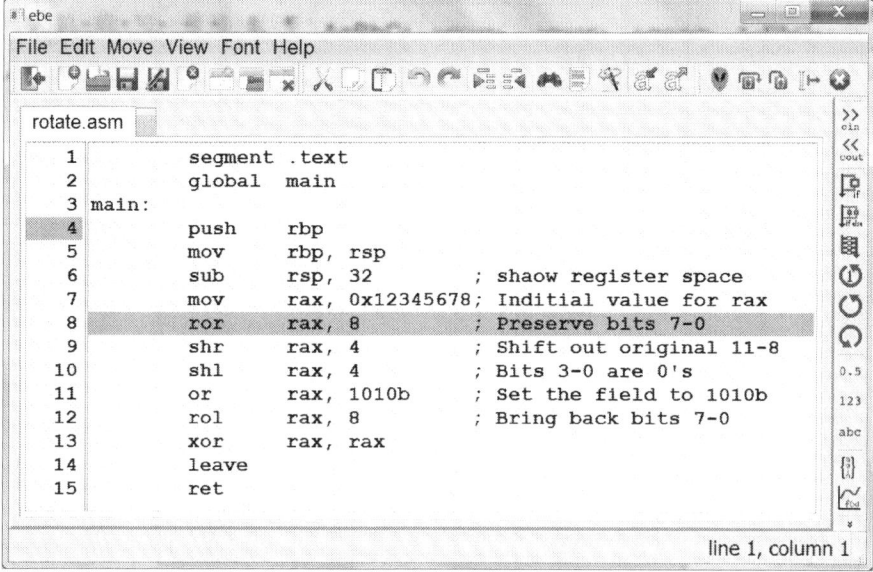

The x86-64 instruction set also includes rotate left (`rol`) and rotate right (`ror`) instructions. These could be used to shift particular parts of a bit string into proper position for testing while preserving the bits. After rotating the proper number of bits in the opposite direction, the original bit string will be left in the register or memory location.

The rotate instructions offer a nice way to clear out some bits. The code below clears out bits 11-8 of `rax` and replaces these bits with `1010b`.

```
1          segment .text
2          global  main
3  main:
4          push    rbp
5          mov     rbp, rsp
6          sub     rsp, 32         ; shaow register space
7          mov     rax, 0x12345678 ; Inditial value for rax
8          ror     rax, 8          ; Preserve bits 7-0
9          shr     rax, 4          ; Shift out original 11-8
10         shl     rax, 4          ; Bits 3-0 are 0's
11         or      rax, 1010b      ; Set the field to 1010b
12         rol     rax, 8          ; Bring back bits 7-0
13         xor     rax, rax
14         leave
15         ret
```

Observe that a breakpoint has been placed on line 4 and the program run and stepped to line 8. In the register display below we see that 0x12345678 has been placed in rax.

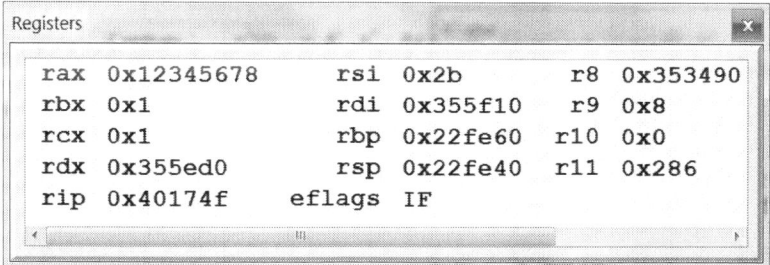

Executing the rotate instruction on line 7 moves the 0x78 byte in rax to the upper part of the register.

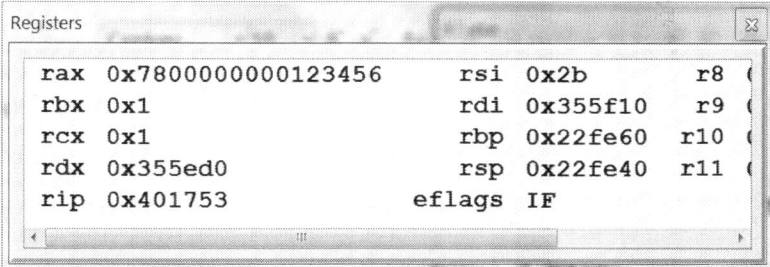

Next the shift instruction on line 8 wipes out bits 3-0 (original 11-8).

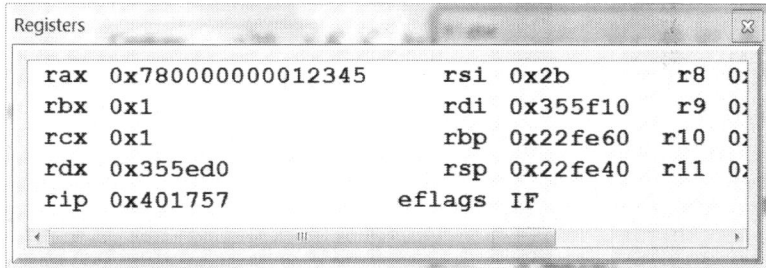

The shift instruction on line 9 introduces four 0 bits into rax.

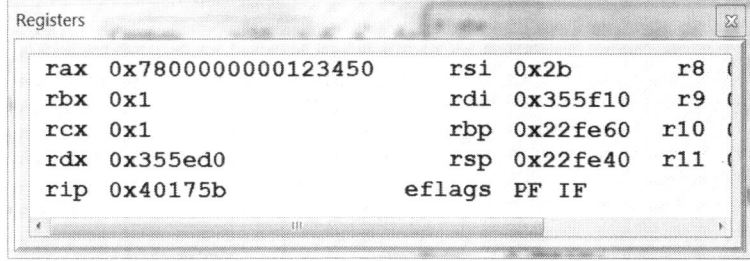

Now the or instruction at line 10 places 1010b into bits 3-0.

79

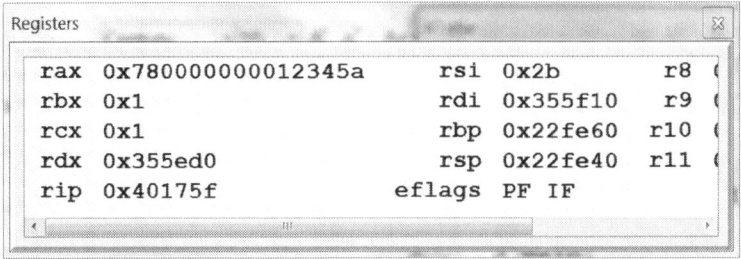

Finally the rotate left instruction at line 11 realigns all the bits as they were originally.

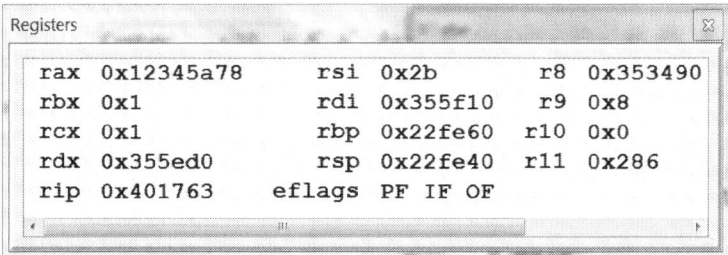

Interestingly C provides shift left (<<) and shift right (>>) operations, but does not provide a rotate operation. So a program which does a large amount of bit field manipulations might be better done in assembly. On the other hand a C struct can have bit fields in it and thus the compiler can possibly use rotate instructions with explicit bit fields.

7.6 Bit testing and setting

It takes several instructions to extract or insert a bit field. Sometimes you need to extract or insert a single bit. This can be done using masking and shifting as just illustrated. However it can be simpler and quicker to use the bit test instruction (**bt**) and either the bit test and set instruction (**bts**) or the bit test and reset instruction (**btr**).

The **bt** instruction has 2 operands. The first operand is a 16, 32 or 64 bit word in memory or a register which contains the bit to test. The second operand is the bit number from 0 to the number of bits minus 1 for the word size which is either an immediate value or a value in a register. The **bt** instructions set the carry flag (**CF**) to the value of the bit being tested.

The **bts** and **btr** instructions operate somewhat similarly. Both instructions test the current bit in the same fashion as **bt**. They differ in that **bts** sets the bit to 1 and **btr** resets (or clears) the bit to 0.

One particular possibility for using these instructions is to implement a set of fairly large size where the members of the set are integers from 0

80

to $n - 1$ where n is the universe size. A membership test translates into determining a word and bit number in memory and testing the correct bit in the word. Following the **bt** instruction the **setc** instruction can be used to store the value of the carry flag into an 8 bit register. There are **setCC** instructions for each of the condition flags in the **eflags** register. Insertion into the set translates into determining the word and bit number and using **bts** to set the correct bit. Removal of an element of the set translates into using **btr** to clear the correct bit in memory.

In the code below we assume that the memory for the set is at a memory location named **set** and that the bit number to work on is in register **rax**. The code preserves **rax** and performs testing, insertion and removal.

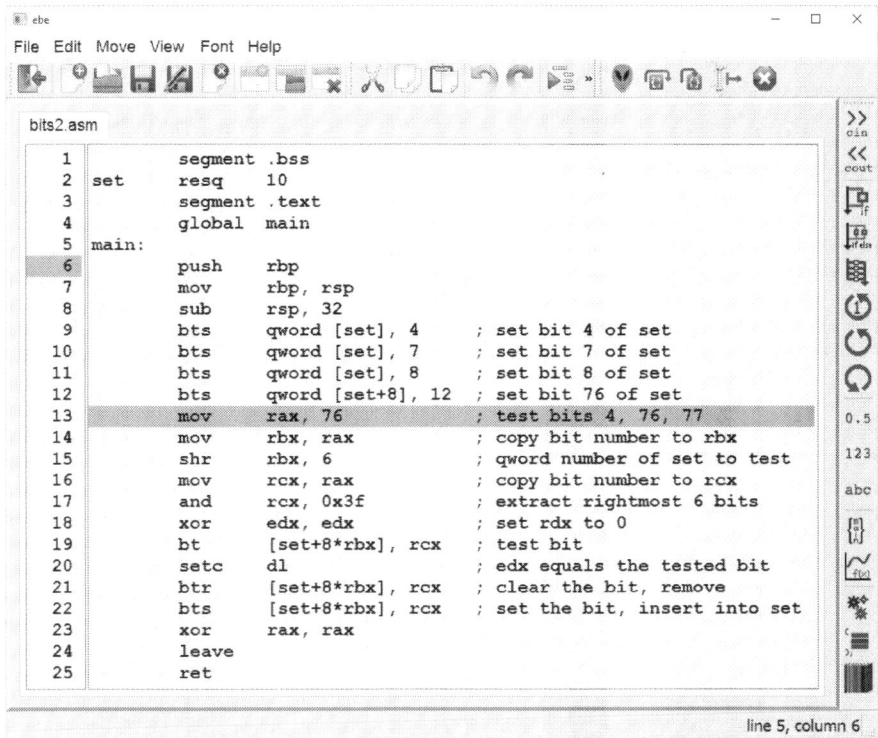

Lines 9 through 12 set bits 4, 7, 8 and 76 in the array **set**. To set bit 76, we use **[set+8]** in the instruction to reference the second quad-word of the array. You will also notice the use of **set+8*rbx** in lines 18, 20 and 21. Previously we have used a variable name in brackets. Now we are using a variable name plus a constant or plus a register times 8. The use of a register times 8 allows indexing an array of 8 byte quantities. The instruction format includes options for multiplying an index register by 2, 4 or 8 to be added to the address specified by **set**. Use 2 for a word array,

4 for a double word array and 8 for a quad-word array. Register **rbx** holds the quad-word index into the **set** array.

Operating on the quad-word of the set in memory as opposed to moving to a register is likely to be the fastest choice, since in real code we will not need to test, insert and then remove in 1 function call. We would do only one of these operations.

Here we trace through the execution of this program. We start by observing the **set** array in hexadecimal after setting 4, 7, 8 and 76. Setting bit 4 yields **0x10**, setting bit 7 yields **0x90** and setting bit 8 yields **0x190**. Bit 76 is bit 12 of the second quad-word in the array and yields **0x1000**.

```
Assembly Data
0x408280   set   190  1000  00  00
                 00   00    00  00
                 00   00    00  00
                 00   00
```

Next lines 13 and 14 move 76 into **rax** and **rbx**.

```
Registers
rax  76             rsi  0x2a       r8   0x3e34c0
rbx  76             rdi  0x3e5f70   r9   0x8
rcx  0x1            rbp  0x22fe60   r10  0x0
rdx  0x3e5f30       rsp  0x22fe40   r11  0x286
rip  0x40177a       eflags  IF
```

Shifting the bit number (76) right 6 bits will yield the quad-word number of the array. This works since $2^6 = 64$ and quad-words hold 64 bits. This shift leaves a 1 in **rbx**.

```
Registers
rax  76             rsi  0x2a       r8   0x3e34c0
rbx  1              rdi  0x3e5f70   r9   0x8
rcx  0x1            rbp  0x22fe60   r10  0x0
rdx  0x3e5f30       rsp  0x22fe40   r11  0x286
rip  0x40177e       eflags  IF
```

We make another copy of the bit number in **rcx**.

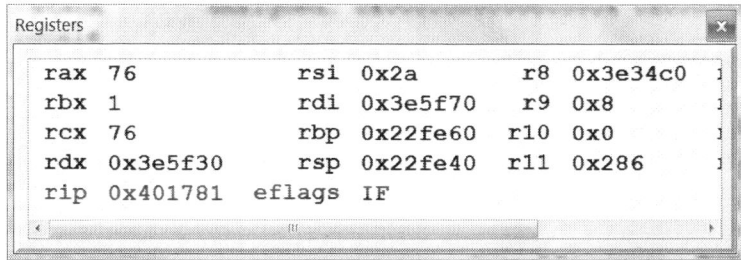

The bit number and'ed with `0x3f` will extract the rightmost 6 bits of the bit number. This will be the bit number of the quad-word containing the bit.

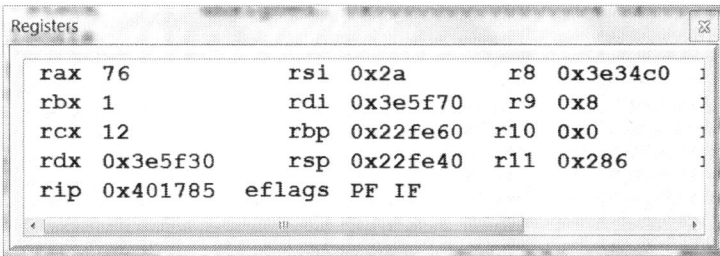

Next we use **xor** to zero out **rdx**.

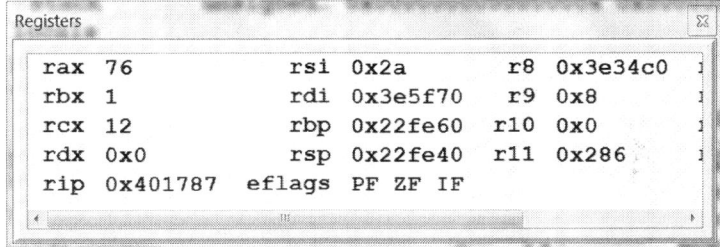

Line 19 tests the bit we wish to test from the array. You will notice that the carry flag (**CF**) is set.

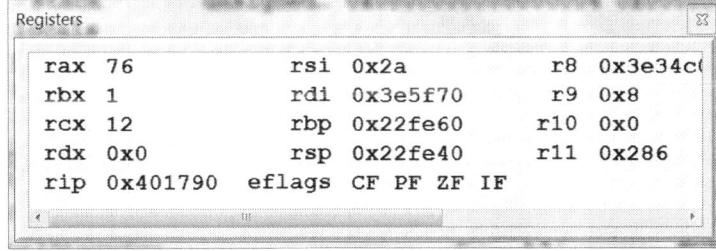

Line 20 uses the **setc** instruction to set **dl** which is now a 1 since 76 was in the set.

83

```
Registers
rax   76            rsi  0x2a           r8   0x3e34c(
rbx   1             rdi  0x3e5f70       r9   0x8
rcx   12            rbp  0x22fe60       r10  0x0
rdx   1             rsp  0x22fe40       r11  0x286
rip   0x401793      eflags  CF PF ZF IF
```

Line 21 clears (resets) the bit in the set, effectively removing 76 from the set.

```
Assembly Data
0x408280   set   190   00   00   00
                 00    00   00   00
                 00    00   00   00
                 00    00
```

Line 22 sets bit 76 again, restoring it to the set.

```
Assembly Data
0x408280   set   190   1000   00   00
                 00    00     00   00
                 00    00     00   00
                 00    00
```

7.7 Extracting and filling a bit field

To extract a bit field you need to shift the field so that its least significant bit is in position 0 and then bit mask the field with an **and** operation with the appropriate mask. Let's suppose we need to extract bits 51-23 from a quad-word stored in a memory location. Then, after loading the quad-word, we need to shift it right 23 bits to get the least significant bit into the proper position. The bit field is of length 29. The simplest way to get a proper mask (29 bits all 1) is using the value `0x1fffffff`. Seven **f**'s is 28 bits and the 1 gives a total of 29 bits. Here is the code to do the work:

```
        mov    rax, [sample]       ; move qword into rax
        shr    rax, 23             ; align bit 23 at 0
        and    rax, 0x1fffffff     ; select 29 low bits
        mov    [field], rax        ; save the field
```

Of course it could be that the field width is not a constant. In that case you need an alternative. One possibility is to generate a string of 1 bits based on knowing that $2^n - 1$ is a string of n 1 bits. You can generate 2^n by shifting 1 to the left n times or use **bts**. Then you can subtract 1 using **dec**.

Another way to extract a bit field is to first shift left enough bits to clear out the bits to the left of the field and then shift right enough bits to wipe out the bits to the right of the field. This will be simpler when the field position and width are variable. To extract bits 51-23, we start by shifting left 12 bits. Then we need to shift right 35 bits. In general if the field is bits m through n where m is the higher bit number, we shift left $63 - m$ and then shift right $n + (63 - m)$.

```
mov     rax, [sample]   ; move qword into rax
shl     rax, 12         ; wipe out higher bits
shr     rax, 35         ; align the bit field
mov     [field], rax    ; save the field
```

Now suppose we wish to fill in bits 51-23 of **sample** with the bits in **field**. The easy method is to rotate the value to align the field, shift right and then left to clear 29 bits, or in the field, and then rotate the register to get the field back into bits 23-51. Here is the code:

```
mov     rax, [sample]   ; move qword into rax
ror     rax, 23         ; align bit 23 at 0
shr     rax, 29         ; wipe out 29 bits
shl     rax, 29         ; align bits again
or      rax, [field]    ; trust field is 29 bits
rol     rax, 23         ; realign the bit fields
mov     [sample], rax   ; store fields in memory
```

Exercises

1. Write an assembly program to count all the 1 bits in a byte stored in memory. Use repeated code rather than a loop.

2. Write an assembly program to swap 2 quad-words in memory using **xor**. Use the following algorithm:

   ```
   a = a ^ b
   b = a ^ b
   a = a ^ b
   ```

3. Write an assembly program to use 3 quad-words in memory to represent 3 sets: A, B and C. Each set will allow storing set values 0-63 in the corresponding bits of the quad-word. Perform these steps:

   ```
   insert 0 into A
   insert 1 into A
   insert 7 into A
   insert 13 into A
   insert 1 into B
   insert 3 into B
   insert 12 into B
   store A union B into C
   store A intersect B into C
   store A - B into C
   remove 7 from C
   ```

4. Write an assembly program to move a quad-word stored in memory into a register and then compute the exclusive-or of the 8 bytes of the word. Use either **ror** or **rol** to manipulate the bits of the register so that the original value is retained.

5. Write an assembly program to dissect a double stored in memory. This is a 64 bit floating point value. Store the sign bit in one memory location. Store the exponent after subtracting the bias value into a second memory location. Store the fraction field with the implicit 1 bit at the front of the bit string into a third memory location.

6. Write an assembly program to perform a product of 2 float values using integer arithmetic and bit operations. Start with 2 float values in memory and store the product in memory.

Chapter 8
Branching and looping

So far we have not used any branching statements in our code. Using the conditional move instructions added a little flexibility to the code while preserving the CPU's pipeline contents. We have seen that it can be tedious to repeat instructions to process each byte in a quad-word or each bit in a byte. In the next chapter we will work with arrays. It would be fool-hardy to process an array of 1 million elements by repeating the instructions. It might be possible to do this, but it would be painful coping with variable sized arrays. We need loops.

In many programs you will need to test for a condition and perform one of 2 actions based on the results. The conditional move is efficient if the 2 actions are fairly trivial. If each action is several instructions long, then we need a conditional jump statement to branch to one alternative while allowing the CPU to handle the second alternative by not branching. After completing the second alternative we will typically need to branch around the code for the first alternative. We need conditional and unconditional branch statements.

8.1 Unconditional jump

The unconditional jump instruction (`jmp`) is the assembly version of the `goto` statement. However there is clearly no shame in using `jmp`. It is a necessity in assembly language, while `goto` can be avoided in higher level languages.

The basic form of the `jmp` instruction is

```
jmp     label
```

where `label` is a label in the program's text segment. The assembler will generate a `rip` relative jump instruction, meaning that the flow of control will transfer to a location relative to the current value of the instruction pointer. The simplest relative jump uses an 8 bit signed immediate value and is encoded in 2 bytes. This allows jumping forwards or backwards about 127 bytes. The next variety of relative jump in 64 bit mode uses a 32 bit signed immediate value and requires a total of 5 bytes. Fortunately the assembler figures out which variety it can use and chooses the shorter form. The programmer simply specifies a label.

The effect of the `jmp` statement is that the CPU transfers control to the instruction at the labeled address. This is generally not too exciting except when used with a conditional jump. However, the `jmp` instruction can jump to an address contained in a register or memory location. Using a conditional move one could manage to use an unconditional jump to an address contained in a register to implement a conditional jump. This isn't sensible, since there are conditional jump statements which handle this more efficiently.

There is one more possibility which is more interesting - implementing a switch statement. Suppose you have a variable `i` which is known to contain a value from 0 to 2. Then you can form an array of instruction addresses and use a `jmp` instruction to jump to the correct section of code based on the value of `i`. Here is an example:

```
        segment .data
switch:
        dq      main.case0
        dq      main.case1
        dq      main.case2
i:      dq      2
        segment .text
        global  main
main:
        mov     rax, [i]            ; move i to rax
        jmp     [switch+rax*8]      ; switch ( i )
.case0:
        mov     rbx, 100            ; go here if i == 0
        jmp     .end
.case1:
        mov     rbx, 101            ; go here if i == 1
        jmp     .end
.case2:
        mov     rbx, 102            ; go here if i == 2
.end:
        xor     eax, eax
        ret
```

In this code we have used a new form of label with a dot prefix. These labels are referred to as "local" labels. They are defined within the range of enclosing regular labels. Basically the local labels could be used for all labels inside a function and this would allow using the same local labels in multiple functions. Also we used `main.case0` outside of main to refer to the `.case0` label inside main.

From this example we see that an unconditional jump instruction can be used to implement some forms of conditional jumps. Though conditional jumps are more direct and less confusing, in larger switch statements it might be advantageous to build an array of locations to jump to.

8.2 Conditional jump

To use a conditional jump we need an instruction which can set some flags. This could be an arithmetic or bit operation. However doing a subtraction just to learn whether 2 numbers are equal might wipe out a needed value in a register. The x86-64 CPU provides a compare instruction (`cmp`) which subtracts its second operand from its first and sets flags without storing the difference.

There are quite a few conditional jump instructions with the general pattern:

```
jCC    label   ; jump to location
```

The `CC` part of the instruction name represents any of a wide variety of condition codes. The condition codes are based on specific flags in `eflags` such as the zero flag, the sign flag, and the carry flag. Below are some useful conditional jump instructions.

instruction	meaning	aliases	flags
`jz`	jump if zero	`je`	ZF=1
`jnz`	jump if not zero	`jne`	ZF=0
`jg`	jump if > 0	`jnle`	ZF=0 and SF=0
`jge`	jump if ≥ 0	`jnl`	SF=0
`jl`	jump if > 0	`jnge js`	SF=1
`jle`	jump if ≤ 0	`jng`	ZF=1 or SF=1
`jc`	jump if carry	`jb jnae`	CF=1
`jnc`	jump if not carry	`jnb jae`	

It is possible to generate "spaghetti" code using jumps and conditional jumps. It is probably best to stick with high level coding structures translated to assembly language. The general strategy is to start with C code and translate it to assembly. The rest of the conditional jump section discusses how to implement C if statements.

Simple if statement

Let's consider how to implement the equivalent of a C simple `if` statement. Suppose we are implementing the following C code:

```
if ( a < b ) {
    temp = a;
    a = b;
    b = temp;
}
```

Then the direct translation to assembly language would be

```
;         if ( a < b ) {
          mov     rax, [a]
          mov     rbx, [b]
          cmp     rax, rbx
          jge     in_order
;             temp = a;
              mov     [temp], rax
;             a = b;
              mov     [a], rbx
;             b = temp
              mov     [b], rax
;         }
in_order:
```

The most obvious pattern in this code is the inclusion of C code as comments. It can be hard to focus on the purpose of individual assembly statements. Starting with C code which is known to work makes sense. Make each C statement an assembly comment and add assembly statements to achieve each C statement after the C statement. Indenting might help a little though the indentation pattern might seem a little strange.

You will notice that the `if` condition was less than, but the conditional jump used greater than or equal to. Perhaps it would appeal to you more to use `jnl` rather than `jge`. The effect is identical but the less than mnemonic is part of the assembly instruction (with not). You should select the instruction name which makes the most sense to you.

If/else statement

It is fairly common to do 2 separate actions based on a test. Here is a simple C `if` statement with an `else` clause:

```
if ( a < b ) {
    max = b;
```

```
        } else {
            max = a;
        }
```

This code is simple enough that a conditional move statement is likely to be a faster solution, but nevertheless here is the direct translation to assembly language:

```
;       if ( a < b ) {
        mov     rax, [a]
        mov     rbx, [b]
        cmp     rax, rbx
        jnl     else ;
            max = b;
            mov     [max], rbx
            jmp     endif
;       } else {
else:
;           max = a;
            mov     [max], rax
;       }
endif:
```

If/else-if/else statement

Just as in C/C++ you can have an **if** statement for the **else** clause, you can continue to do tests in the **else** clause of assembly code conditional statements. Here is a short **if/else-if/else** statement in C:

```
if ( a < b ) {
    result = 1;
} else if ( a > c ) {
    result = 2;
} else {
    result = 3;
}
```

This code is possibly a good candidate for 2 conditional move statements, but simplicity is bliss. Here is the assembly code for this:

```
;       if ( a < b ) {
        mov     rax, [a]
        mov     rbx, [b]
        cmp     rax, rbx
        jnl     else_if
;           result = 1;
            mov     qword [result], 1
            jmp     endif
;       } else if ( a > c ) {
```

92

```
    else_if:
            mov     rcx, [c]
            cmp     rax, rcx
            jng     else
;           result = 2;
            mov     qword [result], 2
            jmp     endif
;       } else {
    else:
;           result = 3;
            mov     qword [result], 3
;       }
    endif:
```

It should be clear that an arbitrary sequence of tests can be used to simulate multiple **else-if** clauses in C.

8.3 Looping with conditional jumps

The jumps and conditional jumps introduced so far have been jumping forward. By jumping backwards, it is possible to produce a variety of loops. In this section we discuss **while** loops, **do-while** loops and counting loops. We also discuss how to implement the effects of C's **continue** and **break** statements with loops.

While loops

The most basic type of loop is possibly the **while** loop. It generally looks like this in C:

```
    while ( condition ) {
        statements;
    }
```

C **while** loops support the **break** statement which gets out of the loop and the **continue** statement which immediately goes back to the top of the loop. Structured programming favors avoiding **break** and **continue**. However they can be effective solutions to some problems and, used carefully, are frequently clearer than alternatives based on setting condition variables. They are substantially easier to implement in assembly than using condition variables and faster.

Counting 1 bits in a memory quad-word

The general strategy is to shift the bits of a quad-word 1 bit at a time and add bit 0 of the value at each iteration of a loop to the sum of the 1 bits. This loop needs to be done 64 times. Here is the C code for the loop:

```c
sum = 0;
i = 0;
while ( i < 64 ) {
    sum += data & 1;
    data = data >> 1;
    i++;
}
```

The program below implements this loop with only the minor change that values are in registers during the execution of the loop. It would be pointless to store these values in memory during the loop. The C code is shown as comments which help explain the assembly code.

```
        segment .data
; long long data;
data    dq      0xfedcba9876543210
; long long sum;
sum     dq      0
        segment .text
        global  main

; int main() ; {
main:
        push    rbp
        mov     rbp, rsp
        sub     rsp, 32

;       int i;              in register rcx
;       Register usage
;
;       rax: bits being examined
;       rbx: carry bit after bt, setc
;       rcx: loop counter i, 0-63
;       rdx: sum of 1 bits

        mov     rax, [data]
        xor     ebx, ebx
;       i = 0;
        xor     ecx, ecx
;       sum = 0;
        xor     edx, edx
;       while ( i < 64 ) {
```

```
while:
        cmp     rcx, 64
        jnl     end_while
;       sum += data & 1;
        bt      rax, 0
        setc    bl
        add     edx, ebx
;       data >>= 1;
        shr     rax, 1
;       i++;
        inc     rcx
;       }
        jmp     while
end_while:
        mov     [sum], rdx
        xor     eax, eax
        leave
        ret
```

The first instruction of the loop is `cmp` which is comparing `i` (`rcx`) versus 64. The conditional jump selected, `jnl`, matches the inverse of the C condition. Hopefully this is less confusing than using `jge`. The last instruction of the loop is a jump to the first statement of the loop. This is the typical translation of a `while` loop.

Coding this in C and running

```
gcc -O3 -S countbits.c
```

yields an assembly language file named `countbits.s` which is unfortunately not quite matching our nasm syntax. The assembler for gcc, `gas`, uses the AT&T syntax which differs from the Intel syntax used by nasm. Primarily the source and destination operands are reversed and some slight changes are made to instruction mnemonics. You can also use

```
gcc -O3 -S -masm=intel countbits.c
```

to request that gcc create an assembly file in Intel format (for Linux) which is very close to the code in this book. Here is the loop portion of the program produced by gcc:

```
        mov     rax, QWORD PTR data[rip]
        mov     ecx, 64
        xor     edx, edx
.L2:
        mov     rsi, rax
        sar     rax
        and     esi, 1
        add     rdx, rsi
```

```
sub     ecx, 1
jne     .L2
```

You will notice that the compiler eliminated one jump instruction by shifting the test to the end of the loop. Also the compiler did not do a compare instruction. In fact it discovered that the counting up to 64 of `i` was not important. Only the number of iterations mattered, so it decremented down from 64 to 0. Thus it was possible to do a conditional jump after the decrement. Overall the compiler generated a loop with 6 instructions, while the hand-written assembly loop used 8 instructions. As stated in the introduction a good compiler is hard to beat. You can learn a lot from studying the compiler's generated code. If you are interested in efficiency you may be able to do better than the compiler. You could certainly copy the generated code and do exactly the same, but if you can't improve on the compiler's code then you should stick with C.

There is one additional compiler option, `-funroll-all-loops` which tends to speed up code considerably. In this case the compiler used more registers and did 8 iterations of a loop which added up 8 bits in each iteration. The compiler did 8 bits in 24 instructions where before it did 1 bit in 6 instructions. This is about twice as fast. In addition the instruction pipeline is used more effectively in the unrolled version, so perhaps this is 3 times as fast.

Optimization issues like loop unrolling are highly dependent on the CPU architecture. Using the CPU in 64 bit mode gives 16 general-purpose registers while 32 bit mode gives only 8 registers. Loop unrolling is much easier with more registers. Other details like the Intel Core i series processors' use of a queue of micro-opcodes might eliminate most of the effect of loops interrupting the CPU pipeline. Testing is required to see what works best on a particular CPU.

Do-while loops

We saw in the last section that the compiler converted a `while` loop into a `do-while` loop. The `while` structure translates directly into a conditional jump at the top of the loop and an unconditional jump at the bottom of the loop. It is always possible to convert a loop to use a conditional jump at the bottom.

A C `do-while` loop looks like

```
do {
    statements;
} while ( condition );
```

A `do-while` always executes the body of the loop at least once.

Let's look at a program implementing a search in a character array, terminated by a 0 byte. We will do an explicit test before the loop to not execute the loop if the first character is 0. Here is the C code for the loop:

```
i = 0;
c = data[i];
if ( c != 0 ) {
    do {
        if ( c == x ) break;
        i++;
        c = data[i];
    } while ( c != 0 );
}
n = c == 0 ? -1 : i;
```

Here's an assembly implementation of this code:

```
        segment .data
data    db      "hello world", 0
n       dq      0
needle:
        db      'w'
        segment .text
        global  main
main:
        push    rbp
        mov     rbp, rsp
        sub     rsp, 32

;       Register usage
;
;       rax: c, byte of data array
;       bl:  x, byte to search for
;       rcx: i, loop counter, 0-63

        mov     bl, [needle]
;       i = 0;
        xor     ecx, ecx
;       c = data[i];
        mov     al, [data+rcx]
;       if ( c != 0 ) {
        cmp     al, 0
        jz      end_if
;           do {
do_while:
;               if ( c == x ) break;
            cmp     al, bl
            je      found
;               i++;
```

```
;                 inc     rcx
;                 c = data[i];
                  mov     al, [data+rcx];
;               } while ( c != 0 );
                  cmp     al, 0
                  jnz     do_while
;         }
end_if:
;         n = c == 0 ? -1 : i;
          mov     rcx, -1 ; c == 0 if you reach here
found:
          mov     [n], rcx
;         return 0;
          xor     eax, eax
          leave
          ret
```

The assembly code (if stripped of the C comments) looks simpler than the C code. The C code would look better with a **while** loop. The conditional operator in C was not necessary in the assembly code, since the conditional jump on finding the proper character jumps past the movement of -1 to **rcx**.

It might seem rational to try to use more structured techniques, but the only reasons to use assembly are to improve efficiency or to do something which can't be done in a high level language. Bearing that in mind, we should try to strike a balance between structure and efficiency.

Counting loops

The normal counting loop in C is the **for** loop, which can be used to implement any type of loop. Let's assume that we wish to do array addition. In C we might use

```
for ( i = 0; i < n; i++ ) {
    c[i] = a[i] + b[i];
}
```

Translated into assembly language this loop might be

```
          mov     rdx, [n]
          xor     ecx, ecx
for:      cmp     rcx, rdx
          je      end_for
          mov     rax, [a+rcx*8]
          add     rax, [b+rcx*8]
          mov     [c+rcx*8], rax
          inc     rcx
```

```
        jmp     for
end_for:
```

Once again it is possible to do a test on **rdx** being 0 before executing the loop. This could allow the compare and conditional jump statements to be placed at the end of the loop. However it might be easier to simply translate C statements without worrying about optimizations until you improve your assembly skills. Perhaps you are taking an assembly class. If so, does performance affect your grade? If not, then keep it simple.

8.4 Loop instructions

There is a **loop** instruction along with a couple of variants which operate by decrementing the **rcx** register and branching until the register reaches 0. Unfortunately, it is about 4 times faster to subtract 1 explicitly from **rcx** and use **jnz** to perform the conditional jump. This speed difference is CPU specific and only true for a trivial loop. Generally a loop will have other work which will take more time than the loop instruction. Furthermore the **loop** instruction is limited to branching to an 8 bit immediate field, meaning that it can branch backwards or forwards about 127 bytes. All in all, it doesn't seem to be worth using.

Despite the forgoing tale of gloom, perhaps you still wish to use **loop**. Consider the following code which looks in an array for the right-most occurrence of a specific character:

```
        mov     ecx, [n]
more:   cmp     [data+rcx-1],al
        je      found
        loop    more
found:  sub     ecx, 1
        mov     [loc], ecx
```

8.5 Repeat string (array) instructions

The x86-64 repeat instruction (**rep**) repeats a string instruction the number of times specified in the count register (**rcx**). There are a handful of variants which allow early termination based on conditions which may occur during the execution of the loop. The repeat instructions allow setting array elements to a specified value, copying one array to another, and finding a specific value in an array.

String instructions

There are a handful of string instructions. The ones which step through arrays are suffixed with **b**, **w**, **d** or **q** to indicate the size of the array elements (1, 2, 4 or 8 bytes).

The string instructions use registers **rax**, **rsi** and **rdi** for special purposes. Register **rax** or its sub-registers **eax**, **ax** and **al** are used to hold a specific value. Resister **rsi** is the source address register and **rdi** is the destination address. None of the string instructions need operands.

All of the string operations working with 1, 2 or 4 byte quantities are encoded in 1 byte, while the 8 byte variants are encoded as 2 bytes. Combined with a 1 byte repeat instruction, this effectively encodes some fairly simple loops in 2 or 3 bytes. It is hard to beat a repeat.

The string operations update the source and/or destination registers after each use. This updating is managed by the direction flag (**DF**). If **DF** is 0 then the registers are increased by the size of the data item after each use. If **DF** is 1 then the registers are decreased after each use.

Move

The **movsb** instruction moves bytes from the address specified by **rsi** to the address specified by rdi. The other **movs** instructions move 2, 4 or 8 byte data elements from [**rsi**] to [**rdi**]. The data moved is not stored in a register and no flags are affected. After each data item is moved, the **rdi** and **rsi** registers are advanced 1, 2, 4 or 8 bytes depending on the size of the data item.

Below is some code to move 100000 bytes from one array to another:
```
    lea     rsi, [source]
    lea     rdi, [destination]
    mov     rcx, 100000
    rep     movsb
```

Store

The **stosb** instruction moves the byte in register **al** to the address specified by **rdi**. The other variants move data from **ax**, **eax** or **rax** to memory. No flags are affected. A repeated store can fill an array with a single value. You could also use **stosb** in non-repeat loops taking advantage of the automatic destination register updating.

Here is some code to fill an array with 1000000 double words all equal to 1:
```
    mov     eax, 1
    mov     ecx, 1000000
    lea     rdi, [destination]
    rep     stosd
```

Load

The `lodsb` instruction moves the byte from the address specified by `rsi` to the `al` register. The other variants move more bytes of data into `ax`, `eax` or `rax`. No flags are affected. Repeated loading seems to be of little use. However you can use `lods` instructions in other loops taking advantage of the automatic source register updating.

Here is a loop which copies data from 1 array to another removing characters equal to 13:

```
        lea     rsi, [source]
        lea     rdi, [destination]
        mov     ecx, 1000000
more:   lodsb
        cmp     al, 13
        je      skip
        stosb
skip:   sub     ecx, 1
        jnz     more
end
```

Scan

The `scasb` instruction searches through an array looking for a byte matching the byte in `al`. It uses the `rdi` register. Here is an implementation of the C `strlen` function:

```
        segment .text
        global  strlen
strlen:
        mov     rdi, rcx  ; first parameter is rcx
        cld               ; prepare to increment rdi
        mov     rcx, -1   ; maximum iterations
        xor     al, al    ; will scan for 0
        repne   scasb     ; repeatedly scan for 0
        mov     rax, -2   ; start at -1
                          ; end 1 past the end
        sub     rax, rcx
        ret
```

The function sets `rcx` to -1, which would allow quite a long repeat loop since the code uses `repne` to loop. It would decrement `rcx` about 2^{64} times in order to reach 0. Memory would run out first.

The first parameter in a 64 bit Windows program in `rcx` which must be copied to `rdi` to prepare for the scan instruction. Interestingly the first parameter for Linux and OS X is placed in `rdi` which makes this function 1 instruction shorter. The standard way to return an integer value is to place it in `rax`, so we place the length there.

Compare

The **cmpsb** instruction compares values of 2 arrays. Typically it is used with **repe** which will continue to compare values until either the count in **ecx** reaches 0 or two different values are located. At this point the comparison is complete.

This is almost good enough to write a version of the C **strcmp** function, but **strcmp** expects strings terminated by 0 and lengths are not usually known for C strings. It is good enough for **memcmp**:

```
        segment .text
        global  memcmp
memcmp: mov     rdi, rcx  ; first array address
        mov     rsi, rdx  ; second array address
        mov     rcx, r8   ; count: third parameter
        repe    cmpsb     ; compare until end or difference
        cmp     rcx, 0
        jz      equal     ; reached the end
        movzx   eax, byte [rdi-1]
        movzx   ecx, byte [rsi-1]
        sub     rax, rcx
        ret
equal:  xor     eax, eax
        ret
```

In the **memcmp** function the repeat loop advances the **rdi** and **rsi** registers one too many times. Thus there is a -1 in the move and zero extend instructions to get the 2 bytes. Subtraction is sufficient since **memcmp** returns 0, a positive or a negative value. It was designed to be implemented with a subtraction yielding the return value. The first 2 parameters to **memcmp** are **rdi** and **rsi** with the proper order.

Set/clear direction

The clear direction **cld** instruction clears the direction flag to 0, which means to process increasing addresses with the string operations. The set direction **std** instruction sets the direction flag to 1. Programmers are supposed to clear the direction flag before exiting any function which sets it.

Exercises

1. Write an assembly program to compute the dot product of 2 arrays, i.e:
$$p = \sum_{i=0}^{n-1} a_i * b_i$$

   Your arrays should be double word arrays in memory and the dot product should be stored in memory.

2. Write an assembly program to compute Fibonacci numbers storing all the computed Fibonacci numbers in a quad-word array in memory. Fibonacci numbers are defined by

   ```
   fib(0) = 0
   fib(1) = 1
   fib(i) = fib(i-1) + fib(i-2) for i > 1
   ```

   What is the largest i for which you can compute `fib(i)`?

3. Write an assembly program to sort an array of double words using bubble sort. Bubble sort is defined as

   ```
   do {
       swapped = false;
       for ( i = 0; i < n-1; i++ ) {
           if ( a[i] > a[i+1] ) {
               swap a[i] and a[i+1]
               swapped = true;
           }
       }
   } while ( swapped );
   ```

4. Write an assembly program to determine if a string stored in memory is a palindrome. A palindrome is a string which is the same after being reversed, like "**refer**". Use at least one repeat instruction.

5. Write an assembly program to perform a "find and replace" operation on a string in memory. Your program should have an input array and an output array. Make your program replace every occurrence of "**amazing**" with "**incredible**". A Pythagorean triple is a set of three integers a, b and c such that $a^2 + b^2 = c^2$. Write an assembly program to determine if an integer, c stored in memory has 2 smaller integers a and b making the 3 integers a Pythagorean triple. If so, then place a and b in memory.

Chapter 9
Functions

In this chapter we will discuss how to write assembly functions which can be called from C or C++ and how to call C functions from assembly. Since the C or C++ compiler generally does a very good job of code generation, it is usually not important to write complete programs in assembly. There might be a few algorithms which are best done in assembly, so we might write 90% of a program in C or C++ and write a few functions in assembly language.

It is also useful to call C functions from assembly. This gives your assembly programs full access to all C libraries. We will use **scanf** to input values from **stdin** and we will use **printf** to print results. This will allow us to write more useful programs.

9.1 The stack

So far we have had little use for the run-time stack, but it is an integral part of using functions. The default stack size under Windows is 1 MB and the location is generally in lower addresses than the code or data for a program.

Items are pushed onto the stack using the **push** instruction. The effect of **push** is to subtract 8 from the stack pointer **rsp** and then place the value being pushed at that address. We tend to refer to the latest item placed on the stack as the "top" of the stack, while the address is actually the lowest of all items on the stack. Most CPUs use stacks which grow downwards, but there have been exceptions.

Many different values are pushed onto the stack by the operating system. These include the environment (a collection of variable names and values defining things like the search path) and the command line parameters for the program.

Values can be removed from the stack using the **pop** instruction. **pop** operates in the reverse pattern of **push**. It moves the value at the location specified by the stack pointer (**rsp**) to a register or memory location and then adds 8 to **rsp**.

You can push and pop smaller values than 8 bytes, at some peril. It works as long as the stack remains bounded appropriately for the current operation. So if you push a word and then push a quad-word, the quad-word push may fail. It is simpler to push and pop only 8 byte quantities.

9.2 Call instruction

The assembly instruction to call a function is **call**. A typical use would be like

```
call    my_function
```

The operand **my_function** is a label in the text segment of a program. The effect of the **call** instruction is to push the address of the instruction following the call onto the stack and to transfer control to the address associated with **my_function**. The address pushed onto the stack is called the "return address". Another way to implement a call would be

```
    push    next_instruction
    jmp     my_function
next_instruction:
```

While this does work, the **call** instruction has more capability which we will generally ignore.

Ebe has a macro named **frame** which defines a few variables and helps a lot in using functions. It enables the proper display of the stack frame which can be enabled from the View menu. It is called with 3 parameters. The first is the number of parameters to the function. The second is the number of local variables to use in the function. The third parameter is the maximum number of parameters used in calls within the current function. The **frame** macro does not generate any instructions, so the assembly code used is normal. It is valuable enough that it will be used from here on out in nearly all functions. Here is a short program using **frame** within **main**.

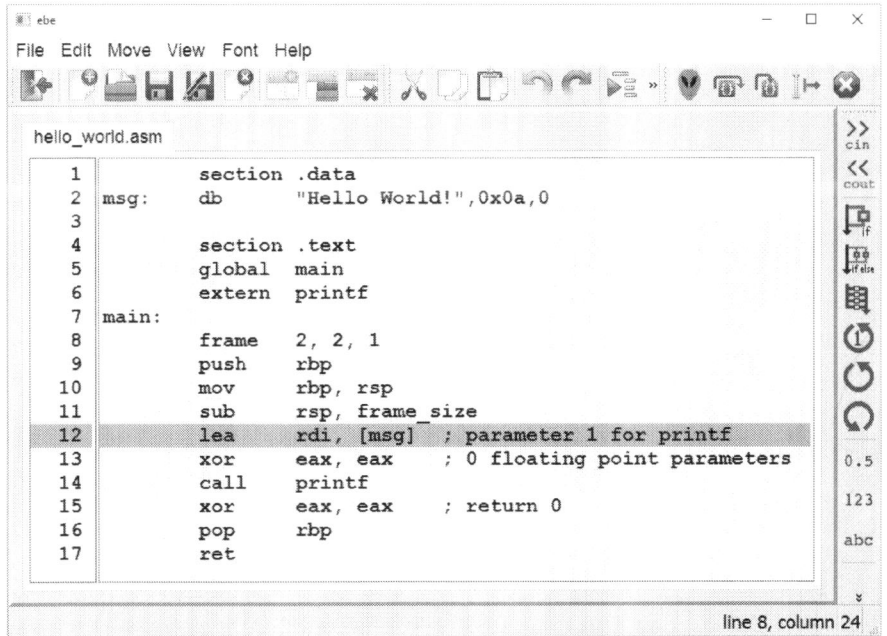

This program tells the **frame** macro that **main** has 2 parameters, 2 local variables and there will be at most 1 parameter to called functions. Below we can see the stack frame created for **main** after hitting the breakpoint on line 12.

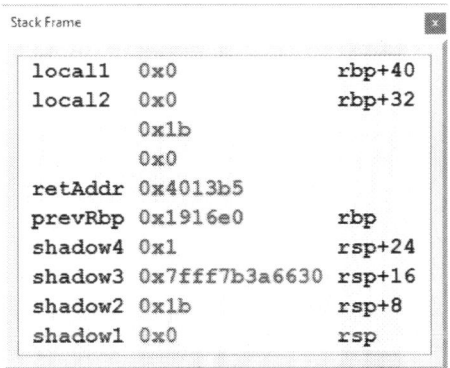

Notice that the 2 local variables are at the top of the frame. Also there are 2 unlabeled locations below the 2 locals and there are 4 mysterious shadow locations as well. On Windows the first 4 parameters to a function are passed in registers, so the 2 parameters to **main** are expected in registers and also the 1 parameter to **printf**. If a function requires more than 4 parameters the additional parameters are placed on the stack. To simplify coding for functions with a variable number of parameters, the calling function must have space on the stack for the 4 register-based parameters. This allows the function to copy these registers to the stack and then it can have all its parameters in a contiguous block on the stack. So the shadow locations are there for **printf** to use to copy its 4 register parameters onto the stack. Since **printf** is variadic (variable number of parameters) it might very well start its execution by copying the 4 registers to the stack. The main function is called the same way and the 4 locations above the return address as shadow space for **main**. In general it is up to the called function to decide what to do with these 4 locations. In this book we will use this space for the first 4 local variables.

Before **main** was called, the calling function had prepared a space of 32 bytes (four 8-byte quadwords) on the stack with **rsp** pointing to the lowest address of these 4 quadwords. Executing the **call** instruction will place the return address (**retAddr**) just below the 4 shadow locations. Within main the **push rbp** instruction will save the **rbp** register as the previous **rbp**, to be restored later. The **mov rbp, rsp** will set a new "base" value for **rbp**. This would logically be termed the "frame pointer register". The value of **frame_size** for this example is 32, so the **sub rsp, frame_size** instruction moves **rsp** to point to the **shadow1** location. The simplest way to manage the stack is to subtract the required value from **rsp** in the beginning of a function and restore it at the end. The **leave** instruction copies the current value of **rbp** to **rsp** and pops the previous **rbp** value from the stack. This restores the stack and the **rbp** register to the values in the calling function. After leave **main** is ready to return using the **ret** instruction.

The return address on the stack is **0x4013b5**. Normal text segment addresses tend to be a little past **0x400000** in Windows programs as illustrated by **rip** in the register display below taken from the same program when it enters **main**. The return address is an address in a function provided by the compiler (probably in a DLL), which prepares the environment and command line parameters for a C main function. For a C++ program this DLL function will also call all constructors for global objects. Note also that the value of **rsp** ends in a 0 which means that it is a multiple of 16.

Registers

rax	0x7fff7b4d47a8	rsi	0x1b	r8	0x181de0	r12	0x1
rbx	0x1	rdi	0x404010	r9	0x1816e0	r13	0x8
rcx	0x1	rbp	0x61fe50	r10	0x0	r14	0x0
rdx	0x1816e0	rsp	0x61fe00	r11	0x246	r15	0x0
rip	0x401840	eflags	PF		0		0

For functions with more parameters, the **frame** macro will accommodate more space on the stack. Below we see the stack frame from

main with 7 parameters to **main** (pretended), 6 local variables and 7 for the maximum number of parameters to called functions.

Stack Frame		
	0x0	
currPar7	0x0	rbp+64
currPar6	0x0	rbp+56
currPar5	0x0	rbp+48
local1	0x0	rbp+40
local2	0x0	rbp+32
local3	0x1b	rbp+24
local4	0x0	rbp+16
retAddr	0x4013b5	
prevRbp	0x10616e0	rbp
local5	0x1	rbp-8
local6	0x7fff7b3a6630	rbp-16
	0x1b	
newPar7	0x0	rsp+48
newPar6	0x401949	rsp+40
newPar5	0x1	rsp+32
shadow4	0x4019c5	rsp+24
shadow3	0xffffffffffffffff	rsp+16
shadow2	0x1	rsp+8
shadow1	0x1061720	rsp

The stacked parameters to **main** are labeled **currPar5**, **currPar6** and **currPar7**. There is an unlabeled location above **currPar7** in the stack frame which is required in order to keep **rsp** bounded at addresses which are a multiple of 16. This is done to maintain maximum efficiency for instructions which operate on 16 byte quantities. The first four locals are placed in the space which corresponds to the first 4 parameters if they had been stacked. Below this is the return address and the saved **rbp** value. Below the saved **rbp** value are the 2 remaining local variables. Since the number of locals plus the number of new parameters is odd, the bounding concept applies again and there is another unlabeled location. Following that are the 3 stacked parameters followed by the shadow register space.

Note carefully that the rightmost column gives the preferred way to address these items in the stack frame. The **currPar** locations and locals are all addressed with respect to rbp while the **newPar** locations are addressed with respect to **rsp**. In addition ebe defines macros for each of the parameters and locals as shown, so you could address **currPar7** using **rbp+currPar7** and **local5** using **rbp+local5**. The new parameters are addressed by adding to **rsp**, such as **rsp+newPar5**. The macros for locals which are shown as negative offsets from **rbp** are defined as negative values so in all cases you can add a stack frame label to **rbp** or **rsp**.

9.3 Linux Function calls

Recent versions of Linux have implemented an improved address randomization scheme which changes the way functions in shared libraries are called. Previously shared library functions were at addresses known at compile time which made it easy to link in the address. Now the system will randomize the addresses and to keep things relatively simple it uses a table of addresses within the program (global offsets table or "GOT") and the programmer must call the functions using the GOT. Ebe invokes the C/C++ compiler forcing the non-randomization of calls keeping programming simpler. Using the GOT requires **rip**-relative addressing which means that addresses are offsets from the **rip** register. Here is a sample call using the GOT.

```
default rel    ; force rip-relative
call [printf wrt ..got]
```

9.4 Return instruction

To return from a function you use the **ret** instruction. This instruction pops the address from the top of the stack and transfers control to that address. In the example in section 9.2 **next_instruction** is the label for the return address.

Below is shown a very simple program which illustrates the steps of a function call and return. The first instruction in **main** is a call to the **doit** function. I have violated my suggestion to use the frame macro for all functions. This simple code is easy to understand, though when **main** calls **doit** it upsets the multiple of 16 bounding rule for **rsp**, but **doit** is very simple and there will be no ill effects in executing simple instructions in **doit** with **rsp** not a multiple of 16.

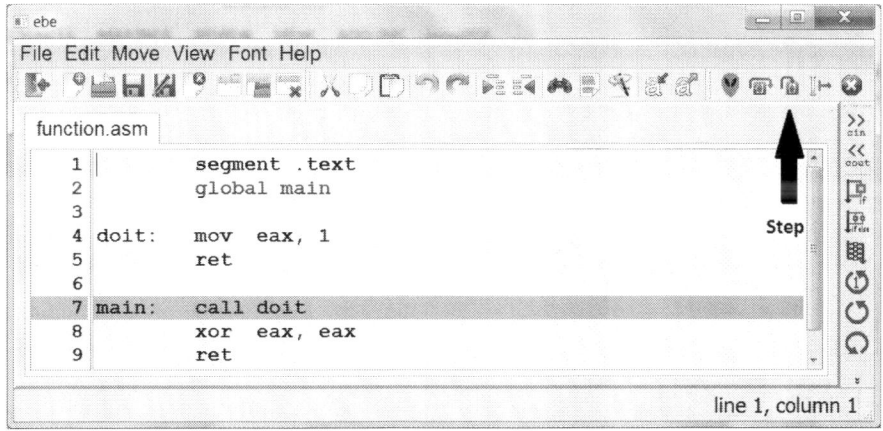

You can see that there is a breakpoint on line 7 and the call to `doit` has not yet been made. I have added an arrow pointing to the "Step" button which is immediately to the right of the "Next" button. In the register display below you can see that `rip` is `0x401836`.

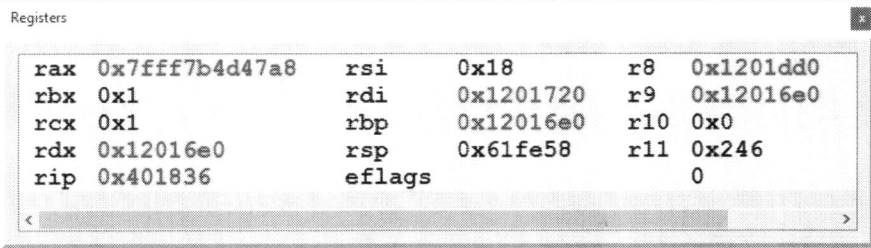

Previously we have used the "Next" button to execute the current instruction. However, if we use "Next" now, the debugger will execute the `doit` call and control will be returned after the function returns and the highlighted line will be line 8. In order to study the function call, I have clicked on "Step" which will step into the `doit` function.

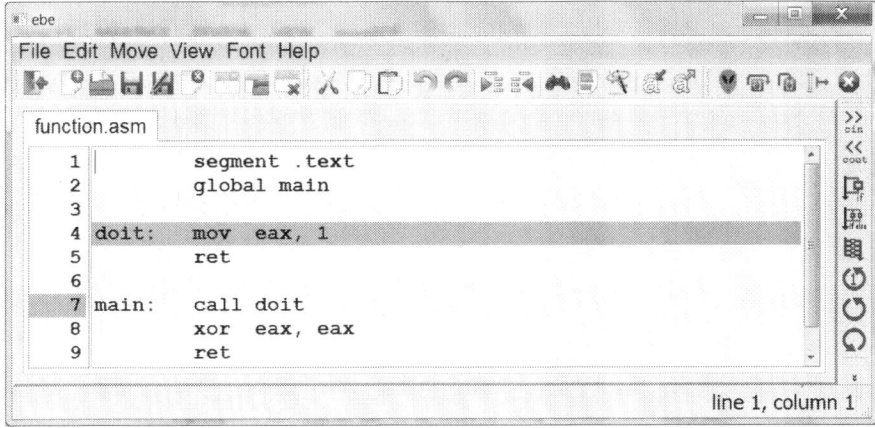

Now we see that the next instruction to execute is on line 4. It is instructive to view the registers at this point and the stack.

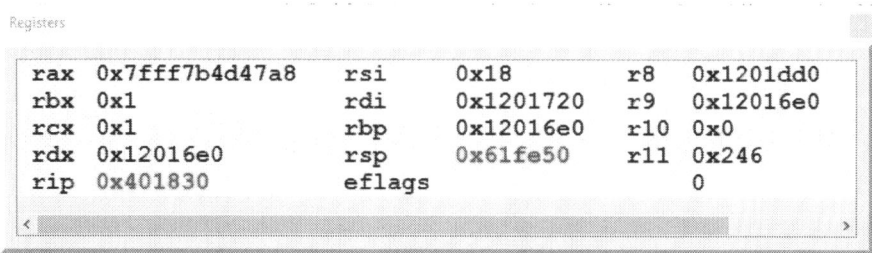

You can see that `rip` is now `401830` which is at a lower address than the call at line 7. The addresses within an assembly file will increase with line number.

After using "Step" two more times the debugger executes the return from `doit`. Below are the registers after executing the return.

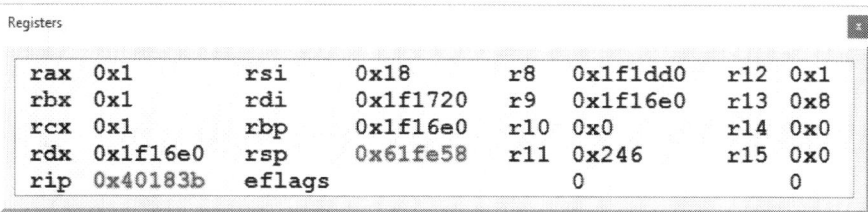

Here we see that `rip` is now `0x40183b` which was the value placed on the stack by the call to `doit`.

9.5 Function parameters and return value

Most function have parameters which might be integer values, floating point values, addresses of data values, addresses of arrays, or any other type of data or address. The parameters allow us to use a function to operate on different data with each call. In addition most functions have a return value which is commonly an indicator of success or failure.

Windows uses a function call protocol called the "Microsoft x64 Calling Convention", while Linux and OS X use a different protocol called the "System V Application Binary Interface" or System V ABI. In both protocols some of the parameters to functions are passed in registers. Windows allows the first 4 integer parameters to be passed in registers, while Linux allows the first 6 (using different registers). Windows allows the first 4 floating point parameters to be passed in floating pointer registers `xmm0-xmm3`, while Linux allows the first 8 floating point parameters to be passed in registers `xmm0-xmm7`.

There is one peculiarity in calling functions with a variable number of parameters in Windows. The central idea in the ABI is that there can be 4 parameters in registers and that these 4 can be easily moved into position on the stack as if they had been pushed. To make this even easier the caller must copy any floating point registers to the corresponding general purpose register prior to the call. This is needed to make it possible to copy just the general purpose to the stack early in the called function. The most likely function to exhibit this situation is **printf**. Below is a code segment illustrating how to print the double value in register **xmm0**. The address of the format string will be placed in **rcx** and then the value in **xmm0** must be copied to **xmm1** and also to **rdx**.

```
           segment  .data
format     db       "x is %lf", 0x0a, 0
           segment  .text
           lea      rcx, [format]
           movsd    xmm1, xmm0    ; discussed in chapter 11
           movq     rdx, xmm1     ; copies from xmm1
           call     printf
```

Windows, Linux and OS X use register **rax** for integer return values and register **xmm0** for floating point return values. Register **xmm0** is used to return 128 bit results while larger structs are allocated and a pointer to the struct is passed in register **rax**.

Linux uses a different strategy for returning larger values. It returns large integers in **rdx:rax**, while the calling function must provide a hidden first parameter for larger structs. This means the caller allocates memory and places the address of this memory in **rdi**.

Both Windows and Linux expect the stack pointer to be maintained on 16 byte boundaries in memory. This means that the hexadecimal value for **rsp** should end in 0. The reason for this requirement is to allow local variables in functions to be placed at 16 byte alignments for SSE and AVX instructions. Executing a **call** would then decrement **rsp** leaving it ending with an 8. Conforming functions should either push something or subtract from **rsp** to get it back on a 16 byte boundary. It is common for a function to push **rbp** as part of establishing a stack frame which reestablishes the 16 byte boundary for the stack. If your function calls any external function, it seems wise to stick with the 16 byte bounding requirement.

The first 4 parameters in a function under Windows are passed in registers with **rcx**, **rdx**, **r8** and **r9** being used for integer values and **xmm0-xmm3** for floating point values. For example if a function used parameters which were int, float, int and float it would use registers **rcx**, **xmm1**, **r8** and **xmm3**. By contrast Linux and OS X use up to 6 integer parameters in registers **rdi**, **rsi**, **rdx**, **rcx**, **r8** and **r9** and up to 8 floating point parameters in registers **xmm0-xmm7**. This means that a Linux or OSX function could have as many as 14 register parameters. If a function requires more parameters, they are pushed onto the stack in reverse order.

Under Linux and OS X functions like **scanf** and **printf** which have a variable number of parameters pass the number of floating point parameters in the function call using the **rax** register. This is not required for Windows.

A final requirement for making function calls in Windows is that the calling function must leave 32 bytes free at the top of the stack at the point of the call. This space is intended to make it easy for a function to move its four register parameters onto the stack making it possible to access all the function's parameters as an array. This is quite handy for functions which have a variable number of parameters. Technically the called function can use the space however it wishes, but the caller must make sure that this "shadow" space is available.

For 32 bit programs the protocol is different. Registers **r8-r15** are not available, so there is not much value in passing function parameters in registers. These programs use the stack for all parameters.

We are finally ready for "Hello World!"

```
        segment  .data
msg:    db       "Hello World!",0x0a,0
        segment  .text
        global   main
        extern   printf
main:
        push   rbp
        mov    rbp, rsp
        frame  2, 0, 1
        sub    rsp, frame_size ; will be 32
                               ; shadow parameter space
        lea    rcx, [msg] ; parameter 1 for printf
        call   printf
        xor    eax, eax    ; return 0
        leave
        ret
```

We use the "load effective address" instruction (**lea**) to load the effective address of the message to print with **printf** into **rcx**. This could also be done with **mov**, but **lea** allows specifying more items in the brackets so that we could load the address of an array element. Furthermore, under OS X **mov** will not allow you to move an address into a register. There the problem is that static addresses for data have values which exceed the capacity of 32 bit pointers and to save space the software is designed to use 32 bit fields for addresses which must then be relative to `rip`. The easy assessment is to use `lea` to load addresses.

9.6 Stack frames

One of the most useful features of the gdb debugger is the ability to trace backwards through the stack functions which have been called using command `bt` or `backtrace`. To perform this trick each function must keep a pointer in `rbp` to a 2 quad-word object on the stack identifying the previous value of `rbp` along with the return address. You might notice the sequence "`push rbp; mov rbp, rsp`" in the hello world program. The first instruction pushes `rbp` immediately below the return address. The second instruction makes `rbp` point to that object.

Assuming all functions obey this rule of starting with the standard 2 instructions, there will be a linked list of objects on the stack - one for each function invocation. The debugger can traverse through the list to identify the function (based on the location of the return address) called and use other information stored in the executable to identify the line number for this return address (for C/C++).

These 2 quad-word objects are simple examples of "stack frames". In functions which do not call other functions (leaf functions), the local variables for the function might all fit in registers. If there are too many local variables or if the function calls other functions, then there might need to be some space on the stack for these local variables in excess of the shadow parameter space in the active stack frame. To allocate space for the local variables, you simply subtract from `rsp`. For example to leave 32 bytes for local variables and 32 bytes for shadow space for calling functions in the stack frame do this:

```
push    rbp
mov     rbp, rsp
sub     rsp, 64
```

Be sure to subtract a multiple of 16 bytes to avoid possible problems with stack alignment.

To establish a stack frame, you use the following 2 instructions at the start of a function:

```
push    rbp
mov     rbp, rsp
```

The effect of the these 2 instructions and a possible subtraction from `rsp` can be undone using

```
leave
```

just before a **ret** instruction. For a leaf function there is no need to do the standard 2 instruction prologue and no need for the **leave** instruction. They can also be omitted in general though it will prevent gdb from being able to trace backwards though the stack frames.

The **frame** macro will be used in this book to manage stack frames. It is called with 3 integer parameters which define the number of parameters to the function, the number of local variables and the maximum number of parameters to any called functions. It completely manages the computation of sizes and makes sure that **rsp** is maintained on a 16 byte boundary.

Below is a diagram of the stack contents of after preparing a stack frame in a function with 6 parameters, 2 local variables and 3 for the number of parameters to called functions:

```
Stack Frame
currPar6   0x0                rbp+56
currPar5   0x0                rbp+48
local1     0x0                rbp+40
local2     0x0                rbp+32
           0x1b
           0x0
retAddr    0x4013b5
prevRbp    0x9e16e0           rbp
shadow4    0x1                rsp+24
shadow3    0x7ffbc5ab6630     rsp+16
shadow2    0x1b               rsp+8
shadow1    0x0                rsp
```

In the diagram the bottom 4 cells are reserved for shadow space for the functions which are called by this function. Normally this space will be left unused by the current function. The previous value of **rbp** which was pushed at the start of the function is located where rbp currently points. At **rbp+8** is the return address which was placed on the stack in the process of making the call. The 4 locations above the return address are for copying the register parameters of the current function with 2 of these to be used as **local1** and **local2**. Above these four values might be are **currPar5** and **currPar6** which are placed on the stack by the calling function. In the third column are the address references to use when accessing the current parameters and locals for this function. There is generally no need to use the shadow space for called functions. Note that **frame_size** was 32 in this example.

To save registers in the shadow space you would move values into the memory references from the diagram. If you want to save **rcx** on the stack, I suggest using one of the locals.

```
        mov     [rbp+local1], rcx
```

Perhaps you would prefer to use a name for the spot rather than using 16. Then you could use something like

```
count   equ     local1
        mov     [rbp+count], rcx
```

The **equ** pseudo-op stands for "equate" and it gives you a symbolic name for a number – in the previous case: 16. The stack frame window will display the first local as **count**.

```
Stack Frame
    currPar6    0x0                     rbp+56
    currPar5    0x0                     rbp+48
    count       0x0                     rbp+40
    local2      0x0                     rbp+32
                0x1b
                0x0
    retAddr     0x4013b5
    prevRbp     0x216e0                 rbp
    shadow4     0x1                     rsp+24
    shadow3     0x7ffbc5ab6630          rsp+16
    shadow2     0x1b                    rsp+8
    shadow1     0x0                     rsp
```

Sometimes you may need more local space than the 32 bytes in the shadow parameter space. Let's assume that you wish to use 2 local variables named **x** and **y** in addition to 4 variables in the shadow space. Using the following code we can set this up nicely.

```
        frame   6, 6, 3
count   equ     local1
x       equ     local5
y       equ     local6
```

Here is a diagram of how this might look:

Stack Frame

currPar6	0x0	rbp+56
currPar5	0x0	rbp+48
count	0x0	rbp+40
local2	0x0	rbp+32
local3	0x1b	rbp+24
local4	0x0	rbp+16
retAddr	0x4013b5	
prevRbp	0x12016e0	rbp
x	0x1	rbp-8
y	0x7ffbc5ab6630	rbp-16
shadow4	0x1b	rsp+24
shadow3	0x0	rsp+16
shadow2	0x401949	rsp+8
shadow1	0x1	rsp

You can see that we need to subtract 48 from `rsp` rather than 32 to leave room for 6 local variables. The frame macro will correctly set `frame_size` to 48. Also had the number of locals been 7, it would set the value to 64 to maintain `rsp` at a 16 byte boundary. The memory reference for `x` would be `[rbp+x]` and for `y` we would use `[rbp+y]` as in this code which saves `r8` and `r9` in `x` and `y`.

```
mov     [rbp+x], r8
mov     [rbp+y], r9
```

Using the `frame` macro we can have all the variables in the stack frame addressed as `rbp` plus a label or as `rsp` plus a label. We do need to be careful to use `rbp` for current parameters and locals and `rsp` for new parameters.

Now suppose we decide to call a function with 5 parameters. Then we change the frame macro call to

```
frame 6, 6, 5
```

Again we can give a more meaningful name to newPar5 by

new_count equ   newPar5

Then we have the fifth parameter placed just above `shadow4` in the stack frame and it is labeled as we wish. You must use `rsp+new_count` to refer to the fifth parameter.

Stack Frame

currPar6	0x0	rbp+56
currPar5	0x0	rbp+48
count	0x0	rbp+40
local2	0x0	rbp+32
local3	0x1b	rbp+24
local4	0x0	rbp+16
retAddr	0x4013b5	
prevRbp	0x216e0	rbp
x	0x1	rbp-8
y	0x7ffbc5ab6630	rbp-16
	0x1b	
new_count	0x0	rsp+32
shadow4	0x401949	rsp+24
shadow3	0x1	rsp+16
shadow2	0x4019c5	rsp+8
shadow1	0xffffffffffffffff	rsp

With any function protocol you must specify which registers must be preserved in a function. The Windows calling convention requires that registers rbx, rbp, rsp, rsi, rdi and r12-15 must be preserved, while for the System V ABI (Linux and OS X) registers rbx, rbp and r12-15 must be preserved. The registers which you preserve would be copied into the stack frame like count, x and y from the previous examples and copied back to the appropriate registers before returning.

So we have rax used for function return values; rcx, rdx, r8 and r9 used for parameters; and registers rbx, rbp, rsp, rsi, rsi, and r12-r15 which must be preserved across function calls. That's nearly all of them. We are left with r10 and r11 which can be used without preservation. The list of registers to save is a bit long. So anytime you need a register other than the parameter registers, choose r10 and r11 if not already in use. If you have to choose another one, it will be one that you must preserve on the stack and restore before returning.

Function to print the maximum of 2 integers

The program listed below calls a function named print_max to print the maximum of 2 longs passed as parameters. It calls printf so it uses the extern pseudo-op to inform nasm and ld that printf will be loaded from a library. You can see the original C code as comments which help to translate into assembly. No effort has been made to save instructions by maintaining values in registers while calling `printf`. The saving of a few instructions is a quite small time compared to the time spent calling `printf` and printing some text in a terminal window.

```
        segment .text
        global  main
        extern  printf

; void print_max ( long a, long b )
; {
a    equ    local1       ; parameter a (rcx) in local1
b    equ    local2       ; parameter b (rdx) in local2
print_max:
        push rbp;         ; normal stack frame
        mov  rbp, rsp
        sub  rsp, frame_size
;       int max;
max  equ    local3       ; max will be local3
        mov  [rbp+a], rcx ; save a
        mov  [rbp+b], rdx ; save b
;       max = a;
        mov  [rbp+max], rcx
;       if ( b > max ) max = b;
        cmp  rdx, rcx
        jng  skip
        mov  [rbp+max], rdx
skip:
;       printf ( "max(%ld,%ld) = %ldn", a, b, max );
        segment .data
fmt  db     'max(%ld,%ld) = %ld',0xa,0
        segment .text
        lea  rcx, [fmt]
        mov  rdx, [rbp+a]
        mov  r8,  [rbp+b]
        mov  r9,  [rbp+max]
        call printf
; }
        leave
        ret

main:
        push rbp
        mov  rbp, rsp
        frame 0, 0, 2
        sub  rsp, frame_size   ; shadow parameter space
;       print_max ( 100, 200 )
        mov  rcx, 100    ; first parameter
        mov  rdx, 200    ; second parameter
```

```
        call  print_max
        xor   eax, eax        ; to return 0
        leave
        ret
```

In **main** you first see the standard 2 instructions to establish a stack frame. There are no local variables in **main** and we aren't using any parameters to main, so frame is called with 0 for the number of current parameters. Also there are no locals in main, so that value for the **frame** call is also 0. There are 2 parameters to **print_max**, so the **frame** call has parameters 0, 0 and 2. Just subtracting 32 sounds easy enough but perhaps the code will change.

The C **print_max** function has 2 parameters and 1 local variable. We will save the 2 parameters as locals and there is a local variable, **max**, so the frame call has 2 for the number of parameters and 3 as the number of locals. The **printf** call has 4 parameters so the **frame** call parameters are 2, 3, and 4. We subtract **frame_size** from **rsp** to provide the shadow parameter space for the **printf** call. It would be possible to avoid storing the 3 variables in memory, but it would be more confusing and less informative. According to Donald Knuth "premature optimization is the root of all evil." It is not worth the bother for code which will not executed enough time to measure.

Immediately after the comment for the heading for **print_max**, I have 2 equates to establish meaningful labels for **a** and **b**. After the comment for the declaration for **max**, I have an equate for it too.

Before doing any of the work of **print_max** I have 2 **mov** instructions to save **a** and **b** onto the stack. Both variables will be parameters to the **printf** call, but they will be the second and third parameters so they will need to be different registers at that point.

The computation for **max** is done using the stack location for **max** rather than using a register. It would have been possible to use **r9** which is the register for **max** in the **printf** call, but would be less clear and the goal of this code is to show how to handle parameters and local variables in functions simply. The easy technique for writing assembly is to translate C code one line at a time.

The call to **printf** requires a format string which should be in the data segment. It would be possible to have a collection of data prior to the text segment for the program, but it is nice to have the definition of the format string close to where it is used. It is possible to switch back and forth between the text and data segments, which seems easier to maintain.

9.7 Recursion

One of the fundamental problem solving techniques in computer programming is recursion. A recursive function is a function which calls itself. The focus of recursion is to break a problem into smaller problems. Frequently these smaller problems can be solved by the same function. So you break the problem into smaller problems repeatedly and eventually you reach such a small problem that it is easy to solve. The easy to solve problem is called a "base case". Recursive functions typically start by testing to see if you have reached the base case or not. If you have reached the base case, then you prepare the easy solution. If not you break the problem into sub-problems and make recursive calls. As you return from recursive calls you assemble solutions to larger problems from solutions to smaller problems.

Recursive functions generally require stack frames with local variable storage for each stack frame. Using the complete stack frame protocol can help in debugging.

Using the function call protocol it is easy enough to write recursive functions. As usual, recursive functions test for a base case prior to making a recursive call.

The factorial function can be defined recursively as

$$f(n) = \begin{cases} 1 & \text{if } n \leq 1 \\ n * f(n-1) & \text{if } n > 1 \end{cases}$$

Here is a program to read an integer n, compute n! recursively and print n!.

```
        segment .data
x       dq          0
scanf_format:
        db          "%ld",0
printf_format:
        db          "fact(%ld) = %ld",0x0a,0

        segment .text
        global  main            ; tell world about main
        global  fact            ; tell world about fact
        extern  scanf           ; resolve scanf and
        extern  printf          ; printf from libc
main:
        push    rbp
        mov     rbp, rsp
        frame   0, 0, 3
        sub     rsp, frame_size
        lea     rcx, [scanf_format] ; set arg 1
        lea     rdx, [x]            ; set arg 2 for scanf
        call    scanf
```

```
            mov       rcx, [x]         ; move x for fact call
            call      fact
            lea       rcx, [printf_format]; set arg 1
            mov       rdx, [x]         ; set arg 2 for printf
            mov       r8, rax          ; set arg 3 to be x!
            call      printf
            xor       eax, eax         ; set return value to 0
            leave
            ret

fact:                                  ; recursive function
n           equ       local1
            push      rbp
            mov       rbp, rsp
            frame     1, 1, 1
            sub       rsp, frame_size
            cmp       rcx, 1           ; compare n with 1
            jg        greater          ; if n <= 1, return 1
            mov       eax, 1           ; set return value to 1
            leave
            ret
greater:
            mov       [rbp+n], rcx     ; save n
            dec       rcx              ; call fact with n-1
            call      fact
            mov       rcx, [rbp+n]     ; restore original n
            imul      rax, rcx         ; multiply fact(n-1)*n
            leave
            ret
```

In the **fact** function I have used an equate for the variable n. The **equ** statement defines the label n to have the same value as **local1**. In the body of the function I save the value of **n** on the stack prior to making a recursive call to **fact**. After the call I retrieve n from the stack and multiply the return value from the **fact** call by n.

Exercises

1. Write an assembly program to produce a billing report for an electric company. It should read a series of customer records using scanf and print one output line per customer giving the customer details and the amount of the bill. The customer data will consist of a name (up to 64 characters not including the terminal 0) and a number of kilowatt hours per customer. The number of kilowatt hours is an integer. The cost for a customer will be $20.00 if the number of kilowatt hours is less than or equal to 1000 or $20.00 plus 1 cent per kilowatt hour over 1000 if the usage is greater than 1000. Use quotient and remainder after dividing by 100 to print the amounts as normal dollars and cents. Write and use a function to compute the bill amount (in pennies).

2. Write an assembly program to generate an array of random integers (by calling the C library function **random**), to sort the array using a bubble sort function and to print the array. The array should be stored in the **.bss** segment and does not need to be dynamically allocated. The number of elements to fill, sort and print should be stored in a memory location. Write a function to loop through the array elements filling the array with random integers. Write a function to print the array contents. If the array size is less than or equal to 20, call your print function before and after printing.

3. A Pythagorean triple is a set of three integers, a, b and c, such that $a^2 + b^2 = c^2$. Write an assembly program to print all the Pythagorean triples where $c <= 500$. Use a function to test whether a number is a Pythagorean triple.

4. Write an assembly program to keep track of 10 sets of size 1000000. Your program should read accept the following commands: **"add"**, **"union"**, **"print"** and **"quit"**. The program should have a function to read the command string and determine which it is and return 0, 1, 2 or 3 depending on the string read. After reading **"add"** your program should read a set number from 0 to 9 and an element number from 0 to 999999 and insert the element into the proper set. You need to have a function to add an element to a set. After reading **"union"** your program should read 2 set numbers and make the first set be equal to the union of the 2 sets. You need a set union function. After

reading "`print`" your program should print all the elements of the set. You can assume that the set has only a few elements. After reading "`quit`" your program should exit.

5. A sequence of numbers is called bitonic if it consists of an increasing sequence followed by a decreasing sequence or if the sequence can be rotated until it consists of an increasing sequence followed by a decreasing sequence. Write an assembly program to read a sequence of integers into an array and print out whether the sequence is bitonic or not. The maximum number of elements in the array should be 100. You need to write 2 functions: one to read the numbers into the array and a second to determine whether the sequence is bitonic. Your bitonic test should not actually rotate the array.

6. Write an assembly program to read two 8 byte integers with `scanf` and compute their greatest common divisor using Euclid's algorithm, which is based on the recursive definition

$$\gcd(a,b) = \begin{cases} a & \text{if } b = 0 \\ \gcd(b, a \bmod b) & \text{otherwise} \end{cases}$$

7. Write an assembly program to read a string of left and right parentheses and determine whether the string contains a balanced set of parentheses. You can read the string with `scanf` using "`%79s`" into a character array of length 80. A set of parentheses is balanced if it is the empty string or if it consists of a left parenthesis followed by a sequence of balanced sets and a right parenthesis. Here's an example of a balanced set of parentheses: "`( ( ( ) ( ) ) ( ) )`".

Chapter 10
Arrays

An array is a contiguous collection of memory cells of a specific type. This means that an array has a start address. The start address is the lowest address in the array and is identified by the label used when defining an array in the data or bss segment.

Elements of the array are accessed by index with the smallest index being 0 as in C. Subsequent indices access higher memory addresses. The final index of an array of size n is n-1.

It would be possible to define arrays with different starting indices. In fact the default for FORTRAN is for arrays to start at index 1 and you can define the range of indices in many high level languages. However it is quite natural to use 0 as the first index for arrays. The assembly code is simpler in this way which helps with efficiency in C and C++.

10.1 Array address computation

There can be arrays of many types of data. These include the basic types: bytes, words, double words, and quad-words. We can also have arrays of structs (defined later).

Array elements are of a specific type so each array element occupies the same number of bytes of memory. This makes it simple to compute the location of any array element. Suppose that the array **a** with base address **base** uses **m** bytes per element, then element **a[i]** is located at **base + i*m**.

Let's illustrate the indexing of arrays using the following program:

```
        segment .bss
a       resb    20      ; array of 20 bytes
b       resd    9       ; array of 9 double words
        align   8
c       resq    10      ; array of 10 quad-words
```

```
        segment .text
        global  main
main:
        push    rbp
        mov     rbp, rsp
        frame   0,0,0
        sub     rsp, frame_size
        leave
        ret
```

Assembly Data

0x408280	a	0x00	00	00	00	00	00	00	00	00	00	00	00	00	00	00	00
		0x00	00	00	00	00	00	00	00	00	00	00	00	00	00	00	00
0x4082a0	b	00				00				00				00			
		00				00				00				00			
		00															
0x4082c8	c	00				00				00				00			
		00				00				00				00			
		00				00											

We see that array a is at location 0x408280. So a[0] is at 0x408280, a[1] is at 0x408281, etc. Array b is placed right after a so b[0] is at 0x4082a0, b[1] is at 0x4082a4, etc. The locations in b are 4 bytes each since b is defined by resd meaning "reserve doubleword". Array b is 9 elements long which is 36 bytes = 0x24. This means the next available address after b is 0x4082c4, which is misaligned for 8 byte instructions. It is more efficient to access quadword data items placed at addresses which are multiples of 8. Using alignb 8 for .bss data causes the assembler to use 0x4082c8 for c which is the next multiple of 8. Thus c[0] is at 0x4082c8, c[1] is at 0x4082d0, etc. You can use "align 8" for aligning data in the .data segment.

10.2 General pattern for memory references

So far we have used array references in sample code without discussing the options for memory references. A memory reference can be expressed as

[label]   the value contained at label

[label+2*ind]   the value contained at the memory address obtained by adding the label and index register times 2

[label+4*ind]   the value contained at the memory address obtained by adding the label and index register times 4 [label+8*ind]   the value contained at the memory address obtained by adding the label and index register times 8

[reg]   the value contained at the memory address in the register

[reg+k*ind]   the value contained at the memory address obtained by adding the register and index register times k

[label+reg+k*ind]   the value contained at the memory address obtained by adding the label, the register and index register times k

With any of these references we could optionally add a number. So we could use [c+16] to refer to c[2]. Frequently you would access an array in a loop where the loop index is in a register. So if 2 is in register **rbx**, we could access c[2] using [c+rbx*8].

This allows a lot of flexibility in array accesses. For arrays in the data and bss segments it is possible to use the label along with an index register with a multiplier for the array element size (as long as the array element size is 1, 2, 4 or 8). With arrays passed into functions, the address must be placed in a register (or stacked if the parameter is past 4). Therefore the form using a label is not possible. Instead we can use a base register along with an index register. With array **c** passed as the first parameter (**rcx**) and 2 in register **rbx**, we could access c[2] using [rcx+8*rbx]. Any of the 16 general purpose registers may be used as a base register or an index register, however it is unlikely that you would use the **rsp** or **rbp** as an index register.

Let's look at an example using a base register and an index register. Let's suppose we wish to copy an array to another array in a function. Then the two array addresses could be the first 2 parameters (**rcx** and **rdx**) and the number of array elements could be the third parameter **r8**. Let's assume that the arrays are double word arrays.

```
copy_array.asm
1           segment  .data
2   a:      dd       1, 2, 3, 4, 5
3           segment  .bss
4   b:      resd     10
5           segment  .text
6           global   main, copy_array
7   main:
8           push     rbp
9           mov      rbp, rsp
10          frame    2, 0, 3
11          sub      rsp, frame_size
12          lea      rcx, [b]         ; destination
13          lea      rdx, [a]         ; source
14          mov      r8d, 5           ; count
15          call     copy_array
16          xor      eax, eax         ; return 0
17          leave
18          ret
19  copy_array:
20          push     rbp
21          mov      rbp, rsp
22          frame    3, 0, 0
23          sub      rsp, frame_size
24          xor      r9d, r9d         ; start with 0 for index
25  more:   mov      eax, [rdx+4*r9]  ; load dword
26          mov      [rcx+4*r9], eax  ; store qword
27          add      r9d, 1           ; increment index register
28          cmp      r9, r8           ; index vs count register
29          jne      more             ; if not equal, more to do
30          leave
31          ret
```

Ready   line 30, column 1

It is easy to monitor data processed in a function with ebe. You can see that a breakpoint was placed on line 24 and the program was run. At this point the `copy_array` function has been called and the parameters are in registers `rcx`, `rdx`, and `r8`.

```
Registers
rax  0x7fff5dca47a8   rsi     0x1a          r8   0x5         r12  0x1
rbx  0x1              rdi     0x1a1720      r9   0x1a16e0    r13  0x8
rcx  0x408280         rbp     0x61fe20      r10  0x0         r14  0x0
rdx  0x404010         rsp     0x61fe00      r11  0x246       r15  0x0
rip  0x40185f         eflags  0x0                0                0
```

I have right-clicked on b in the assembly data window and selected 4 byte decimals. The default is 4 byte hexadecimal for resd used in .bss. Here is the data for the program.

129

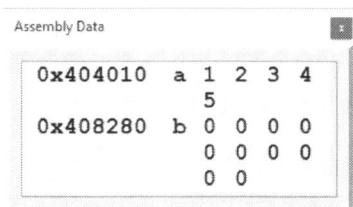

It would be a useful exercise to single step through this program and observe **rax** as data is loaded from **a** and also to watch the successive values from **a** being placed in **b**. You should also observe the changes to **r9**.

In the **copy_array** function we used the parameters as they were provided. We used **rdx** as the base address register for the source array and **rcx** as the base address register for the destination array. For both accesses we used **r9** as the index register with a multiplier of 4 since the arrays have 4 byte elements. This allows us to compare **r9** versus **r8** to see if there are more elements to copy. Register **r9** was chosen since it was one which is considered "volatile" and a function is not required to preserve its original value.

Note that multiplying by 2, 4 or 8 is a shift of 1, 2 or 3 bits, so there is effectively 0 cost to using the multiplier. Alternatively we could add 4 to **r9** in each loop iteration after shifting **r8** left 2 positions.

The last pattern would be useful for accessing an array of structs. If you had an array of structs with each struct having a character array and a pointer, then the number part of the reference could be the offset of the struct element within the struct, while the base register and index register could define the address of a particular struct in the array.

10.3 Allocating arrays

The simplest way to allocate memory in assembly is probably to use the C library **malloc** function. The prototype for **malloc** is

```
void *malloc ( long size );
```

On success **malloc** returns a pointer to the allocated memory, while failure results in **malloc** returning 0. The memory returned by **malloc** is bounded on 16 byte boundaries, which is useful as an address for any type of object (except for arrays needing to be on 32 byte boundaries for AVX instructions). The memory can be returned for potential reuse by calling the **free** function with the pointer returned by **malloc**

```
void free ( void *ptr );
```

Here is an assembly segment to allocate an array of 1,000,000,000 bytes

```
extern    malloc
...
mov       rcx, 1000000000
call      malloc
mov       [pointer], rax
```

There are several advantages to using allocated arrays. The most obvious one is that you can have arrays of exactly the right size. Frequently you can compute the size of array needed in your code and allocate an array of the correct size. If you use statically defined arrays either in the data or bss segment, you have to know the size needed before running the program (or guess).

Another less obvious reason for using allocated arrays is due to size limitations imposed on the data and bss segments by either the assembler, linker or operating system. Nasm reports "**FATAL: out of memory**" when you try to declare an array of much more than 2 billion bytes. It succeeds with an array of 2 billion bytes in the **bss** segment. It took approximately 104 seconds on a 2.4 GHz Opteron system to assemble and link a test program with a 2 GB array. In addition both the object file and the executable file exceeded 2 billion bytes in size. It is much faster (less than 1 second) to assemble and link a program using **malloc** and the executable size was about 10 thousand bytes.

The program using **malloc** was modified to allocate 20 billion bytes and still assembled and linked in less than 1 second. It executed in 3 milliseconds. There is no more practical way to use large amounts of memory than using allocated memory.

The user should be cautioned not to attempt to assemble programs with large static memory needs on a computer with less RAM than required. This will cause disk thrashing while assembling and linking, using far more than 100 seconds and nearly crippling the computer during the process. Also it can be quite painful to use arrays larger than memory even if they are allocated. Disk thrashing is not cool.

10.4 Processing arrays

Here we present an example application with several functions which process arrays. This application allocates an array using **malloc**, fills the array with random numbers by calling **random** and computes the minimum value in the array. If the array size is less than or equal to 20, it prints the values in the array.

Creating the array

The array is created using the `create` function shown below. This function is perhaps too short to be a separate function. It multiplies the array size by 4 to get the number of bytes in the array and then calls `malloc`.

```
;          array = create ( size );
create:
        push    rbp
        mov     rbp, rsp
        frame   1, 0, 1
        sub     rsp, frame_size
        sal     rcx, 2          ; multiply size by 4
        call    malloc
        leave
        ret
```

Filling the array with random numbers

The `fill` function uses storage on the stack for local copies of the array pointer and its size. It also stores a local variable on the stack. These 3 variables require 24 bytes of storage, which we can use from the shadow space prepared by the calling function. We store data in the array using "`mov [rdx+rcx*4], rax`", where `rdx` holds the address of the start of the array and `rcx` contains the index of the current array element.

Here we use several local labels. A local label is a label beginning with a dot. Their scope is between normal labels. So in the `fill` function, labels `.array`, `.size`, `.i` and `.more` are local. This allows reusing these same labels in other functions, which simplifies the coding of this application.

```
;          fill ( array, size );
fill:
.array equ     local1      ; using .array instead of local1
.size  equ     local2      ; using .size instead of local2
.i     equ     local3      ; using .i instead of local3
        push    rbp
        mov     rbp, rsp
        frame   2, 3, 0
        sub     rsp, frame_size
        mov     [rbp+.array], rcx   ; save array on stack
        mov     [rbp+.size], rdx    ; save size on stack
```

```
              xor        ecx, ecx              ; zero index register
.more         mov        [rbp+.i], rcx         ; save index register
              call       rand
              mov        rcx, [rbp+.i]         ; load index register
              mov        rdx, [rbp+.array]     ; load array address
              mov        [rdx+rcx*4], eax      ; store random value
              inc        rcx                   ; increment rcx
              cmp        rcx, [rbp+.size]      ; compare rcx & size
              jl         .more                 ; more if rcx is less
              leave
              ret
```

Printing the array

Printing the array is done with `printf`. The `print` function, just like `fill`, needs to save 3 values on the stack since it calls another function. The code is somewhat similar to `fill`, except that array values are loaded into a register rather than values being stored in the array. You will notice that the data segment is used to store the `printf` format in a spot near the `printf` call. You will also notice that I have reused several local labels.

```
;             print ( array, size );
print:
.array  equ   local1
.size   equ   local2
.i      equ   local3
        push  rbp
        mov   rbp, rsp
        frame 2, 3, 2
        sub   rsp, frame_size
        mov   [rbp+.array], rcx   ; save array
        mov   [rbp+.size],  rdx   ; save size
        xor   r8d, r8d            ; zero index register
        mov   [rbp+.i], r8        ;
        segment .data
.format:
        db    "%10d",0x0a,0
        segment .text
.more   lea   rcx, [.format]      ; first parameter
        mov   rdx, [rbp+.array]   ; get array address
        mov   r8, [rbp+.i]        ; get index register
        mov   edx, [rdx+r8*4]     ; get array[i]
        call  printf
        mov   rcx, [rbp+.i]       ; get index register
        inc   rcx                 ; increment index
        mov   [rbp+.i], rcx       ; save index register
```

```
            cmp     rcx, [rbp+.size]    ; compare index & size
            jl      .more               ; more if index is <
            leave
            ret
```

Finding the minimum value

The `min` function is a leaf function (does not call any other functions), so there is no real need for a stack frame and no need to align the stack at a 16 byte boundary. I have included the stack frame code as a good habit. The 5 extra instructions are probably a small overhead in a function with a loop. A conditional move instruction is used to avoid interrupting the instruction pipeline.

```
    ;           x = min ( array, size );
    min:
            push    rbp
            mov     rbp, rsp
            frame   2, 0, 0
            sub     rsp, frame_size
            mov     eax, [rcx]          ; get array[0]
            mov     r8d, 1              ; set index register = 1
    .more   mov     r9d, [rcx+r8*4]     ; get array[r8]
            cmp     r9d, eax            ; is array[r8] < eax
            cmovl   eax, r9d            ; if so, move to eax
            inc     r8                  ; increment index
            cmp     r8, rdx             ; compare r8 vs size
            jl      .more               ; more if r8 < size
            leave
            ret
```

Main program for the array minimum

The main program is shown below. It uses stack space for the local variables `.array` and `.size`. It uses a command line parameter for the array size, which is discussed in the next section. Comments in the code outline the behavior.

```
    main:
    .array  equ     local1
    .size   equ     local2
            push    rbp
            mov     rbp, rsp
            frame   2, 2, 2
            sub     rsp, frame_size
            mov     r8d, 10             ; set default size
```

```
                mov     [rbp+.size], r8

;               check for argv[1] providing a size
                cmp     ecx, 2          ; rcx = argc
                jl      .nosize
                mov     rcx, [rdx+8]    ; get argv[1]
                call    atoi
                mov     [rbp+.size], rax

.nosize:
;               create the array
                mov     rcx, [rbp+.size]
                call    create

                mov     [rbp+.array], rax
;               fill the array with random numbers
                mov     rcx, rax
                mov     rdx, [rbp+.size]
                call    fill

;               if size <= 20 print the array
                mov     rdx, [rbp+.size]
                cmp     rcx, 20
                jg      .toobig
                mov     rcx, [rbp+.array]
                call    print

.toobig:
;               print the minimum
                segment .data
.format:
                db      "min: %ld",0xa,0
                segment .text
                mov     rcx, [rbp+.array]
                mov     rdx, [rbp+.size]
                call    min
                lea     rcx, [.format]
                mov     rdx, rax
                call    printf
                leave
                ret
```

10.5 Command line parameter array

The command line parameters are available to a C program as parameters to **main**. The number of command line parameters is the first argument to **main** and an array of character pointers is the second argument to **main**. The first parameter is always the name of the executable file being run. The remaining parameters are the expansion by the user's shell of the rest of the command line. This expansion makes it convenient to use patterns like "*.dat" on the command line. The shell replaces that part of the command line with all the matching file names.

Here is a simple C program to print the command line parameters:

```
#include <stdio.h>

int main ( int argc, char *argv[] )
{
    int i;
    for ( i = 0; i < argc; i++ ) {
        printf("%sn", argv[i]);
    }
    return 0;
}
```

When executed as "./args hello world", it prints

```
./args
hello
world
```

The **argv** array is passed like all C arrays by placing the address of the first element of the array in a register or on the stack. In the case of **argv** its address is in register **rdx**. Below is a translation of the program to assembly, though the assembly code takes advantage of the fact that there is a **NULL** pointer at the end of the **argv** array.

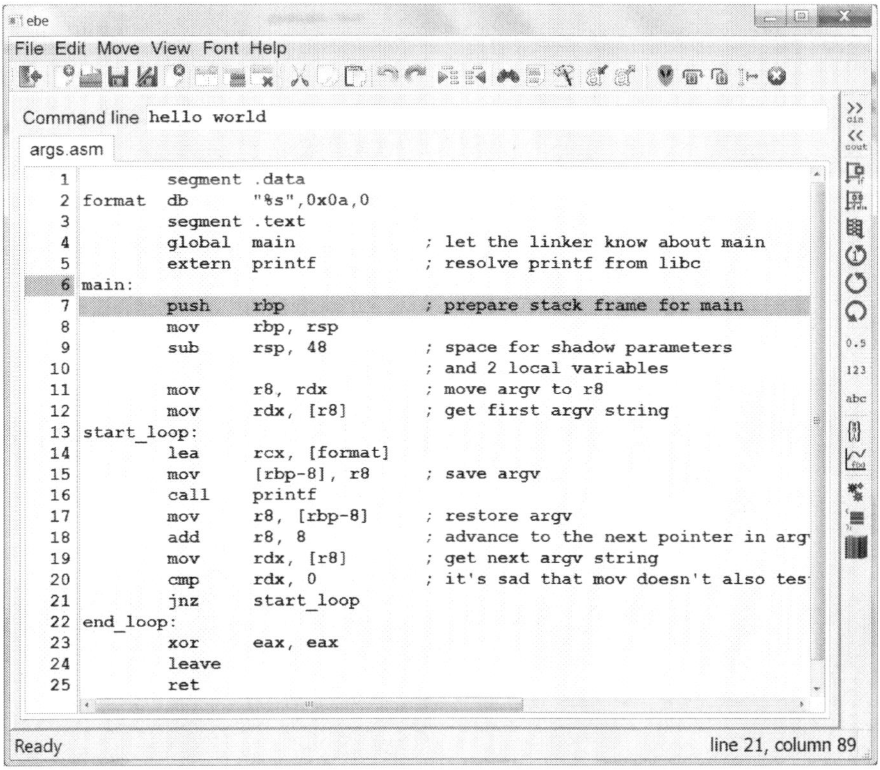

```
                        * ebe                                                                    _ □ x
                        File Edit Move View Font Help

                        Command line hello world
                        args.asm
                          1           segment  .data
                          2 format    db       "%s",0x0a,0
                          3           segment  .text
                          4           global   main                ; let the linker know about main
                          5           extern   printf              ; resolve printf from libc
                          6 main:
                          7           push     rbp                 ; prepare stack frame for main
                          8           mov      rbp, rsp
                          9           sub      rsp, 48             ; space for shadow parameters
                         10                                        ; and 2 local variables
                         11           mov      r8, rdx             ; move argv to r8
                         12           mov      rdx, [r8]           ; get first argv string
                         13 start_loop:
                         14           lea      rcx, [format]
                         15           mov      [rbp-8], r8         ; save argv
                         16           call     printf
                         17           mov      r8, [rbp-8]         ; restore argv
                         18           add      r8, 8               ; advance to the next pointer in arg
                         19           mov      rdx, [r8]           ; get next argv string
                         20           cmp      rdx, 0              ; it's sad that mov doesn't also tes
                         21           jnz      start_loop
                         22 end_loop:
                         23           xor      eax, eax
                         24           leave
                         25           ret

                        Ready                                                              line 21, column 89
```

You will notice that "`hello world`" has been entered in the "Command line" text box. When this program executes it will print the program name followed by "`hello`" and "`world`" on separate lines in the ebe terminal window. This terminal window will also be used by ebe for all reads from standard input.

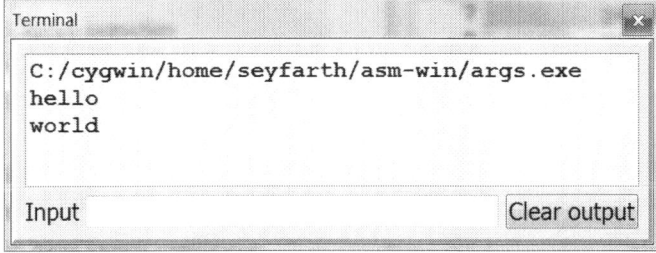

Exercises

1. Write 2 test programs: one to sort an array of random 4 byte integers using bubble sort and a second program to sort an array of random 4 bytes integers using the **qsort** function from the C library. Your program should use the C library function **atol** to convert a number supplied on the command line from ASCII to **long**. This number is the size of the array (number of 4 byte integers). Then your program can allocate the array using **malloc** and fill the array using **rand**. You call **qsort** like this

    qsort (array, n, 4, compare);

    The second parameter is the number of array elements to sort and the third is the size in bytes of each element. The fourth parameter is the address of a comparison function. Your comparison function will accept two parameters. Each will be a pointer to a 4 byte integer. The comparison function should return a negative, 0 or positive value based on the ordering of the 2 integers. All you have to do is subtract the second integer from the first.

2. Write a program to use **qsort** to sort an array of random integers and use a binary search function to search for numbers in the array. The size of the array should be given as a command line parameter. Your program should use **rand()%1000** for values in the array. This will make it simpler to enter values to search for. After building the array and sorting it, your program should enter a loop reading numbers with **scanf** until **scanf** fails to return a 1. For each number read, your program should call your binary search function and either report that the number was found at a particular index or that the number was not found.

3. Write an assembly program to compute the Adler-32 checksum value for the sequence of bytes read using **fgets** to read 1 line at a time until end of file. The prototype for **fgets** is

    char *fgets(char *s, int size, FILE *fp);

    The parameter **s** is a character array which should be in the **bss** segment. The parameter **size** is the number of bytes in the array **s**.

The parameter `fp` is a pointer and you need `stdin`. Place the following line in your code to tell the linker about `stdin`

    extern stdin

`fgets` will return the parameter `s` when it succeeds and will return 0 when it fails. You are to read until it fails. The Adler-32 checksum is computed by

```
long adler32(char *data, int len)
{
    long a = 1, b = 0;
    int i;
        for ( i = 0; i < len; i++ ) {
            a = (a + data[i]) % 65521;
            b = (b + a) % 65521;
        }
    return (b << 16) | a;
}
```

Your code should compute 1 checksum for the entire file. If you use the function shown for 1 line, it works for that line, but calling it again restarts.

4. Write a test program to evaluate how well the hashing function below works.

```
int multipliers[] = {
    123456789,
    234567891,
    345678912,
    456789123,
    567891234,
    678912345,
    789123456,
    891234567
};

int hash ( unsigned char *s )
{
    unsigned long h = 0;
    int i = 0;

    while ( s[i] ) {
        h = h + s[i] * multipliers[i%8];
        i++;
    }
    return h % 99991;
}
```

Your test program should read a collection of strings using `scanf` with the format string "%79s" where you are reading into a character array of 80 bytes. Your program should read until `scanf` fails to return 1. As it reads each string it should call `hash` (written in assembly) to get a number h from 0 to 99990. It should increment location h of an array of integers of size 99991. After entering all the data, this array contains a count of how many words mapped to each location in the array. What we want to know is how many of these array entries have 0 entries, how many have 1 entry, how many have 2 entries, etc. When multiple words map to the same location, it is called a "collision". So the next step is to go through the array collision counts and increment another array by the index there. There should be no more than 1000 collisions, so this could be done using

```
for ( i = 0; i < 99991; i++ ) {
    k = collisions[i];
    if ( k > 999 ) k = 999;
    count[k]++;
}
```

After the previous loop the `count` array has interesting data. Use a loop to step through this array and print the index and the value for all non-zero locations. An interesting file to test is "/usr/share/dict/words" from a Linux system which can also be downloaded from "https://github.com/dwyl/english-words". Write an assembly program to read a sequence of integers using `scanf` and determine if the first number entered can be formed as a sum of some of the other numbers and print a solution if it exists. You can assume that there will be no more than 20 numbers. Suppose the numbers are 20, 12, 6, 3, and 5. Then 20 = 12 + 3 + 5. Suppose the numbers are 25, 11, 17 and 3. In this case there are no solutions.

Chapter 11
Floating point instructions

The 8086 CPU used a floating point coprocessor called the 8087 to perform floating point arithmetic. Many early personal computers lacked the 8087 chip and performed floating point operations in software. This arrangement continued until the 486 which contained a coprocessor internally. The 8087 used instructions which manipulated a stack of 80 bit floating point values. These instructions are still part of modern CPUs, though there is a completely separate floating point facility available which has sixteen 128 bit registers (256 bits for the Intel Core i series) in 64 bit mode. We will study the newer instructions.

If you study the Intel 64 and IA-32 Architectures Software Developer's Manual, you will find many instructions such as **fadd** which work with registers named **ST0**, **ST1**, ... These instructions are for the math coprocessor. There are newer instructions such as **addsd** which work with Streaming SIMD Extensions (SSE) registers **xmm0**, **xmm1**, ..., **xmm15**. SIMD is an acronym for "Single Instruction - Multiple Data". These instructions are the focus of this chapter.

11.1 Floating point registers

There are 16 floating point registers which serve multiple purposes holding either 1 value or multiple values. The names for these registers are **xmm0**, **xmm1**, ..., **xmm15**. These registers can be used with instructions operating on a single value in each register or on a vector of values. When used as a vector an XMM register can be used as either 4 **float**s or 2 **double**s. The registers can also be used for collections of integers of various sizes, though the SSE integer instructions are basically ignored in this book.

The Core i series of computers introduced the Advanced Vector Extensions (AVX) which doubled the size of the floating point registers and added some new instructions. To use the full 256 bits (8 **float**s or 4 **double**s) you need to use a register name from **ymm0**, **ymm1**, ... **ymm15**. Each XMM register occupies the first 128 bits of the corresponding YMM register.

For most of this chapter the discussion refers only to XMM registers. In all cases the same instruction (prefixed by the letter "**v**") can be used with YMM registers to operate on twice as many data values. Stating this repeatedly would probably be more confusing than accepting it as a rule.

Ebe makes it easy to view the contents of floating point registers. The floating point register window displays the floating point registers in a variety of different formats. Consider this simple program which loads 2 float values and adds them:

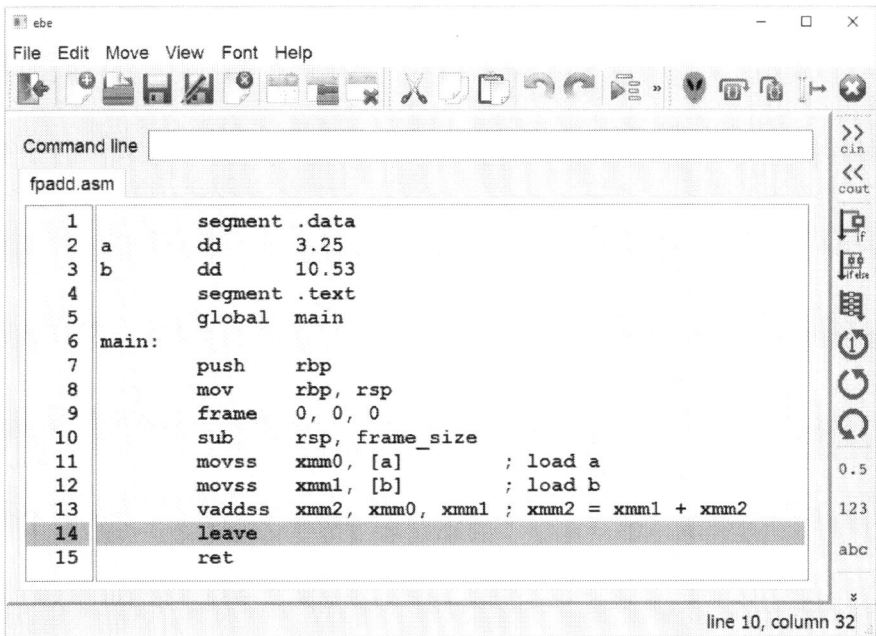

Below are the floating point registers after executing the **vaddss** instruction at line 13.

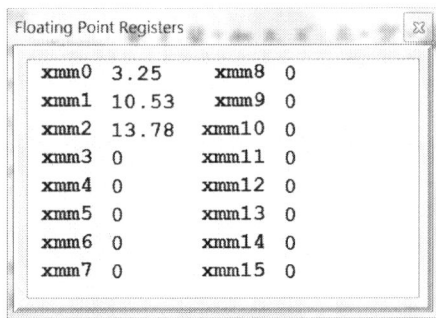

11.2 Moving floating point data

The SSE registers are 128 bits on most x86-64 CPUs (256 bits for the AVX registers). These registers can be used to do 1 operation at a time or multiple operations at a time. There are instructions for moving 1 data value and instructions from moving multiple data items, referred to as "packed" data.

Moving scalars

There are two instructions for moving scalar (1 value) floating point values to/from SSE registers: **movss** which moves 32 bit floating point values (**floats**) and **movsd** which moves 64 bit floating point values (**doubles**). These two instructions move a floating point value from memory to/from the lower part of a XMM register or from one XMM register to another. There is no implicit data conversion - after **movss** a 32 bit value exists in the destination. Here is a sample:

```
movss    xmm0, [x]      ; xmm0 = value at x
movsd    [y], xmm1      ; move xmm1 to y
movss    xmm2, xmm0     ; xmm2 = xmm0
```

Moving packed data

There are instructions for loading integer packed data and floating point packed data. We will concentrate here on packed floating point data. You can move packed **floats** or packed **doubles**. There are instructions for moving aligned or unaligned packed data. The aligned instructions are **movaps** for moving four **floats** and **movapd** for moving two **doubles** using XMM registers. The unaligned versions are **movups** and **movupd**. Moving packed data to/from YMM registers moves twice as many values.

Aligned data means that it is on a 16 byte boundary in memory. This can be arranged by using `align 16` for an array in the **data** segment or `alignb 16` in the **bss** segment[3]. Arrays allocated by **malloc** will be on 16 byte boundaries. Your program will fail with a segmentation fault if you attempt to use an aligned move to an unaligned address. Fortunately on the Core i series of CPUs the unaligned moves are just as fast as the aligned moves when the data is aligned. Note that the instructions using AVX registers begin with "**v**". Also the "**v**" instructions can have 3 register

---

[3] The nasm manual warns about alignment not always working, though it has always worked for me. In case of problems add align=16 to segment commands.

parameters, so you could subtract **ymm1** from **ymm2** and store the difference in **ymm0**. Here is a sample.

```
movups  xmm0, [x]       ; move 4 floats to xmm0
vmovups ymm0, [x]       ; move 8 floats to ymm0
vmovupd ymm1, [x]       ; move 4 doubles to ymm1
movupd  [a], xmm15      ; move 2 doubles to a
```

11.3 Addition

The instructions for adding floating point data come in scalar and packed varieties. The scalar add instructions are **addss** to add two **float**s and **addsd** to add two **double**s. Both these operate on a source operand and destination operand. The source can be in memory or in an XMM register while the destination must be in an XMM register. Unlike the integer add instruction the floating point add instructions do not set any flags, so testing must be done using a compare instruction.

The packed add instructions are **addps** which adds 4 **float**s from the source to 4 **float**s in the destination and **addpd** which adds 2 **double**s from the source to 2 **double**s in the destination using XMM registers. Like the scalar adds the source can be either memory or an XMM register, while the destination must be an XMM register. Using packed adds (**vaddps** or **vaddpd**) with YMM registers adds either 8 pairs of **float**s or 4 pairs of **double**s.

```
movss   xmm0, [a]       ; load a
addss   xmm0, [b]       ; add b to a
movss   [c], xmm0       ; store sum in c
movapd  xmm0, [a]       ; load 2 doubles from a
addpd   xmm0, [b]       ; a[0]+b[0], a[1]+b[1]
movapd  [c], xmm0       ; store 2 sums in c
vmovupd ymm0, [a]       ; load 4 doubles from a
vaddpd  ymm0, [b]       ; add 4 pairs of doubles
movupd  [c], ymm0       ; store 4 sums in c
vsubpd  ymm0, ymm2, ymm1
```

11.4 Subtraction

Subtraction operates like addition on either scalar **float**s or **double**s or packed **float**s or **double**s. The scalar subtract instructions are **subss** which subtracts the source **float** from the destination **float** and **subsd** which subtracts the source **double** from the destination **double**. The source can be either in memory or in an XMM register, while the destination must be an XMM register. No flags are affected by the floating point subtraction instructions.

The packed subtract instructions are **subps** which subtracts 4 source **float**s from 4 **float**s in the destination and **subpd** which subtracts 2 source **double**s from 2 **double**s in the destination using XMM registers. Again the source can be in memory or in an XMM register, while the destination must be an XMM register. Using packed subtracts (**vsubps** or **vsubpd**) with YMM registers subtracts either 8 pairs of **float**s or 4 pairs of **double**s.

```
movss    xmm0, [a]   ; load a
subss    xmm0, [b]   ; subtract b from a
movss    [c], xmm0   ; store a-b in c
movapd   xmm0, [a]   ; load 2 doubles from a
subpd    xmm0, [b]   ; a[0]-b[0], a[1]-b[1]
movapd   [c], xmm0   ; store 2 results in c
vmovapd  ymm0, [a]   ; load 4 doubles from a
vmovapd  [c], ymm0   ; store 4 results in c
```

11.5 Multiplication and division

Multiplication and division follow the same pattern as addition and subtraction in that they operate on memory or register operands. They support **float**s and **double**s and they support scalar and packed data. The basic mathematical instructions for floating point data are

instruction	effect
addsd	add scalar double
addss	add scalar float
addpd	add packed double
addps	add packed float
subsd	subtract scalar double
subss	subtract scalar float
subpd	subtract packed double
subps	subtract packed float
mulsd	multiple scalar double
mulss	multiply scalar float
mulpd	multiple packed double
mulps	multiple packed float
divsd	divide scalar double
divss	divide scalar float
divpd	divide packed double
divps	subtract packed float

11.6 Conversion

It is relatively common to need to convert numbers from one length integer to another, from one length floating point to another, from integer to floating point or from floating point to integer. Converting from one length integer to another is accomplished using the various move instructions presented so far. The other operations take special instructions.

Converting to a different length floating point

There are 2 instructions to convert floats to doubles: **cvtss2sd** which converts one **float** to a **double** and **cvtps2pd** which converts 2 packed **floats** to 2 packed **doubles**. The source can be a memory location or an XMM register while the destination must be an XMM register.

Similarly 2 instructions convert **doubles** to **floats**: **cvtsd2ss** which converts a **double** to a **float** and **cvtpd2ps** which converts 2 packed **doubles** to 2 packed **floats**. It has the same restriction that the destination must be an XMM register.

```
cvtss2sd xmm0, [a]    ; convert a to double in xmm0
addsd    xmm0, [b]    ; add a double to a
```

```
cvtsd2ss xmm0, xmm0    ; convert to float
movss    [c], xmm0     ; move float sum to c
```

Converting floating point to/from integer

There are 2 instructions which convert floating point to integers by rounding: `cvtss2si` which converts a `float` to a double or quad word integer and `cvtsd2si` which converts a `double` to a double or quad word integer. The `mxcsr` register controls the type of conversion. Set it to `0x1f80` to specify rounding. The source can be an XMM register or a memory location, while the destination must be a general purpose register. There are 2 instructions which convert by truncating: `cvttss2si` and `cvttsd2si`.

There are 2 instructions which convert integers to floating point: `cvtsi2ss` which converts a double or quad word integer to a `float` and `cvtsi2sd` which converts a double or quad word integer to a `double`. The source can be a general purpose register or a memory location, while the destination must be an XMM register. When using a register for the source the size is implicit in the register name. When using a memory location you need to add "`dword`" or "`qword`" to the instruction to specify the size.

```
         segment    .data
round dd            0x1f80
         segment    .text
         ldmxcsr    [round]              ; default to rounding
         cvtss2si   eax, xmm0            ; convert to int (round)
         cvtsi2sd   xmm0, rax            ; long to double
         cvtsi2sd   xmm0, dword [x]      ; dword to double
```

11.7 Floating point comparison

The IEEE 754 specification for floating point arithmetic includes 2 types of "Not a Number" or NaN. These 2 types are quiet NaNs and signaling NaNs. A quiet NaN (QNaN) is a value which can be safely propagated through code without raising an exception. A signaling NaN (SNaN) always raises an exception when it is generated. Perhaps you have witnessed a program failing with a divide by 0 error which is caused by a signal.

Floating point comparisons are considered to be either "ordered" or "unordered". An ordered comparison causes a floating point exception if either operand is a QNaN or SNaN. An unordered comparison causes an exception for only an SNaN. The gcc compiler uses unordered comparisons, so I will do the same.

The unordered floating point comparison instructions are `ucomiss` for comparing `float`s and `ucomisd` for comparing `double`s. The first operand must be an XMM register, while the second operand can be memory or an XMM register. They set the zero flag, parity flag and carry flag to indicate the type of result: unordered (at least 1 operand is NaN), less than, equal or greater than. A conditional jump seems like a natural choice after a comparison, but we need some different instructions for floating point conditional jumps. It will look good to use an instruction like `jge` (jump if greater than or equal), but the effect is different from `jae` (jump if above or equal).

instruction	meaning	aliases	flags
jb	jump if <	jc jnae	CF=1
jbe	jump if ≤	jna	CF=1 or ZF=1
ja	jump if >	jnbe	ZF=0 and CF=0
jae	jump if ≥	jnc jnb	CF=0

Here is an example

```
movss    xmm0, [a]
mulss    xmm0, [b]
ucomiss  xmm0, [c]
jbe      less_eq    ; jmp if a*b <= c
                    ; jmp below or equal
```

11.8 Mathematical functions

The 8087 coprocessor implemented a useful collection of transcendental functions like sine, cosine and arctangent. These instructions still exist in modern CPUs, but they use the floating point register stack and are no longer recommended. Instead efficient library functions exist for these functions.

The SSE instructions include floating point functions to compute minimum and maximum, perform rounding, and compute square roots and reciprocals of square roots.

Minimum and maximum

The minimum and maximum scalar instructions are **minss** and **maxss** to compute minimums and maximums for **float**s and **minsd** and **maxsd** to do the same for **double**s. The first operand (destination) must be an XMM register, while the second operand (source) can be either an XMM register or a memory location. The result is placed in the destination register.

There are packed versions of the minimum and maximum instructions: **minps**, **maxps**, **minpd** and **maxpd** which operate on either 4 **float**s (the **ps** versions) or 2 **double**s (the **pd** versions). The packed instructions require an XMM register for the first operand and either an XMM register or memory for the second. The **float** versions compute 4 results while the **double** versions compute 2 results.

```
        movss   xmm0, [x]   ; move x into xmm0
        maxss   xmm0, [y]   ; xmm0 has max(x,y)
        movapd  xmm0, [a]   ; move a[0], a[1] to xmm0
        minpd   xmm0, [b]   ; xmm0[0] = min(a[0],b[0])
                            ; xmm0[1] = min(a[1],b[1])
```

Rounding

The SSE instructions include 4 instructions for rounding floating point numbers to whole numbers: **roundss** which rounds 1 **float**, **roundps** which rounds 4 **float**s, **roundsd** which rounds 1 **double** and **roundpd** which rounds 2 **double**s. The first operand must be an XMM register, while the second operand can be either an XMM register or a memory location. There is a third operand which selects a rounding mode. A simplified view of the possible rounding modes is in the table below:

mode	meaning
0	round, giving ties to even numbers
1	round up
2	round toward 0 (truncate)

Here is an example of rounding normally

```
a       dq      1.5
b       dq      1.45
c       dq      1.99
        segment .text
        roundsd xmm0, [a], 0   ; xmm0 = 2.0
        roundsd xmm1, [b], 0   ; xmm1 = 1.0
        roundsd xmm2, [c], 0   ; xmm2 = 2.0
```

Square roots

The SSE instructions include 4 square root instructions: **sqrtss** which computes 1 **float** square root, **sqrtps** which computes 4 **float** square roots, **sqrtsd** which computes 1 **double** square root and **sqrtpd** which computes 2 **double** square roots. As normal the first operand (destination) must be an XMM register, and the second operand can be either an XMM register or a memory location. Bounding to 16 byte boundaries is required for a packed instruction with a memory reference.

11.9 Sample code

Here we illustrate some of the instructions we have covered in some fairly practical functions.

Distance in 3D

We can compute distance in 3D using a function which accepts 2 **float** arrays with x, y and z coordinates. The 3D distance formula is

$$d = \sqrt{(x_1 - x_2)^2 + (y_1 - y_2)^2 + (z_1 - z_2)^2}$$

Here is assembly code for 3D distance:

```
distance3d:
        movss    xmm0, [rcx]      ; x of first point
        subss    xmm0, [rdx]      ; - x of second point
        mulss    xmm0, xmm0       ; (x1-x2)^2
        movss    xmm1, [rcx+4]    ; y of first point
        subss    xmm1, [rdx+4]    ; - y of second point
        mulss    xmm1, xmm1       ; (y1-y2)^2
        movss    xmm2, [rcx+8]    ; z of first point
        subss    xmm2, [rdx+8]    ; - z of second point
        mulss    xmm2, xmm2       ; (z1-z2)^2
        addss    xmm0, xmm1       ; add x and y parts
        addss    xmm0, xmm2       ; add z part
        sqrtss   xmm0, xmm0
        ret
```

Dot product of 3D vectors

The dot product of two 3D vectors is used frequently in graphics and is computed by

$$x_1x_2 + y_1y_2 + z_1z_2$$

Here is a function computing the dot product of 2 **float** vectors passed as 2 arrays

```
dot_product:
        push    rbp
        mov     rbp, rsp
        frame   2, 0, 0
        sub     rsp, frame_size
        movss   xmm0, [rcx]     ; get x1
        mulss   xmm0, [rdx]     ; times x2
        movss   xmm1, [rcx+4]   ; get y1
        mulss   xmm1, [rdx+4]   ; times y2
        addss   xmm0, xmm1      ; x1*x2+y1*y2
        movss   xmm2, [rcx+8]   ; get z1
        mulss   xmm2, [rdx+8]   ; times z2
        addss   xmm0, xmm2      ; dot product
        leave
        ret
```

Polynomial evaluation

The evaluation of a polynomial of 1 variable could be done at least 2 ways. First is the obvious definition:

$$P(x) = p_0 + p_1 x + p_2 x^2 + \cdots + p_n x^n$$

A more efficient way to compute the value is using Horner's Rule:

$$
\begin{aligned}
b_n &= p_n \\
b_{n-1} &= p_{n-1} + b_n x \\
b_{n-2} &= p_{n-2} + b_{n-1} x \\
&\cdots \\
b_0 &= p_0 + b_1 x
\end{aligned}
$$

Then $P(x) = b_0$.

Written as a function with an array of double coefficients as the first parameter (**rcx**), a value for x as the second parameter (**xmm1**) and the degree of the polynomial as the third parameter (**r8**) we have:

```
horner:
;       first parameter (rcx) is array of coefficients
;       second parameter (xmm1) is a value for x (double)
;       third parameter (r8) is the polynomial degree
        push    rbp
        mov     rbp, rsp
        frame   3, 0, 0
```

```asm
            sub     rsp, frame_size
            movsd   xmm0, [rcx+r8*8]    ; xmm0 = b_k
            cmp     r8d, 0              ; is the degree 0
            jz      done
more:
            sub     r8d, 1
            mulsd   xmm0, xmm1          ; b_k * x
            addsd   xmm0, [rcx+r8*8]    ; add p_k
            jnz     more
done:
            leave
            ret
```

Exercises

1. Write a program testing a function to compute $\sin x$. The formula for $\sin x$ is given as the Taylor's series:

$$\sin x = x - \frac{x^3}{3!} + \frac{x^5}{5!} - \frac{x^7}{7!} \cdots$$

   Your function should work with doubles. Your program should read 2 numbers at a time using **scanf**. The first number is x and the second number is the number of terms of the expansion to compute. Your program should call your sine function and print the value it computes using **scanf**. The reading and computing should continue until **scanf** fails to return 2.

2. Write a program to compute the area of a polygon. You can use this formula for the area

$$A = \frac{1}{2} \sum_{i=0}^{n-1} (x_i y_{i+1} - x_{i+1} y_i)$$

   Your area function should have 3 parameters. The first parameter is an array of doubles holding x values. The second is an array of doubles holding y values. The third is the value n. Your arrays should be size $n + 1$ and location n of both arrays should be repeats of location 0. The number of vertices will be read using **scanf**. Then your program should allocate arrays of size $n + 1$ and read the coordinates using **scanf**. Lastly your program should compute and print the area.

3. Write a program to approximate the definite integral of a polynomial function of degree 5 using the trapezoidal rule. A polynomial of degree 5 is defined by 6 coefficients $p_0, p_1, \cdots, p_5$, where

$$p(x) = p_0 + p_1 x + p_2 x^2 + p_3 x^3 + p_4 x^4 + p_5 x^5$$

   The trapezoidal rule states that the integral from c to d of a function $f(x)$ can be approximated as

$$(d - c) \frac{f(c) + f(d)}{2}$$

   To use this to get a good approximation you divide the interval from a to b into a collection of sub-intervals and use the trapezoidal rule on each sub-interval. Your program should read the values of a and b. Then it should read the number of sub-intervals n. Last it should read the coefficients of the polynomial in the order p_0, p_1, $\cdots$ p_5. Then it should perform the computation and print the approximate integral.

4. Write a program to perform integration and differentiation of polynomials. The program should prompt for and read the degree of the polynomial. Then it should allocate arrays of the correct size for a polynomial, its derivative and its integral. Then the program should prompt for and read the coefficients of the polynomial. The last input will be two values from the domain, a and b. The program should evaluate and print the polynomial and its derivative at a and b. Last it should print the integral from a to b.

Chapter 12
Accessing Files

A system call is essentially a function call which changes the CPU into kernel mode and executes a function which is part of the kernel. When you run a process on Windows it runs in user mode which means that it is limited to executing only "safe" instructions. It can move data within the program, do arithmetic, do branching, call functions, ... , but there are instructions which your program can't do directly. For example it would be unsafe to allow any program to read or write directly to the disk device, so this is avoided by preventing user programs from executing input or output instructions. Another prohibited action is directly setting page mapping registers.

When a user program needs to do something like open a disk file, it makes a system call. This changes the CPU's operating mode to kernel mode where the CPU can execute input and output instructions. The kernel open call will verify that the user program has permission to open the file and then open it, performing any input or output instructions required on behalf of the program

Windows uses the `syscall` instruction much like Linux and OS X do to make system calls. A process places up to 4 parameters for the system call into registers and places any additional parameters on the stack like a normal function call. Then the process places the system call number into register `rax` and issues the `syscall` instruction. Unfortunately Microsoft regularly changes the numbers for system calls and recommends that programmers use the Windows API functions instead. So in this chapter we will discuss a little about file access using the Windows API and also using similar functions from the C library. The C library functions are much easier to use, though a Windows programming adventure would be incomplete without a little of the Windows API. Anyone interested in more Windows API programming should be able to use the online documentation at `http://msdn.microsoft.com` to learn more details.

In this chapter we give a brief introduction to using the Windows API to perform file access and present an alternative more portable low level file access collection. Learning how to use the Windows API file access functions is sufficient for explaining basic concepts involved in using Windows functions for GUI design and process control.

12.1 File access with the Windows API

Here we discuss how to create, read and write disk files using the Windows API. We will present one program to create a file and write "Hello world!" to the file and a second program to copy a file to a new file. The copy program uses command line parameters for file names and for the size of the array used in the copy. We also present timing based on a variety of array sizes.

Creating a file

The primary function for creating or opening a file in the Windows API is CreateFile. There are actually 2 variants: a Unicode version named CreateFileW and an ASCII one name CreateFileA. We will use CreateFileA which uses ASCII characters for the file name. In truth CreateFile can create and open many other things in addition to disk files, but we won't be trying that. The prototype taken from http://msdn.microsoft.com is

```
    HANDLE WINAPI CreateFileA(
      _In_        LPCTSTR lpFileName,
      _In_        DWORD dwDesiredAccess,
      _In_        DWORD dwShareMode,
      _In_opt_    LPSECURITY_ATTRIBUTES lpSecurityAttributes,
      _In_        DWORD dwCreationDisposition,
      _In_        DWORD dwFlagsAndAttributes,
      _In_opt_    HANDLE hTemplateFile
    );
```

The return type is a HANDLE which is a synonym for a double-word. This will be placed in register **rax** by **CreateFileA**, so it could be regarded as a quad-word. This value is an integer which is used in subsequent Windows API calls to refer to this created or opened file.

The first parameter is an input parameter which points to a normal C character string with a terminal 0. This pointer will be placed in register **rcx**.

The second parameter is a double-word which contains the access mode for the file. In the programs we present we will use `GENERIC_READ` and `GENERIC_WRITE` modes. The access mode will be placed in register `rdx` and it is adequate to treat it either as a double-word or a quad-word.

Technically the other double-word parameters can also be considered as quad-words since they are either placed in registers or on the stack in 64 bit locations. We will include the file "`win32n.inc`" prepared by Tamas Kaproncai to facilitate assembly programming using the Windows API. In addition to equates for values like `GENERIC_READ`, the include file includes struct definitions for many Windows API functions.

The third parameter defines the sharing mode for the function. A 0 means that there will be no sharing. One could also choose `FILE_SHARE_READ` or `FILE_SHARE_WRITE`. The third parameter is placed in register `r8`.

The fourth parameter is an optional pointer to a `SECURITY_ATTRIBUTES` struct. Leaving this as 0 will result in default security and prevents this file handle from being inherited by any child processes. The fourth parameter is placed in register `r9`.

The fifth parameter defines what should happen with a call to `CreateFileA`. You may want to only succeed with creation if the file currently does not exist (`CREATE_NEW`), open an existing file and delete its current data (`CREATE_ALWAYS`), open the file and keep its data (`OPEN_ALWAYS`), open the file only if it already exists (`OPEN_EXISTING`) or a handful of other options. The fifth parameter in placed on the stack at position `rsp+0x40` which leaves spaces for the shadow parameters in before the fifth parameter.

The sixth parameter can specify a collection of flags and attributes which are each single bits and can be or'ed together. For our programs we will use `FILE_ATTRIBUTE_NORMAL`. This parameter will be placed on the stack at location `rsp+0x48`.

The seventh parameter is an optional `HANDLE` which can be used to copy file attributes from another file. We will leave this as 0 to not use a template file.

Writing to a file

The Windows API function to write to a file is `WriteFile`. Though the example program writes text to the file, the file can contain any bytes and the writing is an exact copy of the array of bytes used in the `WriteFile` call. In particular in the program below a carriage-return (`0x0d`) and a new-line character (`0x0a`) are written to the file to make it a valid text file. The prototype for `WriteFile` is

```
BOOL WINAPI WriteFile(
    _In_        HANDLE hFile,
    _In_        LPCVOID lpBuffer,
    _In_        DWORD nNumberOfBytesToWrite,
    _Out_opt_   LPDWORD lpNumberOfBytesWritten,
    _Inout_opt_ LPOVERLAPPED
);
```

`WriteFile` returns true when it succeeds and false otherwise. It is generally necessary to use the fourth parameter to receive the number of bytes written to test for complete success.

The first parameter to `WriteFile` is the `HANDLE` returned from `CreateFile`. It is placed in register `rcx`.

The second parameter is the address of the data to be written to the file. This can be the address of any type of data. It is placed in register `rdx`.

The third parameter is the number of bytes to write. This is placed in register `r8`. Since this is a 32 bit integer it is not possible to write more than 2^{31}-1 bytes in one call. Perhaps this is unsigned and you could write more.

The fourth parameter is a pointer to a double-word which will receive back the number of bytes that CreateFile actually writes which can be less than requested for a variety of reasons. The web site describes this as optional, but I had problems leaving this as 0.

The fifth parameter is described as a struct pertaining to "overlapping" which means issuing a write and returning before it completes. This generally requires writing a "call-back" function to be called when the write completes. Another term for this is "asynchronous I/O". We will leave this as 0 indicating no asynchronous I/O.

Complete program to create a file

Below is a program to create a file named "sample.txt" and write "Hello world!" to it. When the program was written I copied the prototype for `CreateFileA` and `WriteFile` into the source as comments, but these comments are omitted from here.

```
%include "win32n.inc"

            segment .data
handle      dq      0
written     dq      0
filename    db      "sample.txt", 0
hello       db      "Hello world!", 0x0d, 0x0a, 0
length      equ     $-hello-1
```

```nasm
        segment .text
        global  main
        extern  CreateFileA, WriteFile, CloseHandle
main:
        push    rbp
        mov     rbp, rsp
        frame   2, 0, 7
        sub     rsp, frame_size
        xor     eax, eax
        mov     [rsp+newPar7], rax      ; hTemplateFile
        mov     qword [rsp+newPar6], FILE_ATTRIBUTE_NORMAL
        mov     qword [rsp+newPar5], CREATE_ALWAYS
        xor     r9d, r9d                ; lpSecurityAttributes
        xor     r8d, r8d                ; dwShareMode
        mov     rdx, GENERIC_WRITE      ; dwDesiredAccess
        lea     rcx, [filename]         ; lpFileName
        call    CreateFileA
        mov     [handle], rax

        xor     eax, eax
        mov     [rsp+newPar5], eax      ; not asynchronous I/O
        lea     r9, [written]           ; pointer to dword
        mov     r8d, length             ; # bytes to write
        lea     rdx, [hello]            ; pointer to text
        mov     rcx, [handle]           ; file handle
        call    WriteFile

        mov     rcx, [handle]
        call    CloseHandle
        xor     eax, eax
        leave
        ret
```

This maximum number of parameters in any called function in this program is 7 for **CreateFile**. Four of those are passed in registers and three on the stack. Providing 4 quad-words of shadow space and room for 3 more parameters means a total of 7 quad-words needed on the stack at the time of the call. This shows the value of the **frame** macro which computes that for 7 parameters, 56 bytes of stack space are needed and rounds the value for frame_size to 64 to maintain the 16 byte alignment of **rsp**.

This program uses an equate for the length of the **hello** array based on the **$** symbol from nasm. **$** means the current position in the code or data. This position is incremented for each byte of **hello**. We don't want to write the terminal 0 byte to the file so we use **$-hello-1**. This would allow changing the text to write while simultaneously adjusting the length value.

Reading from a file

Reading is done using `ReadFile` which has 5 parameters like `WriteFile` and each parameter has similar meanings as the corresponding parameter for `WriteFile`. Here is the prototype

```
BOOL WINAPI ReadFile(
    _In_        HANDLE hFile,
    _Out_       LPVOID lpBuffer,
    _In_        DWORD nNumberOfBytesToRead,
    _Out_opt_   LPDWORD lpNumberOfBytesRead,
    _Inout_opt_ LPOVERLAPPED
);
```

Again I strongly suggest supplying a pointer to a double-word to receive the number of bytes read by `ReadFile`. It is a good habit to check reads and writes for success after each call to discover problems early rather than late, though for simplicity the code in this book omits most error checking.

Program to copy a file

Below is a program to use the command line to accept 3 parameters: an input file name, a name for a new file and the number of bytes to read and write with each `ReadFile` and `WriteFile` call. The reason for varying the number of bytes to read or write is to test performance with various sizes for the data array.

The flow of the program is fairly typical. It starts by testing the number of command line parameters. If this is not 4 it prints a usage message and exits. If this is OK it processes the command line parameters. It saves the pointer to the input file name in variable input which will later hold the hold the HANDLE for the file. It uses the variable output to save the output file name. It uses `atol` to convert the fourth command line parameter to a long which will be the array size. After this it uses malloc to allocate an array of the requested size. Then it opens both files and enters a loop where it attempts to read the number of bytes requested. Upon reading 0 bytes (or less) it breaks out of the loop to close the files and return. After a successful read it writes the same number of bytes as it had read.

```nasm
%include "win32n.inc"

        segment .data
input   dq      0
output  dq      0
read    dq      0
written dq      0
size    dq      0
data    dq      0
usage   db      "usage: copy_file old new bytes_per_read"
        db      0x0a,0

        segment .text
        global  main
        extern  CreateFileA, ReadFile, WriteFile, CloseHandle
        extern  printf, atol, exit, malloc
main:
        push    rbp
        mov     rbp, rsp
        frame   2, 0, 7
        sub     rsp, frame_size

;       if ( argc != 4 ) {
        cmp     rcx, 4
        je      endif

;           print usage message
            lea     rcx, [usage]
            call    printf

;           exit(1)
            mov     ecx, 1
            call    exit
;       }
endif:

;       input = argv[1];
        mov     rcx, [rdx+8]
        mov     [input], rcx

;       output = argv[2];
        mov     rcx, [rdx+16]
        mov     [output], rcx

;       size = atol(argv[3]);
        mov     rcx, [rdx+24]
        call    atoll
```

161

```
                mov     [size], rax
                mov     rcx, rax
                call    malloc
                mov     [data], rax

;               Open input file

                xor     eax, eax
                mov     [rsp+newPar7], rax      ; hTemplateFile
                mov     qword [rsp+newPar6],
FILE_ATTRIBUTE_NORMAL
                mov     qword [rsp+newPar5], OPEN_EXISTING
                xor     r9d, r9d                ;
lpSecurityAttributes
                xor     r8d, r8d                ; dwShareMode
                mov     rdx, GENERIC_READ       ; dwDesiredAccess
                mov     rcx, [input]            ; lpFileName
                call    CreateFileA

;               if ( open fails ) {
                cmp     rax, 0
                jg      opened_input
;               print message
                segment .data
open_failure db         "failed to open %s",0x0a
                segment .text
                lea     rcx, [open_failure]
                mov     rdx, [input]
                call    printf

;               exit(1)
                mov     ecx, 1
                call    exit

;               }
opened_input:
                mov     [input], rax

;               Open output file

                xor     eax, eax
                mov     [rsp+newPar7], rax      ; hTemplateFile
                mov     qword [rsp+newPar6],
FILE_ATTRIBUTE_NORMAL
                mov     qword [rsp+newPar5], CREATE_ALWAYS
                xor     r9d, r9d                ;
lpSecurityAttributes
                xor     r8d, r8d                ; dwShareMode
```

```
                mov     rdx, GENERIC_WRITE      ; dwDesiredAccess
                mov     rcx, [output]           ; lpFileName
                call    CreateFileA

;               if ( open fails ) {
                cmp     rax, 0
                jg      opened_output
;                   print message
                lea     rcx, [open_failure]
                mov     rdx, [output]
                call    printf
                mov     ecx, 1
;                   exit(1)
                call    exit
;               }
opened_output:
                mov     [output], rax

;               while ( 1 )
read_more:
;                   read from input
                xor     eax, eax
                mov     [rsp+newPar5], eax
                lea     r9, [read]
                mov     r8d, [size]
                mov     rdx, [data]
                mov     rcx, [input]
                call    ReadFile
;                   if ( read == 0 ) break;
                mov     r8d, [read]
                cmp     r8, 0
                jle     done
;                   write the same size as read
                xor     eax, eax
                mov     [rsp+newPar5], eax
                lea     r9, [written]
                mov     rdx, [data]
                mov     rcx, [output]
                call    WriteFile
;               }
                jmp     read_more

done:
                mov     rcx, [input]
                call    CloseHandle
                mov     rcx, [output]
                call    CloseHandle
                xor     eax, eax
```

```
leave
ret
```

Below we see a plot of the time taken to copy a 1 million byte file using a variety of different array sizes. Using 1 byte at a time took about 8.5 seconds while using 1000 took about 0.19 seconds. Effectively the performance was almost maximal for 1000 bytes with 100000 and 1000000 requiring 0.18 seconds. These times include the time for running the program which includes program start time and copy time. Interestingly copying an empty file took about 0.175 seconds. The timing was a little erratic and getting more than 2 digits of accuracy would require better timing than afforded by my shell (bash under Cygwin).

Time to copy 1 million bytes
for different array sizes

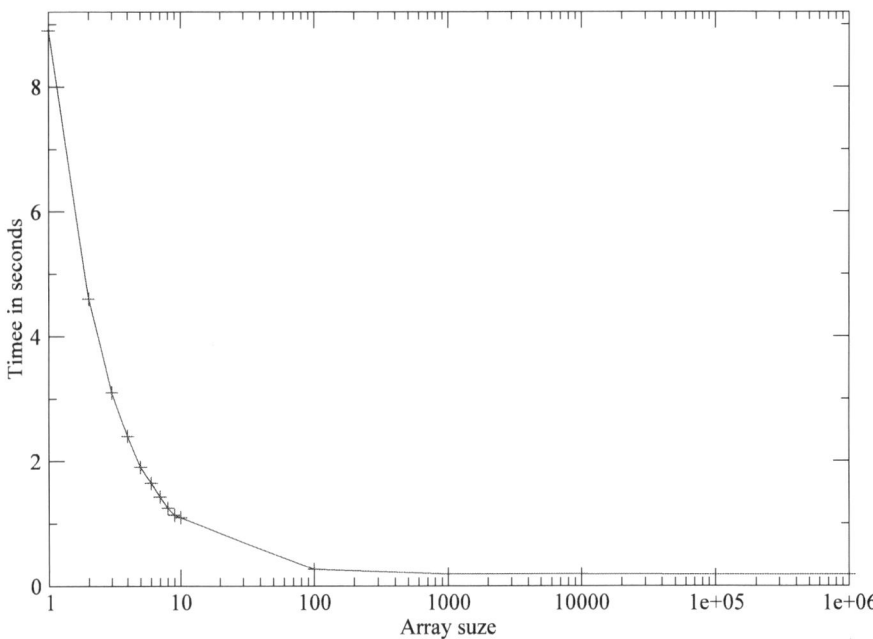

12.2 Portable C file access functions

The *lingua franca* of UNIX is C, so every UNIX system call is usable via a C wrapper function. For example there is a `write` function in the C library which does very little other than use the `syscall` instruction to perform the write request. Using these functions rather than the explicit `syscall` instruction is the preferred way to use the system calls. You won't have to worry about finding the numbers and you won't have to cope with the slightly different register usage.

The UNIX file access functions are available using gcc under Windows. Internally these functions end up calling their Windows API equivalents, so the performance should be slightly worse. Given that it takes a few nanoseconds to make a function call and translate to Windows API calls, the difference should be almost impossible to measure.

The previous "Hello world" program can be rewritten using **write** and **exit** as

```
          segment .data
msg:      db      "Hello World!",0x0a
len:      equ     $-msg        ; Length of the string
          segment .text
          global  main
          extern  write, exit
main:
          push    rbp
          mov     rsp, rsp
          frame   2, 0, 3
          sub     rsp, frame_size
          mov     r8d, len     ; Arg 3 is the length
          mov     rdx, msg     ; Arg 2 is the array
          mov     ecx, 1       ; Arg 1 is the fd
          call    write
          xor     ecx, ecx     ; 0 return = success
          call    exit
          leave                ; Just in case exit fails
          ret                  ; It should not fail, but...
```

Here you will notice that I have used a nasm equate to define **len** to be the current assembly point, $, minus the address of **msg**. **equ** is a pseudo-op which defines a symbolic name for an expression. This saves the trouble of counting characters and insulates the program from slight changes.

You might also have noticed the use of **extern** to tell the linker that **write** and **exit** are to be defined in some other place, in this case from the C library.

open

In order to read and write a file, it must be opened. For ordinary files this is done using the **open** function:

```
int open ( char *pathname, int flags [, int mode ]);
```

The **pathname** is a C string (character array terminated with a 0 byte). The **flags** are a set of bit patterns which are or'ed together to define how the file is to be opened: read-only mode, write mode or read-write mode and other characteristics like whether the file is to be created. If the file is to be created the **mode** parameter defines the permissions to assign to the new file.

The **flags** are defined in the table below:

bits	meaning
0	read-only
1	write-only
2	read and write
0x40	create if needed
0x200	truncate the file
0x400	append

The basic permissions are read, write and execute. A process must have read permission to read an object, write permission to write it, and execute permission to execute it. Execute permission for a file means that the file (either a program or a script) can be executed. Execute permission for a directory allows traversal of the directory.

These three permissions are granted or denied for 3 categories of accounts: user, group and other. When a user logs in to a Linux system the user's shell is assigned the user's user-id which is an integer identifying the user. In addition the user has a group-id (also an integer) which identifies the user as being in a particular group of users. A user can belong to multiple groups though only one is the active group. You can use the "**id**" command in the shell to print your user-id, group-id and the list of groups you belong to.

The basic permissions are 3 permissions for 3 groups. The permissions are 1 bit each for read, write and execute. This makes an ideal situation for using octal numbers. One octal "digit" represents 3 bits. Using 9 bits you can specify the basic permissions for user, group and others. Using nasm an octal number can be represented by a sequence of digits ending in either "**o**" or "**q**". Thus you could specify permissions for read and write for the user as 6, read for the group as 4 and no permissions for others as 0. Putting all these together we get **640o**.

The return value from **open** is a file descriptor if the value is greater than or equal to 0. An error is indicated by a negative return. A file descriptor is an integer identifying the connection made by **open**. File descriptors start at 0 and increase for each opened file. Here is some code to open a file:

```
        segment .data
fd:     dd      0
name:   db      "sample",0
        segment .text
        extern  open
        lea     rcx, [name]   ; pathname
        mov     edx, 0x42     ; read-write|create
        mov     r8d, 600o     ; read-write for me
        call    open
        cmp     eax, 0
        jl      error         ; failed to open
        mov     [fd], eax
```

read and write

The functions to read and write data to files are **read** and **write**. Their prototypes are quite similar:

```
int read(int fd, void *data, long count);
int write(int fd, void *data, long count);
```

The data array can be any type of data. Whatever the type is, the **count** is the number of bytes to read or write. Both functions return the number of bytes read or written. An error is indicated by returning -1 and setting the **extern** variable **errno** to an integer indicating the type of error. You can use the **perror** function call to print a text version of the error.

lseek

When reading or writing files, it is sometimes necessary to position to a specific spot in the file before reading or writing. An example would be writing record number 1000 from a file with records which are 512 bytes each. Assuming that record numbers begin with 0, then record 1000 would start at byte position $1000 * 512 = 512000$. It can be very quick to position to 512000 and write 512 bytes. This is also easier than reading and writing the whole file.

The **lseek** function allows you to set the current position for reading or writing in a file. Its prototype is

```
long lseek(int fd, long offset, int whence);
```

The **offset** parameter is frequently simply the byte position in the file, but the meaning of **offset** depends on the value of **whence**. If **whence** is 0, then **offset** is the byte position. If **whence** is 1, then **offset** is relative to the current position. If **whence** is 2, then **offset** is relative to the end of file. The return value from `lseek` is the position of the next read or write for the file.

Using `lseek` with `offset` 0 and `whence` equal to 2, `lseek` will return a byte position 1 greater than the last byte of the file. This is an easy way to determine the file size. Knowing the size, you could allocate an array and read the entire file (as long as you have enough RAM).

```
mov     rcx, [fd]
xor     edx, edx        ; set offset to 0
mov     r8d, 2          ; set whence to 2
call    lseek           ; determine file size
mov     [size], rax
mov     rcx, rax
call    malloc          ; allocate an array
mov     [data], rax
mov     rcx, [fd]
xor     edx, esi        ; set offset to 0
xor     r8d, r8d        ; set whence to 0
call    lseek           ; seek to start of file
mov     rcx, [fd]
mov     rdx, [data]
mov     r8, [size]
call    read            ; read the entire file
```

With 64 Windows, Linux and OS X, `lseek` uses a 64 bit integer for the `offset` parameter and this makes it possible to seek to positions greater than 2^{32}. Doing the same with 32 bit Windows would require using `lseek64`.

close

When you are done reading or writing a file you should close it. The only parameter for the `close` function is the file descriptor for the file to close. If you exit a program without closing a file, it will be closed by the operating system. Data read or written using file descriptors is not buffered in the user program, so there will not be any unwritten data which might be lost. This is not true for using `FILE` pointers which can result in lost data if there is no close. The biggest advantages to closing files are that it reduces overhead in the kernel and avoids running into the per-process limit on the number of open files.

```
mov     edi, [fd]
call    close
```

Exercises

1. Write a program which processes a collection of files named on the command line. For each file the program should print the number of bytes, words and lines much like the **wc** program does.

2. Write a program which expects 2 strings on the command line. The first string is a string to find and the second is the name of a file to search through for the string. The program should print all matching lines. This is a greatly simplified version of **grep**.

3. Write a version of the file copy program using open, read, write and close rather than the Windows API equivalents. Compare the times for both version for various sizes for the data array.

Chapter 13
Structs

It is fairly simple to use structs compatible with C by defining a struct in nasm. A struct is a compound object which can have data items of different types. Let's consider the C struct **Customer**:

```
struct Customer {
    int  id;
    char name[64];
    char address[64];
    int  balance;
};
```

We could access the customer data using assembly code assuming that we know the offsets for each item of the struct.

```
mov     rcx, 136        ; size of a Customer
call    malloc
mov     [c], rax        ; save the address
mov     [rax], dword 7  ; set the id
lea     rcx, [rax+4]    ; name field
lea     rdx, [name]     ; name to copy to struc
call    strcpy
mov     rax, [c]
lea     rcx, [rax+68]   ; address field
lea     rdx, [address]  ; address to copy
call    strcpy
mov     rax, [c]
mov     edx, [balance]
mov     [rax+132], edx
```

13.1 Symbolic names for offsets

Well that was certainly effective but using specific numbers for offsets within a struct is not really ideal. Any changes to the structure will require code modification and errors might be made adding up the offsets. It is better to have nasm assist you with structure definition. The nasm keyword for starting a struct is "**struc**". Struct components are defined between "**struc**" and "**endstruc**". Here is the definition of Customer:

```
        struc   Customer
id      resd    1
name    resb    64
address resb    64
balance resd    1
        endstruc
```

Using this definition gives us the same effect as using **equ** to set symbolic names for the offsets. These names are globally available, so you would not be permitted to have **id** in multiple structs. Instead you can prefix each of these names with a period like this:

```
         struc   Customer
.id      resd    1
.name    resb    64
.address resb    64
.balance resd    1
         endstruc
```

Now you must use "**Customer.id**" to refer to the offset of the **id** field. A good compromise is to prefix the field names with a short abbreviation of the struct name. In addition to giving symbolic names to the offsets, nasm will also define **Customer_size** to be the number of bytes in the struct. This makes it easy to allocate memory for the struct. Below is a program to initialize a struct from separate variables.

```
          segment .data
name      db      "Calvin", 0
address   db      "12 Mockingbird Lane",0
balance   dd      12500
          struc   Customer
c_id      resd    1
c_name    resb    64
c_address resb    64
c_balance resd    1
          endstruc
c         dq      0
          segment .text
          global  main
```

```
            extern    malloc, strcpy
main:
            push      rbp
            mov       rbp, rsp
            frame     2, 0, 2
            sub       rsp, frame_size
            mov       rcx, Customer_size
            call      malloc
            mov       [c], rax         ; save the pointer
            mov       [rax+c_id], dword 7
            lea       rcx, [rax+c_name]
            lea       rdx, [name]
            call      strcpy
            mov       rax, [c]         ; restore the pointer
            lea       rcx, [rax+c_address]
            lea       rdx, [address]
            call      strcpy
            mov       rax, [c]         ; restore the pointer
            mov       edx, [balance]
            mov       [rax+c_balance], edx
            xor       eax, eax
            leave
            ret
```

Now this is all great but there is a possible alignment problem versus C if we make the address field 1 byte larger. In C this makes the offset of **balance** increase from 132 to 136. In nasm it increases from 132 to 133. It still works but the struct definition does not match the alignment of C. To do so we must place **alignb 4** before the definition of **c_balance**.

Another possibility is to have a static variable of type **Customer**. To do this with default data, simply use this:

```
c           istruc    Customer
            iend
```

If you wish to define the fields, define them all in order.

```
c           istruc    Customer
            at c_id, dd 7
            at c_name, db "Calvin", 0
            at c_address, db "12 Mockingbird Lane", 0
            at c_balance, dd 12500
            iend
```

Let's look at the assembly data for the program which has a static **Customer**, **m**, and an allocated **Customer**, **c**.

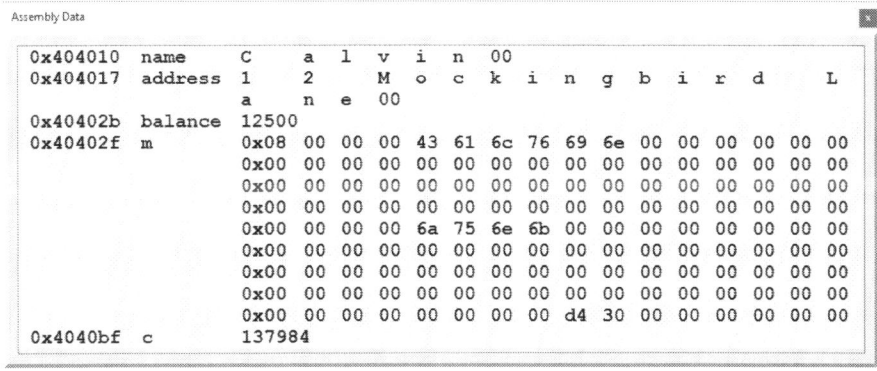

Initially the data for m is displayed as an array of bytes. After right clicking on the **m** variable, ebe displays a menu which allows you to select a format. You will notice "Expand struc *" and "struc". We could use the "Expand struc *" option on **c** and the "struc" option on **m**.

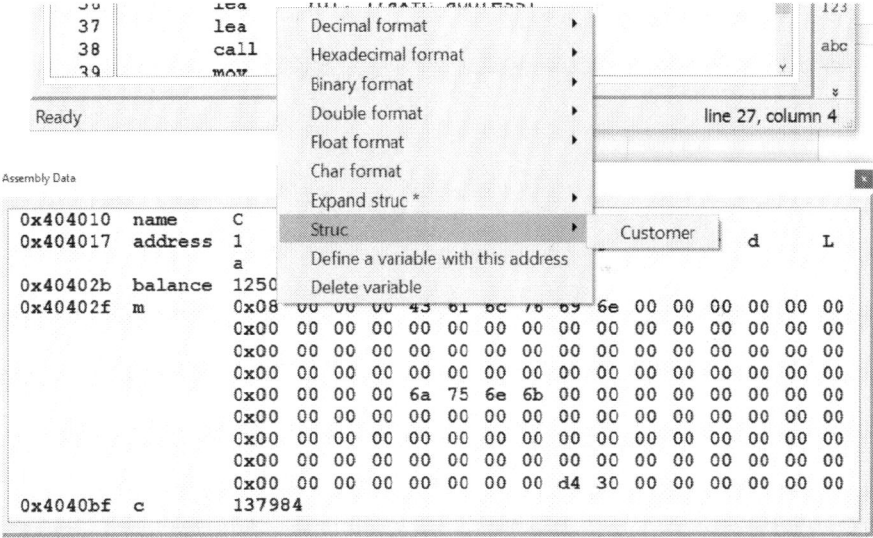

Here we see the data after selecting the appropriate menu choices for **c** and **m** and their components.

```
Assembly Data
0x404010  name        C   a   l   v   i   n   00
0x404017  address     1   2       M   o   c   k   i   n   g   b   i   r   d           L
                      a   n   e   00
0x40402b  balance     12500
0x40402f  m           0x43 61 6c 76 69 6e 00 00 00 00 00 00 00 00 00 00
0x40402f  c_name      C   a   l   v   i   n   00  00  00  00  00  00  00  00  00  00
                      00  00  00  00  00  00  00  00  00  00  00  00  00  00  00  00
                      00  00  00  00  00  00  00  00  00  00  00  00  00  00  00  00
                      00  00  00  00  00  00  00  00  00  00  00  00  00  00  00  00
0x40406f  c_address   1   2       M   o   c   k   i   n   g   b   i   r   d           L
                      a   n   e   00  00  00  00  00  00  00  00  00  00  00  00  00
                      00  00  00  00  00  00  00  00  00  00  00  00  00  00  00  00
                      00
0x4040b3  c_balance   12500
0x4040b7  c           1587632
0x1839b0  c_name      C   a   l   v   i   n   00  ba  \r  f0  ad  ba  \r  f0  ad  ba
                      \r  f0  ad  ba  \r  f0  ad  ba  \r  f0  ad  ba  \r  f0  ad  ba
                      \r  f0  ad  ba  \r  f0  ad  ba  \r  f0  ad  ba  \r  f0  ad  ba
                      \r  f0  ad  ba  \r  f0  ad  ba  \r  f0  ad  ba  \r  f0  ad  ba
0x1839f0  c_address   1   2       M   o   c   k   i   n   g   b   i   r   d           L
                      a   n   e   00  \r  f0  ad  ba  \r  f0  ad  ba  \r  f0  ad  ba
                      \r  f0  ad  ba  \r  f0  ad  ba  \r  f0  ad  ba  \r  f0  ad  ba
                      \r
0x183a34  c_balance   12500
```

13.2 Allocating and using an array of structs

If you wish to allocate an array of structs, then you need to multiply the size of the struct times the number of elements to allocate enough space. But the size given by `Customer_size` might not match the value from `sizeof(struct Customer)` in C. C will align each data item on appropriate boundaries and will report a size which will result in each element of an array having aligned fields. You can assist nasm by adding a terminal `alignb X` where X represents the size of the largest data item in the struct. If the struct has any quad word fields then you need `alignb 8` to force the `_size` value to be a multiple of 8. If the struct has no quad word byte fields but has some double word fields you need `alignb 4`. Similarly you might need `alignb 2` if there are any word fields.

So our code to declare a struct (slightly changed) and allocate an array would look like this

```
           segment .data
           struc   Customer
c_id       resd    1          ; 4 bytes
c_name     resb    65         ; 69 bytes
c_address  resb    65         ; 134 bytes
           alignb  4          ; aligns to 136
c_balance  resd    1          ; 140 bytes
```

```
c_rank      resb    1       ; 141 bytes
            alignb  4       ; aligns to 144
            endstruc
customers   dq      0
            segment .text
            mov     ecx, 100 ; for 100 structs
            mul     ecx, Customer_size
            call    malloc
            mov     [customers], rax
```

Now to work with each array element we can start with a register holding the value of **customers** and add **Customer_size** to the register after we process each customer. We're assuming that the following code is part of a function with at least 2 local variables.

```
            segment .data
format      db      "%s %s %d",0x0a,0
            segment .text
            mov     [rbp+local1], r14
            mov     [rbp+local2], r15

;           We're using r14 and r15 since
;           they are preserved through calls

            mov     r15, 100        ; loop counter
            mov     r14, [customers]
more        lea     ecx, [format]
            lea     edx, [r14+c_name]
            lea     r8, [r14+c_address]
            mov     r9, [r14+c_balance]
            call    printf
            add     r14, Customer_size
            sub     r15, 1
            jnz     more

;           r14 and r15 must be restored
;           for the calling function

            mov     r14, [rbp+local1]
            nov     r15, [rbp+local2]
```

Exercises

1. Design a struct to represent a set. The struct will hold the maximum set size and a pointer to an array holding 1 bit per possible element of the set. Members of the set will be integers from 0 to the set size minus 1. Write a test program to read commands which operate on the set. The commands will be "**add**", "**remove**", and "**test**". Each command will have an integer parameter entered with it. Your program will then be able to add elements to the set, remove elements to the set and test numbers for membership.

2. Using the design for sets from exercise 1, write a program to manipulate multiple sets. Implement commands "**add**", "**union**", "**print**" and "**intersect**". Create 10 sets with size equal to 10000. "**add s k**" will add k to set s. "**union s t**" will replace set s with $s \cup t$. "**intersect s t**" will replace set s with $x \cap t$. "**print s**" will print the elements of s.

3. Design a struct to represent large integers. For simplicity use quad word arrays as the data for the large integers. Each quad word will represent 18 digits of the number. So 1 quad word can store a number up to 999,999,999,999,999,999. 2 quad words can store a number up to 999,999,999,999,999,999,999,999,999,999,999,999. Implement only positive numbers. Implement addition and multiplication (based on addition). Compute 50!. You are permitted to write a main routine and the factorial function in C or C++ using assembly code to perform all long arithmetic.

Chapter 14
Using the C stream I/O functions

The functions callable from C include a wide variety of functions in many areas including process management, file handling, network communications, string processing and graphics programming. Studying much of these capabilities would lead us too far afield from the study of assembly language. The stream input and output facilities provide an example of a higher level library which is also quite useful in many programs.

In the chapter on system calls we focused on **open**, **read**, **write** and **close** which are merely wrapper functions for system calls. In this chapter we will focus on a similar collection of functions which perform buffered I/O. Buffered I/O means that the application maintains a data buffer for each open file.

Reading using a buffered I/O system can be more efficient. Let's suppose you ask the buffered I/O system to read 1 byte. It will attempt to read 1 byte from the buffer of already read data. If it must read, then it reads enough bytes to fill its buffer - typically 8192 bytes. This means that 8192 reads of 1 byte can be satisfied by 1 actual system call. Reading a byte from the buffer is very fast. In fact reading a large file is over 20 times as fast reading 1 byte at a time using the C stream **getchar** function compared to reading one byte at a time using **read**.

You should be aware that the operating system also uses buffers for open files. When you call **read** to read 1 byte, the operating system is forced by the disk drive to read complete sectors, so it must read at least 1 sector (probably 512 bytes). Most likely the operating system reads 4096 bytes and saves the data which has been read in order to make use of the data in subsequent reads. If the operating system did not use buffers, reading 1 byte at a time would require interacting with the disk for each byte which would be perhaps 10 to 20 times slower than using the buffer.

The net result from this discussion is that if your program needs to read or write small quantities of data, it will be faster to use the stream I/O facilities rather than using the system calls. It is generally possible to use the system calls and do your own buffering which is tailored for your needs thereby saving time. You will of course pay for this improved efficiency by working harder. You must weigh the importance of improved performance versus increased labor. Also be sure to test to verify that the assembly version uses less time.

14.1 Opening a file

The function to open a file using the stream I/O functions is **fopen**. It, like the other stream I/O functions, begins with the letter "**f**" to make the name distinct from the system call wrapper function it resembles. The prototype for **fopen** is

```
FILE *fopen ( char *pathname, char *mode );
```

The file to be opened is named in the first parameter and the mode is named in the second parameter. The **mode** can be any of the values from the table below

mode	meaning
r	read-only
r+	read and write, truncates or creates
w	write-only, truncates or creates
w+	read and write, truncates or creates
a	write only, appends or creates
a+	read and write, appends or creates

The return value is a pointer to a **FILE** object. This is an opaque pointer in the sense than you never need to know the components of the **FILE** object. Most likely a **FILE** object is a struct which contains a pointer to the buffer for the file and various "house-keeping" data items about the file. This pointer is used in the other stream I/O functions. In assembly language it is sufficient to simply store the pointer in a quad-word and use that quad-word as needed for function calls. Here is some code to open a file:

```
        segment .data
name    db      "customers.dat",0
mode    db      "w+",0
fp      dq      0
        segment .text
```

```
            global    fopen
            lea       rcx, [name]
            lea       rdx, [mode]
            call      fopen
            mov       [fp], rax
```

14.2 fscanf and fprintf

You have encountered `scanf` and `printf` in previous code. `scanf` is a function which calls `fscanf` with a `FILE` pointer named `stdin` as its first parameter, while `printf` is a function which calls `fprintf` with `FILE` pointer `stdout` as its first parameter. The only difference between these pairs of functions is that `fscanf` and `fprintf` can work with any `FILE` pointer. Their prototypes are

```
int fscanf( FILE *fp, char *format, ... );
int fprintf( FILE *fp, char *format, ... );
```

For simple use consult Appendix B which discusses `scanf` and `printf`. For more information use "`man fscanf`" or "`man fprintf`" or consult a C book.

14.3 fgetc and fputc

If you need to process data character by character, it can be convenient to use `fgetc` to read characters and `fputc` to write characters. Their prototypes are

```
int fgetc ( FILE *fp );
int fputc ( int c, FILE *fp );
```

The return value of `fgetc` is the character which has been read, except for end of file or errors when it returns the symbolic value `EOF` which is -1 as a 32 bit integer. This means that you need to compare `eax` instead of `rax` for a negative value to detect end of file. The function `fputc` writes the character provided in `c` to the file. It returns the same character it has written unless there is an error when it returns `EOF`.

Fairly often it is convenient to get a character and do something which depends on the character read. For some characters you may need to give control over to another function. This can be simplified by giving the character back to the file stream using `ungetc`. You are guaranteed only

1 pushed back character, but having 1 character of look-ahead can be quite useful. The prototype for ungetc is

```
int ungetc ( int c, FILE *fp );
```

Below is a loop copying a file from one stream to another using fgetc and fputc.

```
more:   mov     rcx, [ifp]      ; input file pointer
        call    fgetc
        cmp     eax, -1
        je      done
        mov     rcx, rax
        mov     rdx, [ofp]      ; output file pointer
        call    fputc
        jmp     more
done:
```

14.4 fgets and fputs

Another common need is to read lines of input and process them line by line. The function **fgets** reads 1 line of text (or less if the array is too small) and **fputs** writes 1 line of text. Their prototypes are

```
char *fgets(char *s, int size, FILE *fp);
int fputs(char *s, FILE *fp);
```

The first parameter to **fgets** is an array of characters to receive the line of data and the second parameter is the size of the array. The size is passed into the function to prevent buffer overflow. **fgets** will read up to **size** - 1 characters into the array. It stops reading when it hits a new-line character or end of file. If it reads a new-line it stores the new-line in the buffer. Whether it reads a complete line or not, **fgets** always places a 0 byte at the end of the data it has read. It returns **s** on success and a **NULL** pointer on error or end of file.

fputs writes the string in **s** without the 0 byte at the end of the string. It is your responsibility to place any required new-lines in the array and add the 0 byte at the end. It returns a non-negative number on success or **EOF** on error.

It can be quite useful following **fgets** to use **sscanf** to read data from the array. **sscanf** is like **scanf** except that the first parameter is an array of characters which it will attempt to convert in the same fashion as **scanf**. Using this pattern gives you an opportunity to read the data with sscanf, determine that the data was not what you expected and read it again with sscanf with a different format string.

Here is some code which copies lines of text from one stream to another, skipping lines which start with a ";"

```
more:   lea     rcx, [s]
        mov     edx, 200
        mov     r8, [ifp]
        call    fgets
        cmp     rax, 0
        je      done
        mov     al, [s]
        cmp     al, ';'
        je      more
        lea     rcx, [s]
        mov     rdx, [ofp]
        call    fputs
        jmp     more
done:
```

14.5 fread and fwrite

The **fread** and **fwrite** functions are designed to read and write arrays of data. Their prototypes are

```
int fread(void *p, int size, int nelts, FILE *fp);
int fwrite(void *p, int size, int nelts, FILE *fp);
```

The first parameter to these functions is an array of any type. The next parameter is the size of each element of the array, while the third is the number of array elements to read or write. They return the number of array elements read or written. In the event of an error or end of file, the return value might be less than **nelts** or 0.

Here is some code to write all 100 elements of the **customers** array to a disk file

```
        mov     rcx, [customers] ; allocated array
        mov     edx, Customer_size
        mov     r8d, 100
        mov     r9, [fp]
        call    fwrite
```

14.5 fseek and ftell

Positioning a stream is done using the **fseek** function, while **ftell** is used to determine the current position. The prototype for these functions are

```
int fseek ( FILE *fp, long offset, int whence );
long ftell ( FILE *fp );
```

The second parameter, **offset**, of **fseek** is a byte position value which is dependent on the third parameter, **whence**, to define its meaning. The meaning of **whence** is exactly like in **lseek**. If **whence** is 0, then **offset** is the byte position. If **whence** is 1, then **offset** is relative to the current position. If **whence** is 2, then **offset** is relative to the end of file.

The return value of **fseek** is 0 for success and -1 for errors. If there is an error the variable **errno** is set appropriately. The return value of **ftell** is the current byte position in the file unless there is an error. On error it returns -1.

Here is a function to write a **Customer** record to a file.

```
;          void write_customer(FILE *fp, struct Customer *c,
;                              int record_number );
           segment .text
           global  write_customer:
.fp        equ     local1
.c         equ     local2
.rec       equ     local3
           push    rbp
           mov     rbp, rsp
           sub     rsp, 32          ; shadow parameters
           mov     [rbp+.fp], rcx   ; save parameters in
           mov     [rbp+.c], rdx    ; current stack frame
           mov     [rbp+.rec], r8
           mul     r8, Customer_size
           mov     rdx, r8          ; offset for ftell
           mov     r8, 0            ; whence
           call    fseek            ; position file
           mov     rcx, [rbp+.c]
           mov     rdx, Customer_size
           mov     r8, 1
           mov     r9, [rbp+.fp]
           call    fwrite           ; write the record
           leave
           ret
```

14.6 fclose

`fclose` is used to close a stream. This is important since a stream may have data in its buffer which needs to be written. This data will be written when you call `fclose` and will be forgotten if you fail to call it. A `FILE` pointer is the only parameter to `fclose`.

Exercises

1. Write an assembly program which will create a new **Customer** using the struct definition from this chapter. Your program should prompt for and read the file name, the customer name, address, balance and rank fields. Then your code should scan the data in the file looking for an empty position. An empty position is a record with 0 in the **id** field. In general the **id** value will be 1 greater than the record number for a record. If there is no empty record, then add a new record at the end of the file. Report the customer's id.

2. Write an assembly program to update the balance for a customer. The program should accept from the command line the name of a data file, a customer id and an amount to add to the balance for that customer. The customer's id is 1 greater than the record number. Report an error if the customer record is unused (**id** = 0).

3. Write an assembly program to read the customer data in a file, sort it by balance and print the data in increasing balance order. You should open the file and use **fseek** to seek to the end and use **ftell** to determine the number of records in the file. It should allocate an array large enough to hold the entire file, read the records one at a time, skipping past the unused records (**id** = 0). Then it should sort using **qsort**. You can call **qsort** using

    ```
    qsort(struct Customer *c, int count, int size, compare);
    ```

    The **count** parameter is the number of structs to sort and **size** is the size of each in bytes. The **compare** parameter is the address of a function which will accept 2 parameters, each a pointer to a **struct Customer**. This function will compare the **balance** fields of the 2 structs and return a negative, 0, or positive value based on the order of the 2 balances.

Chapter 15
Data structures

Data structures are widely used in application programming. They are frequently used for algorithmic purposes to implement structures like stacks, queues and heaps. They are also used to implement data storage based on a key, referred to as a "dictionary". In this chapter we discuss implementing linked lists, hash tables, doubly-linked lists and binary trees in assembly.

One common feature of all these data structures is the use of a structure called a "node" which contains data and one or more pointers to other nodes. The memory for these nodes will be allocated using `malloc`.

15.1 Linked lists

A linked list is a structure composed of a chain of nodes. Below is an illustration of a linked list:

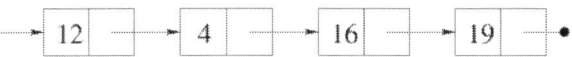

You can see that the list has 4 nodes. Each node has a data value and a pointer to another node. The last node of the list has a **NULL** pointer (value 0), which is illustrated as a filled circle. The list itself is represented as a pointer. We can illustrate the list more completely by placing the list's first pointer in a box and giving it a name:

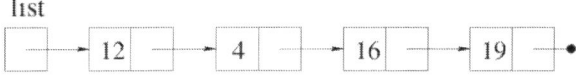

This list has no obvious order to the data values in the nodes. It is either unordered or possibly ordered by time of insertion. It is very easy to insert a new node at the start of a list, so the list could be in decreasing time of insertion order.

The list is referenced using the pointer stored at the memory location labeled `list`. The nodes on the list are not identified with specific labels in the code which maintains and uses the list. The only way to access these nodes is by using the pointers in the list.

List node structure

Our list node will have 2 fields: a data value and a pointer to the next node. The nasm structure definition is

```
        struc   node
n_value resq    1
n_next  resq    1
        alignb  8
        endstruc
```

The alignment instruction is not needed with 2 quad-words in the structure, but it may protect us from confusion later.

Creating an empty list

The first decision in designing a container structure is how to represent an empty container. In this linked list design we will take the simplest choice of using a NULL pointer as an empty list. Despite this simplicity it may be advantageous to have a function to create an empty list. Perhaps later we will change the representation of a empty list. Creating a frame is overkill for a trivial function.

```
newlist:
        xor     eax, eax
        ret
```

Inserting a number into a list

The decision to implement an empty list as a NULL pointer leaves a small issue for insertion. Each insertion will be at the start of the list which means that there will be a new pointer stored in the list start pointer for each insertion. There are 2 possible ways to cope with this. One way is to pass the address of the pointer into the insertion function. A second way is to have the insertion pointer return the new pointer and leave it to the insertion code to assign the new pointer upon return. It is less confusing to dodge the address of a pointer problem. Here is the insertion code:

```
;       list = insert ( list, k );
insert:
```

```
.list   equ     local1
.k      equ     local2
        push    rbp
        mov     rbp, rsp
        frame   2, 2, 1
        sub     rsp, frame_size
        mov     [rbp+.list], rcx    ; save list pointer
        mov     [rbp+.k], rdx       ; and k in stack frame
        mov     ecx, node_size
        call    malloc              ; rax = node pointer
        mov     r8, [rbp+.list]     ; get list pointer
        mov     [rax+n_next], r8    ; r8 is next new node
        mov     r9, [rbp+.k]        ; get k
        mov     [rax+n_value], r9   ; save k in node
        leave
        ret
```

Traversing the list

Traversing the list requires using an instruction like

```
        mov     rbx, [rbx+n_next]
```

to advance from a pointer to one node to a pointer to the next node. We start by inspecting the pointer to see if it is **NULL**. If it is not then we enter the loop. After processing a node we advance the pointer and repeat the loop if the pointer is not **NULL**. The print function below traverses the list and prints each data item. The code shows a good reason why it is nice to have a few registers protected in calls. We depend on **rbx** being preserved by **printf**.

```
print:
        segment .data
.print_fmt:
        db      "%ld ",0
.newline:
        db      0x0a,0
        segment .text
.rbx    equ     local1
        push    rbp
        mov     rbp, rsp
        frame   1, 1, 2
        sub     rsp, frame_size
        mov     [rbp+.rbx], rbx     ; save old rbx
        cmp     rcx, 0              ; skip the loop if
        je      .done               ; list pointer == 0
        mov     rbx, rcx            ; get first node
.more:
```

```
        lea     rcx, [.print_fmt]
        mov     rdx, [rbx+n_value]
        call    printf          ; print node value
        mov     rbx, [rbx+n_next] ; p = p->next
        cmp     rbx, 0          ; end the loop if
        jne     .more           ; node pointer == 0
.done:
        lea     rcx, [.newline]
        call    printf          ; print a new-line
        mov     rbx, [rbp+.rbx] ; restore rbx
        leave
        ret
```

Last we have a main function which creates a list, reads values using **scanf**, inserts the values into the list and prints the list after each insertion.

```
main:
.list   equ     local1
.k      equ     local2
        segment .data
.scanf_fmt:
        db      "%ld",0
        segment .text
        push    rbp
        mov     rbp, rsp
        frame   2, 2, 2
        sub     rsp, frame_size
        call    newlist         ; create a list
        mov     [rbp+.list], rax
.more   lea     rcx, [.scanf_fmt]
        lea     rdx, [rbp+.k]
        call    scanf           ; read k
        cmp     rax, 1          ; if read fails return
        jne     .done
        mov     rcx, [rbp+.list]
        mov     rdx, [rbp+.k]
        call    insert          ; insert k
        mov     [rbp+.list], rax
        mov     rcx, rax
        call    print           ; print the list
        jmp     .more
.done   leave
        ret
```

Here is a sample session using the program, entering the numbers 1 through 5 (input in boldface):

```
1
1

2
2 1

3
3 2 1

4
4 3 2 1

5
5 4 3 2 1
```

You can see the most recently printed number is at the first of the list. By adding a function to get and remove (pop) the first element of the list, we could turn this into a stack. This is one of the exercises for this chapter.

15.2 Doubly-linked lists

A doubly-linked list has 2 pointers for each node: one points to the next node and one points to the previous node. It becomes quite simple to manage a doubly-linked list if you make the list circular and if you retain an unused cell at the start of the list. Here is an example list with 4 data nodes, where the X indicates the value for the unused cell:

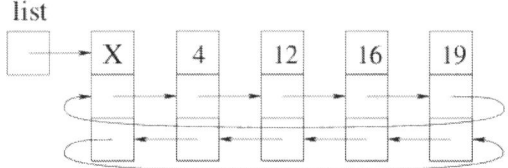

We see that the variable **list** points to the first node of the list, called the "head node". The head node has a value, but we never use the value. The top pointer in each node points to the next node in the list and the bottom pointer points to the previous node in the list. The previous pointer of the head node is the last node in the list. This makes this list capable of implementing a stack (last-in first-out), a queue (first-in first-out) or a double-ended queue (deque). The primary advantage of this design is that the list is never really empty. It can be logically empty but the head node remains. Furthermore, once a list is created, the pointer to the head node never changes.

Doubly-linked list node structure

Our list node will have 3 fields: a data value, a pointer to the next node and a pointer to the previous node. The nasm structure definition is

```
                struc   node
n_value resq    1
n_next  resq    1
n_prev  resq    1
        alignb  8
        endstruc
```

Creating a new list

The code for creating a new doubly-linked list allocates a new node and sets its next and previous pointers to itself. The calling function receives a pointer which does not change during the execution of the program. Here is the creation code:

```
;           list = newlist();
newlist:
        push    rbp
        mov     rbp, rsp
        frame   0, 0, 1
        sub     rsp, frame_size
        mov     ecx, node_size
        call    malloc
        mov     [rax+n_next], rax   ; points forward
        mov     [rax+n_prev], rax   ; and back to itself
        leave
        ret
```

When it returns the empty list looks like the diagram below:

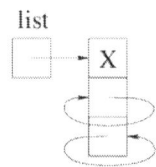

Inserting at the front of the list

To insert a new node at the front of the list you need to place the head node's next pointer in the new node's next slot and place the head pointer into the new node's previous slot. After doing that you can make the head node point forward to the new node and make the head's former next point backwards to the new node. These steps are illustrated in the diagram below. The old links are in dashed lines and the new links are numbered, with bold lines.

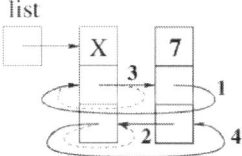

One of the elegant features of the doubly-linked circular list is the elimination of special cases. Inserting the first node is done with exactly the same code as inserting any other node.

The code for insertion is

```
;     insert ( list, k );
insert:
.list  equ    local1
.k     equ    local2
       push   rbp
       mov    rbp, rsp
       frame  2, 2, 1
       sub    rsp, frame_size
       mov    [rbp+.list], rcx    ; save list pointer
       mov    [rbp+.k], rdx       ; and k on stack frame
       mov    ecx, node_size
       call   malloc              ; rax = new node
       mov    r8, [rbp+.list]     ; get list pointer
       mov    r9, [r8+n_next]     ; get head's next
       mov    [rax+n_next], r9    ; p->next = h->next
       mov    [rax+n_prev], r8    ; p->prev = h
       mov    [r8+n_next], rax    ; h->next = p
       mov    [r9+n_prev], rax    ; p->next->prev = p
       mov    r9, [rbp+.k]        ; get k
       mov    [rax+n_value], r9   ; save k in node
       leave
       ret
```

List traversal

List traversal of a doubly-linked list is somewhat similar to traversal of a singly-linked list. We do need to skip past the head node and we need to test the current pointer against the pointer to the head node to detect the end of the list. Here is the code for printing the list:

```
;     print ( list );
print:
       segment .data
.print_fmt:
```

```
            db      "%ld ",0
.newline:
            db      0x0a,0
            segment .text
.list   equ local1
.rbx    equ local2
            push    rbp
            mov     rbp, rsp
            frame   1, 2, 2
            sub     rsp, frame_size
            mov     [rbp+.rbx], rbx    ; save rbx
            mov     [rbp+.list], rcx   ; keep head pointer
            mov     rbx, [rcx+n_next]  ; get first node
            cmp     rbx, [rbp+.list]   ; if it's head node
            je      .done              ; the list is empty
.more:
            lea     rcx, [.print_fmt]
            mov     rdx, [rbx+n_value]
            call    printf             ; print node value
            mov     rbx, [rbx+n_next]  ; get next node
            cmp     rbx, [rbp+.list]   ; if it's head node
            jne     .more              ; end the loop
.done:
            lea     rcx, [.newline]
            call    printf             ; print a newline
            mov     rbx, [rbp+.rbx]    ; restore rbx
            leave
            ret
```

15.3 Hash tables

A hash table is an efficient way to implement a dictionary. The basic idea is that you compute a hash value for the key for each item in the dictionary. The purpose of the hash value is to spread the keys throughout an array. A perfect hash function would map each key to a unique location in the array used for hashing, but this is difficult to achieve. Instead we must cope with keys which "collide".

The simplest way to cope with collisions is to use a linked list for each location in the hash array. Consider the illustration below:

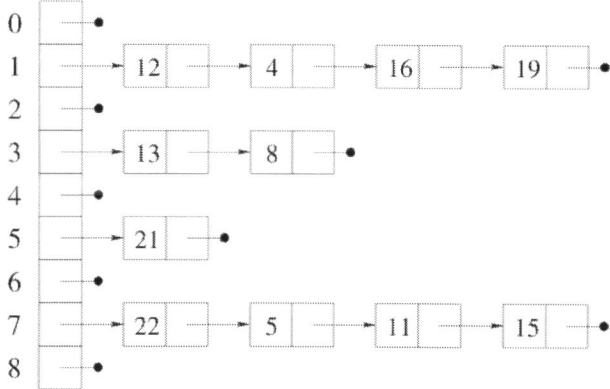

In this hash table, keys 12, 4, 16 and 9 all have hash values of 1 and are placed on the list in location 1 of the hash array. Keys 13 and 8 both have hash values 3 and are placed on the list in location 3 of the array. The remaining keys are mapped to 5 and 7.

One of the critical issues with hashing is to develop a good hashing function. A hashing function should appear almost random. It must compute the same value for a particular key each time it is called for the key, but the hash values aren't really important - it's the distribution of keys onto lists which matters. We want a lot of short lists. This means that the array size should be at least as large as the number of keys expected. Then, with a good hash function, the chains will generally be quite short.

A good hash function for integers

It is generally recommended that a hash table size be a prime number. However this is not very important if there is no underlying pattern to the numbers used as keys. In that case you can simply use n mod t where n is the key and t is the array size. If there is a pattern like many multiples of the same number, then using a prime number for t makes sense. For simplicity I am using a bad hash function. However it is good for debugging.

Here is the hash function for the example code:

```
;           i = hash ( n );
  hash      mov       eax, ecx      ; no stack frame for
            and       eax, 0xff     ; such a simple function
            ret
```

The table size is 256 in the example, so using **and** gives n mod 256.

A good hash function for strings

A good hash function for strings is to treat the string as containing polynomial coefficients and evaluate $p(n)$ for some prime number n. In the code below we use the prime number 191 in the evaluation. After evaluating the polynomial value, you can perform a modulus operation using the table size (100000 in the sample code). Using a prime number in the computation makes it less important that the table size be a prime.

```
int hash ( unsigned char *s )
{
    unsigned long h = 0;
    int i = 0;
    while ( s[i] ) {
        h = h*191 + s[i];
        i++;
    }
    return h % 100000;
}
```

Hash table node structure and array

In the sample hash table the table size is 256, so we need an array of 256 NULL pointers when the program starts. Since this is quite small, it is implemented in the data segment. For a more realistic program, we would need a hash table creation function to allocate an array and fill it with 0's. Below is the declaration of the array and the structure definition for the linked lists at each array location.

```
         segment .data
table    times 256 dq   0
         struc  node
n_value  resq   1
n_next   resq   1
         alignb 8
         endstruc
```

Function to find a value in the hash table

The basic purpose of a hash table is to store some data associated with a key. In the sample hash table we are simply storing the key. The **find** function below searches through the hash table looking for a key. If it is found, the function returns a pointer to the node with the key. If it is not found, it returns 0. A more realistic program would probably return a pointer to the data associated with the key.

The **find** function operates by calling **hash** to compute the index in the hash array for the linked list which might hold the key being sought. Then the function loops through the nodes on the list looking for the key.

```
;       p = find ( n );
;       p = 0 if not found
find:
.n      equ    local1
        push   rbp
        mov    rbp, rsp
        frame  1, 1, 1
        sub    rsp, frame_size
        mov    [rbp+.n], rcx        ; save n
        call   hash                 ; h = hash(n)
        mov    rax, [table+rax*8]   ; p = table[h]
        mov    rcx, [rbp+.n]        ; restore n
        cmp    rax, 0               ; if node pointer
        je     .done                ; is 0 quit
.more:
        cmp    rcx, [rax+n_value]   ; if p->value = n
        je     .done                ; return p
        mov    rax, [rax+n_next]    ; p = p->next
        cmp    rax, 0               ; if node pointer
        jne    .more                ; is 0 quit
.done:
        leave
        ret
```

Insertion code

The code to insert a key into the hash table begins by calling **find** to avoid inserting the key more than once. If the key is found it skips the insertion code. If the key is not found, the function calls **hash** to determine the index for the linked list to add the key to. It allocates memory for a new node and inserts it at the start of the list.

```
;       insert ( n );
insert:
.n      equ    local1
.h      equ    local2
        push   rbp
        mov    rbp, rsp
        frame  1, 2, 1
        sub    rsp, frame_size
        mov    [rbp+.n], rcx        ; save n
        call   find                 ; look for n
        cmp    rax, 0               ; if n id found
```

```
            jne     .found              ; skip insertion
            mov     rcx, [rbp+.n]       ; restore n
            call    hash                ; compute h=hash(n)
            mov     [rbp+.h], rax       ; save h
            mov     rcx, node_size
            call    malloc              ; allocate node
            mov     r9, [rbp+.h]        ; restore h
            mov     r8, [table+r9*8]    ; get first node f from
                                        ; table[h]
            mov     [rax+n_next], r8    ; set next pointer of
                                        ; node to f
            mov     r8, [rbp+.n]        ; set value of new
            mov     [rax+n_value], r8   ; node to n
            mov     [table+r9*8], rax   ; make node first on
                                        ; table[h]
.found:
            leave
            ret
```

Printing the hash table

The **print** function iterates through the indices from 0 through 255, printing the index number and the keys on each non-empty list. It uses registers **r12** and **r13** for safe storage of a loop counter to iterate through the locations of the hash table array and for a pointer to loop through the nodes on each linked list. This is more convenient than using registers which require saving and restoring around each **printf** call. It does require saving and restoring these 2 registers at the start and end of the function to preserve them for calling functions.

You will notice that the code switches back and forth between the data and text segments so that printf format strings will be placed close to their point of use in the code.

```
print:
.r12    equ     local1
.r13    equ     local2
        push    rbp
        mov     rbp, rsp
        frame   1, 2, 2
        sub     rsp, frame_size
        mov     [rbp+.r12], r12   ; i: integer counter
                                  ; for table
        mov     [rbp+.r13], r13   ; p: pointer for list at
                                  ; table[i]
;       for ( i = 0; i < 256; i++ ) {
        xor     r12, r12
```

```
        .more_table:
;               p = table[i];
                mov     r13, [table+r12*8]

;               if ( p != 0 ) {
                cmp     r13, 0
                je      .empty
;                   print the list header
                    segment .data
    .print1:
                    db      "list %3d: ",0
                    segment .text
                    lea     rcx, [.print1]
                    mov     rdx, r12
                    call    printf

;                   do {
    .more_list:
;                       print the node's value
                        segment .data
     .print2            db      "%ld ",0
                        segment .text
                        lea     rcx, [.print2]
                        mov     rdx, [r13+n_value]
                        call    printf

;                       advance to the next node
                        mov     r13, [r13+n_next]

;                   } while ( the node != 0 )
                    cmp     r13, 0

                    jne     .more_list
;                   print new line
                    segment .data
    .print3:    db      0x0a,0
                segment .text
                lea     rcx, [.print3]
                call    printf
    .empty:

;               i++
                inc     r12
                cmp     r12, 256
                jl      .more_table
;           } end of for loop
```

```
        mov     r13, [rbp+.r13]     ; restore r12 and r13
        mov     r12, [rbp+.r12]     ; for calling function
        leave
        ret
```

Testing the hash table

The main function for the hash table reads numbers with **scanf**, inserts them into the hash table and prints the hash table contents after each insertion:

```
main:
.k      equ     local1
        segment .data
.scanf_fmt:
        db      "%ld",0
        segment .text
        push    rbp
        mov     rbp, rsp
        frame   0, 1, 2
        sub     rsp, frame_size
.more:
        lea     rcx, [.scanf_fmt]
        lea     rdx, [rbp+.k]
        call    scanf               ; read k
        cmp     rax, 1              ; if the read fails
        jne     .done               ; end it all
        mov     rcx, [rbp+.k]
        call    insert              ; insert(k);
        call    print               ; print hash table
        jmp     .more
.done:
        leave
        ret
```

Below is the printing of the hash table contents after inserting 1, 2, 3, 4, 5, 256, 257, 258, 260, 513, 1025 and 1028.

```
list    0: 256
list    1: 1025 513 257 1
list    2: 258 2
list    3: 3
list    4: 1028 260 4
list    5: 5
```

15.4 Binary trees

A binary tree is a structure with possibly many nodes. There is a single root node which can have left or right child nodes (or both). Each node in the tree can have left or right child nodes (or both).

Generally binary trees are built with an ordering applied to keys in the nodes. For example you could have a binary tree where every node divides keys into those less than the node's key (in the left sub-tree) and those greater than the node's key (in the right sub-tree). Having an ordered binary tree, often called a binary search tree, makes it possible to do fast searches for a key while maintaining the ability to traverse the nodes in increasing or decreasing order.

Here we will present a binary tree with integer keys with the ordering being lower keys on the left and greater keys on the right. First are the structures used for the tree.

Binary tree node and tree structures

The nodes in the binary tree have an integer value and two pointers. The structure definition below uses a prefix convention in naming the value field as **n_value** and the left and right pointers as **n_left** and **n_right**.

```
        struc   node
n_value resq    1
n_left  resq    1
n_right resq    1
        alignb  8
        endstruc
```

It would be possible to simply use a pointer to the root node to represent the tree. However we could add features to the tree, like node deletion or balancing, which could change the root of the tree. It seems logical to store the root in a structure insulating us from future root changes in a tree. We have also included in the tree structure a count of the number of nodes in the tree.

```
        struc   tree
t_count resq    1
t_root  resq    1
        alignb  8
        endstruc
```

Creating an empty tree

The **new_tree** function allocates memory for a **tree** structure and sets the count and the root of the new tree to 0. By having the root of the tree in a structure the code using the binary tree always refers to a particular tree using the pointer returned by **new_tree**. A more robust function should check the value returned by **malloc**.

```
new_tree:
        push    rbp
        mov     rbp, rsp
        frame   0, 0, 1
        sub     rsp, frame_size
        mov     rcx, tree_size
        call    malloc
        xor     ecx, ecx
        mov     [rax+t_root], rcx
        mov     [rax+t_count], rcx
        leave
        ret
```

Finding a key in a tree

To find a key in a binary search tree you start with a pointer to the root node and compare the node's key with the key being sought. If it's a match you're done. If the target key is less than the node's key you change your pointer to the node's left child. If the target key is greater than the node's key you change the pointer to the node's right child. You then repeat these comparisons with the new node. If you ever reach a **NULL** pointer, the key is not in the tree. Below is the code for finding a key in a binary tree. It returns a pointer to the correct tree node or **NULL** if not found.

```
;               p = find ( t, n );
;               p = 0 if not found
find:
        push    rbp
        mov     rbp, rsp
        frame   2, 0, 0
        sub     rsp, frame_size
        mov     rcx, [rcx+t_root]
        xor     eax, eax
.more   cmp     rcx, 0
        je      .done
        cmp     rdx, [rcx+n_value]
        jl      .goleft
        jg      .goright
        mov     rax, rcx
```

```
            jmp     .done
.goleft:
            mov     rcx, [rcx+n_left]
            jmp     .more
.goright:
            mov     rcx, [rcx+n_right]
            jmp     .more
.done       leave
            ret
```

Inserting a key into the tree

The first step in inserting a key is to use the **find** function to see if the key is already there. If it is, then there is no insertion. If not, then a new tree node is allocated, its value is set to the new key value and its left and right child pointers are set to **NULL**. Then it's time to find where to place this in the tree.

There is a special case for inserting the first node in the tree. If the count of nodes in the tree is 0, then the count is incremented and the tree's root pointer is set to the new node.

If the tree is non-empty then you start by setting a current pointer to point to the root node. If the new key is less than the current node's key, then the new node belongs in the left sub-tree. To handle this you inspect the left child pointer of the current node. If it is null, you have found the insertion point, so set the left pointer to the pointer of the new node. Otherwise update your current node pointer to be the left pointer and start comparisons with this node. If the key is not less than the current node's key, it must be greater than. In that case you inspect the current node's right child pointer and either set it the new node's pointer or advance your current pointer to the right child and repeat the comparison process.

```
;           insert ( t, n );
insert:
.n          equ     16
.t          equ     24
            push    rbp
            mov     rbp, rsp
            frame   2, 2, 2
            sub     rsp, frame_size
            mov     [rbp+.t], rcx
            mov     [rbp+.n], rdx
            call    find                    ; look for n
            cmp     rax, 0                  ; if in the tree
            jne     .done                   ; don't insert it
            mov     rcx, node_size
```

```
            call    malloc                  ; p = new node
            mov     rdx, [rbp+.n]
            mov     [rax+n_value], rdx      ; p->value = n
            xor     eax, eax
            mov     [rax+n_left], rax       ; p->left = NULL
            mov     [rax+n_right], rax      ; p->right = NULL
            mov     r9, [rbp+.t]
            mov     rcx, [r9+t_count]       ; get tree size
            cmp     rcx, 0                  ; count == 0 ?
            jne     .findparent
            inc     qword [r9+t_count]      ; count = 1
            mov     [r9+t_root], rax        ; root = new node
            jmp     .done
.findparent:
            inc     qword [r9+t_count]      ; count++
            mov     r9, [r9+t_root]         ; p = root
.repeatfind:
            cmp     rdx, [r9+n_value]       ; p=>value < n ?
            jl      .goleft
            mov     r8, r9                  ; t = p
            mov     r9, [r8+n_right]        ; p = p->right
            cmp     r9, 0                   ; is p NULL ?
            jne     .repeatfind
            mov     [r8+n_right], rax       ; if so, add node
            jmp     .done                   ; and return
.goleft:
            mov     r8, r9                  ; t = p
            mov     r9, [r8+n_left]         ; p = p->left
            cmp     r9, 0                   ; id p NULL ?
            jne     .repeatfind
            mov     [r8+n_left], rax        ; if so, add node
.done:                                      ; and return
            leave
            ret
```

Printing the keys in order

Printing the keys of a binary tree in order is easily performed by using recursion. The basic idea is to print the keys in the left sub-tree, print the key of the root node and print the keys of the right sub-tree. The use of a special tree structure means that there needs to be a different function to recursively print sub-trees starting with the pointer to the root. The main print function is named **print** and the recursive function is called **rec_print**.

```
rec_print:
    .t      equ     local1
```

```
        push    rbp
        mov     rbp, rsp
        frame   1, 1, 2
        sub     rsp, frame_size
        cmp     rcx, 0
        je      .done
        mov     [rbp+.t], rcx
        mov     rcx, [rcx+n_left]
        call    rec_print
        mov     rcx, [rbp+.t]
        mov     rdx, [rcx+n_value]
        segment .data
.print  db      "%ld ",0
        segment .text
        lea     rcx, [.print]
        call    printf
        mov     rcx, [rbp+.t]
        mov     rcx, [rcx+n_right]
        call    rec_print
.done   leave
        ret

;       print(t);
print:
        push    rbp
        mov     rbp, rsp
        frame   1, 0, 1
        sub     rsp, frame_size
        mov     rcx, [rcx+t_root]
        call    rec_print
        segment .data
.print  db      0x0a, 0
        segment .text
        lea     rcx, [.print]
        call    printf
        leave
        ret
```

Exercises

1. Modify the singly-linked list code to implement a stack of strings. You can use the C **strdup** function to make duplicates of strings that you insert. Write a main routine which creates a stack and enters a loop reading strings. If the string entered equals "**pop**", then pop the top of the stack and print that value. If the string entered equals "**print**", then print the contents of the stack. Otherwise push the string onto the stack. Your code should exit when either **scanf** or **fgets** fails to read a string.

2. Modify the doubly-linked list code to implement a queue of strings. Your main routine should read strings until no more are available. If the string entered equals "**dequeue**", then dequeue the oldest string from the queue and print it. If the string entered equals "**print**", then print the contents of the queue. Otherwise add the string onto the end of the queue. Your code should exit when either **scanf** or **fgets** fails to read a string.

3. Modify the hash table code to implement a hash table where you store strings and integers. The string will be the key and the integer will be its associated value. Your main routine should read lines using **fgets** and read the text again using **sscanf** to get a string and a number. If no number is read, **sscanf** returns 1), then look for the string in the hash table and print its value if it there or else print an error message. If there is a string and a number (**sscanf** returns 2), then add the string or update the string's value in the hash table. Your code should exit when **fgets** fails to read a string

4. Implement a binary tree of strings and use it to read a file of text using **fgets** and then print the lines of text in alphabetical order.

Chapter 16
High performance assembly

In this chapter we discuss some strategies for writing efficient x86-64 assembly language. The gold standard is the efficiency of implementations written in C or C++ and compiled with a good optimizing compiler. The author uses gcc to produce an assembly language file. Studying this generated code may give you some ideas about how to write efficient assembly code.

16.1 Efficient use of cache

One of the goals in high performance computing is to keep the processing units of the CPU busy. A modern CPU like the Intel Core i7 operates at a clock speed around 3 GHz while its main memory maxes out at about 21 GB/sec. If your application ran strictly from data and instructions in memory using no cache, then there would be roughly 7 bytes available per cycle. The CPU has 4 cores which need to share the 21 GB/sec, so we're down to about 2 bytes per cycle per core from memory. Yet each of these cores can have instructions being processed in 3 processing sub-units and 2 memory processing sub-units. Each CPU can complete 4 instructions per cycle. The same is true for the AMD Bulldozer CPUs. It requires much more than 2 bytes per cycle to keep instructions flowing in a modern CPU. To keep these CPUs fed requires 3 levels of cache.

I performed a short test to illustrate the effect of main memory access versus cache on a Core i7 CPU. The test consisted of executing 10 billion exclusive or operations on quad-words in memory. In the plot below you can see that the time depends heavily on the array size. With an array of size 8000 bytes, the time as 1.5 seconds. The time steadily grows through the use of the 8 MB of cache. When the size is 80 million bytes the cache is nearly useless and a maximum of about 5.7 seconds is reached.

Time to Compute XOR

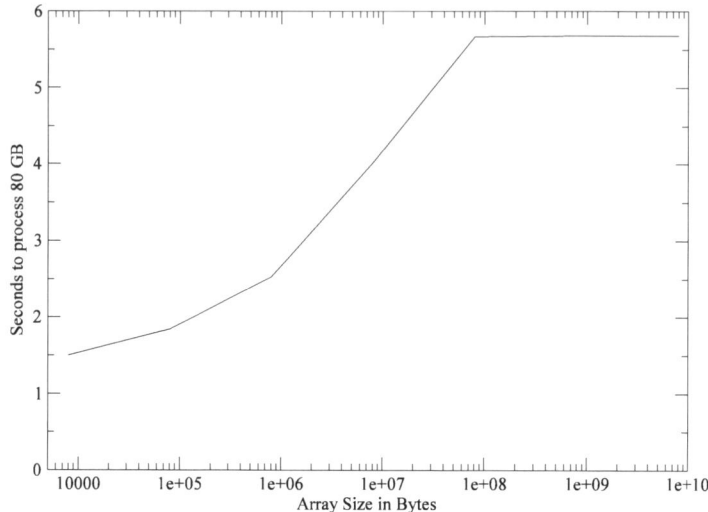

A prime example of making efficient use of cache is in the implementation of matrix multiplication. Straightforward matrix multiplication is $O(n^3)$ where there are n rows and n columns of data. It is commonly coded as 3 nested loops. However it can be broken up into blocks small enough for 3 blocks to fit in cache for a nice performance boost. Below are MFLOPs ratings for various block sizes for multiplying 2 2048x2048 matrices in a C program. There is considerable room for improvement by using assembly language to take advantage of SSE or AVX instructions.

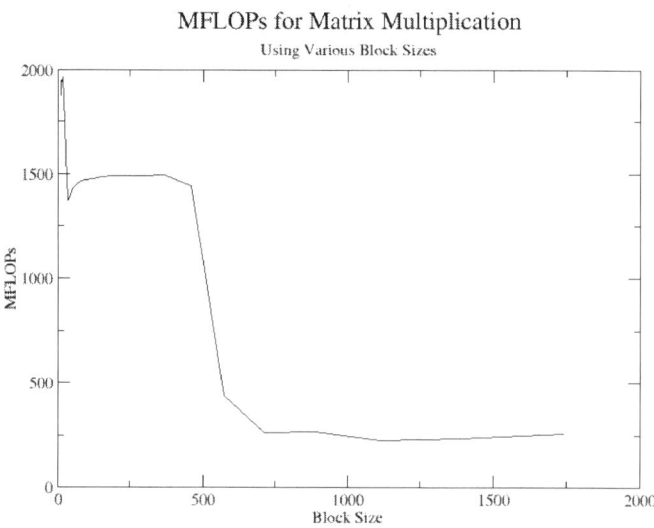

16.2 Common subexpression elimination

Common subexpression eliminations is generally performed by optimizing compilers. If you are to have any hope of beating the compiler, you must do the same thing. Sometimes it may be hard to locate all common subexpressions. This might be a good time to study the compiler's generated code to discover what it found. The compiler is tireless and efficient at its tasks. Humans tend to overlook things.

16.3 Strength reduction

Strength reduction means using a simpler mathematical technique to get an answer. It is possible to compute x^3 using **pow**, but it is probably faster to compute $x * x * x$. If you need to compute x^4, then do it in stages:

```
x2 = x * x;
x4 = x2 * x2;
```

If you need to divide or multiply an integer by a power of 2, this can be done more quickly by shifting. If you need to divide more than one floating point number by x, compute $1/x$ and multiply.

16.4 Use registers efficiently

Place commonly used values in registers. It is nearly always better to place values in registers. I once wrote a doubly nested loop in 32 bit mode where I had all my values in registers. gcc generated faster code by using the stack for a few values. These stack values probably remained in the level 1 cache and were almost as good as being in registers. Testing tells the truth.

16.5 Use fewer branches

Modern CPUs make branch predictions and will prepare the pipeline with some instructions from one of the 2 possibilities when there is a conditional branch. The pipeline will stall when this prediction is wrong, so it will help to try to make fewer branches. Study the generated code from your compiler. It will frequently reorder the assembly code to reduce the number of branches. You will learn some general techniques from the compiler.

16.6 Convert loops to branch at the bottom

If you code a **while** loop as written, there will be a conditional jump at the top of the loop to branch past the loop and an unconditional jump at the bottom of the loop to get back to the top. It is always possible to transform the loop have a conditional branch at the bottom. You may need a one-time use conditional jump before the top of the loop to handle cases where the loop body should be skipped.

Here is a C **for** loop converted to a **do-while** loop. First the **for** loop:

```
for ( i = 0; i < n; i++ ) {
    x[i] = a[i] + b[i];
}
```

Now the **do-while** loop with an additional if:

```
if ( n > 0 ) {
    i = 0;
    do {
        x[i] = a[i] + b[i];
        i++;
    } while ( i < n );
}
```

Please do not adopt this style of coding in C or C++. The compiler will handle **for** loops quite well. In fact the simplicity of the **for** loop might allow the compiler to generate better code. I presented this in C simply to get the point across more simply.

16.7 Unroll loops

Unrolling loops is another technique used by compilers. The primary advantage is that there will be fewer loop control instructions and more instructions doing the work of the loop. A second advantage is that the CPU will have more instructions available to fill its pipeline with a longer loop body. Finally if you manage to use registers with little or no dependencies between the separate sections of unrolled code, then you open up the possibility for a super-scalar CPU (most modern CPUs) to execute multiple original iterations in parallel. This is considerably easier with 16 registers than with 8.

Let's consider some code to add up all the numbers in an array of quad-words. Here is the assembly code for the simplest version:

```
        segment  .text
        global   add_array
:
        xor      eax, eax
.add_words:
        add      rax, [rcx]
        add      rcx, 8
        dec      rdx
        jg       .add_words
        ret
```

Here is a version with the loop unrolled 4 times:

```
        segment  .text
        global   add_array
add_array:
        xor      eax, eax
        mov      r8, rax
        mov      r9, rax
        mov      r10, rax
.add_words:
        add      rax, [rcx]
        add      r8, [rcx+8]
        add      r9, [rcx+16]
        add      r10, [rcx+24]
        add      rcx, 32
        sub      rdx, 4
        jg       .add_words
        add      r9, r10
        add      rax, r8
        add      rax, r9
        ret
```

In the unrolled code I am accumulating partial sums in **rax**, **r8**, **r9** and **r10**. These partial sums are combined after the loop. Executing a test program with 1000000 calls to add up an array of 10000 quad-words took 3.9 seconds for the simple version and 2.44 seconds for the unrolled version. There is so little work to do per data element that the 2 programs start becoming memory bandwidth limited with large arrays, so I tested a size which fit easily in cache.

16.8 Merge loops

If you have 2 `for` loops iterating over the same sequence of values and there is no dependence between the loops, it seems like a no-brainer to merge the loops. Consider the following 2 loops:

```
for ( i = 0; i < 1000; i++ ) {
    a[i] = b[i] + c[i];
}
for ( j = 0; j < 1000; j++ ) {
    d[j] = b[j] - c[j];
}
```

This can easily be merged to get:

```
for ( i = 0; i < 1000; i++ ) {
    a[i] = b[i] + c[i];
    d[i] = b[i] - c[i];
}
```

In general merging loops can increase the size of a loop body, decreasing the overhead percentage and helping to keep the pipeline full. In this case there is additional gain from loading the values of **b** and **c** once rather than twice.

16.9 Split loops

We just got through discussing how merging loops was a good idea. Now we are going to learn the opposite - well for some loops. If a loop is operating on 2 independent sets of data, then it could be split into 2 loops. This can improve performance if the combined loop exceeds the cache capacity. There is a trade-off between better cache usage and more instructions in the pipeline. Sometime merging is better and sometimes splitting is better.

16.10 Interchange loops

Suppose you wish to place 0's in a 2-dimensional array in C. You have 2 choices:

```
for ( i = 0; i < n; i++ ) {
    for ( j = 0; j < n; j++ ) {
        x[i][j] = 0;
```

```
            }
        }
or
        for ( j = 0; j < n; j++ ) {
            for ( i = 0; i < n; i++ ) {
                x[i][j] = 0;
            }
        }
```

Which is better? In C the second index increments faster than the first. This means that `x[0][1]` is immediately after `x[0][0]`. On the other hand `x[1][0]` is n elements after `x[0][0]`. When the CPU fetches data into the cache it fetches more than a few bytes and cache writes to memory behave similarly, so the first loop makes more sense. If you have the extreme misfortune of having an array which is too large for your RAM, then you may experience virtual memory thrashing with the second version. This could turn into a disk access for each array access.

16.11 Move loop invariant code outside loops

This might be a fairly obvious optimization to perform. It's another case where studying the compiler's generated code might point out some loop invariant code which you have overlooked.

16.12 Remove recursion

If it is easy to eliminate recursion then it will nearly always improve efficiency. Often it is easy to eliminate "tail" recursion where the last action of a function is a recursive call. This can generally be done by branching to the top of the function. On the other hand if you try to eliminate recursion for a function like quicksort which makes 2 non-trivial recursive calls, you will be forced to "simulate" recursion using your own stack. This may make things slower. In any case the effect is small, since the time spent making recursive calls in quicksort is small.

16.13 Eliminate stack frames

For leaf functions it is not necessary to use stack frames. In fact if you have non-leaf functions which call your own functions and no others then you can omit the frame pointers from these too. The only real reason for frame pointers is for debugging. There is a requirement for leaving the stack on 16 byte boundaries, but this only becomes an issue with functions which have local variables (on the stack) which participate in aligned 16 or 32 byte accesses which can either fail or be slower. If you know that your own code is not using those instructions, then neither frame pointers nor frame alignment are important other than for debugging.

16.14 Inline functions

As part of optimization compilers can inline small functions. This reduces the overhead significantly. If you wish to do this, you might be interested in exploring macros which can make your code easier to read and write and operate much like a function which has been inlined.

16.15 Reduce dependencies to allow super-scalar execution

Modern CPUs inspect the instruction stream looking ahead for instructions which do not depend upon results of earlier instructions. This is called "out of order execution". If there is less dependency in your code, then the CPU can execute more instructions out of order, allowing multiple independent instructions to execute at one (super-scalar) and your program can run more quickly.

As an example of this I modified the previous **add_array** function with unrolled loops to accumulate all 4 values in the loop into **rax**. This increased the time from 2.44 seconds to 2.75 seconds.

16.16 Use specialized instructions

So far we have seen the conditional move instruction which is fairly specialized and also the packed floating point instructions. There are many specialized instructions in the x86-64 architecture which are more difficult for a compiler to apply. A human can reorganize an algorithm to add the elements of an array somewhat like I did with loop unrolling except to keep 4 partial sums in one AVX register. Combining the 4 parts of the AVX register can be done after the loop. This can make the adding even faster, since 4 adds can be done in one instruction. This technique can also be combined with loop unrolling for additional performance. This will be explored in detail in subsequent chapters.

Exercises

1. Given an array of 3D points defined in a structure with x, y and z components, write a function to compute a distance matrix with the distances between each pair of points.

2. Given a 2D array, M, of floats of dimensions n by 4, and a vector, v, of 4 floats compute Mv.

3. Write a blocked matrix-matrix multiplication using a C main program and an assembly function to perform the multiplication. Try various block sizes to see which block size gives the highest performance.

Chapter 17
Counting bits in an array

In this chapter we explore several solutions to the problem of counting all the 1 bits in an array of quad-word integers. For each test we use the same C main program and implement a different function counting the number of 1 bits in the array. All these functions implement the same prototype:

```
long popcnt_array (unsigned long long *a, int size);
```

17.1 C function

The first solution is a straightforward C solution:

```c
long popcnt_array (unsigned long long *a, int size)
{
    int w, b;
    unsigned long long word;
    long n;

    n = 0;
    for ( w = 0; w < size; w++ ) {
        word = a[w];
        n += word & 1;
        for ( b = 1; b < 64; b++ ) {
            n += (word >> b) & 1;
        }
    }
    return n;
}
```

The testing consists of calling `popcnt_array` 1000 times with an array of 100000 longs (800000 bytes). Compiling with optimization level zero (option -O0) the test took 14.63 seconds. With optimization level 1, it took 5.29 seconds, with level 2 it took 5.29 seconds again, and with level

3 it took 5.37 seconds. Finally adding -funroll-all-loops, it took 4.74 seconds.

The algorithm can be improved by noticing that frequently the upper bits of the quad-words being tested might be 0. We can change the inner for loop into a while loop:

```
long popcnt_array (unsigned long long *a, int size)
{
    int w, b;
    unsigned long long word;
    long n;

    n = 0;
    for ( w = 0; w < size; w++ ) {
        word = a[w];
        while ( word != 0 ) {
            n += word & 1;
            word >>= 1;
        }
    }
    return n;
}
```

Using the maximum optimization options the version takes 3.34 seconds. This is an instance of using a better algorithm.

17.2 Counting 1 bits in assembly

It is not too hard to unroll the loop for working on 64 bits into 64 steps of working on 1 bit. In the assembly code which follows one fourth of the bits of each word are placed in rax, one fourth in rbx, one fourth in rcx and one fourth in rdx. Then each fourth of the bits are accumulated using different registers. This allows considerable freedom for the computer to use out-or-order execution with the loop.

```
        segment .text
        global   popcnt_array
popcnt_array:
        push    rdi
        push    rsi
        push    rbx
        push    rbp
        push    r12
        push    r13
        push    r14
        push    r15
```

```
                mov     rdi, rcx        ; Use rdi and rsi to hold
parameters
                mov     rsi, rdx        ; like Linux to simplify the
coding
                xor     eax, eax
                xor     ebx, ebx
                xor     ecx, ecx
                xor     edx, edx
                xor     r12d, r12d
                xor     r13d, r13d
                xor     r14d, r14d
                xor     r15d, r15d
.count_words:
                mov     r8, [rdi]
                mov     r9, r8
                mov     r10, r8
                mov     r11, r9
                and     r8, 0xffff
                shr     r9, 16
                and     r9, 0xffff
                shr     r10, 32
                and     r10, 0xffff
                shr     r11, 48
                and     r11, 0xffff
                mov     r12w, r8w
                and     r12w, 1
                add     rax, r12
                mov     r13w, r9w
                and     r13w, 1
                add     rbx, r13
                mov     r14w, r10w
                and     r14w, 1
                add     rcx, r14
                mov     r15w, r11w
                and     r15w, 1
                add     rdx, r15

%rep 15
                shr     r8w, 1
                mov     r12w, r8w
                and     r12w, 1
                add     rax, r12
                shr     r9w, 1
                mov     r13w, r9w
                and     r13w, 1
                add     rbx, r13
                shr     r10w, 1
                mov     r14w, r10w
```

```
            and     r14w, 1
            add     rcx, r14
            shr     r11w, 1
            mov     r15w, r11w
            and     r15w, 1
            add     rdx, r15
%endrep
            add     rdi, 8
            dec     rsi
            jg      .count_words
            add     rax, rbx
            add     rax, rcx
            add     rax, rdx
            pop     r15
            pop     r14
            pop     r13
            pop     r12
            pop     rbp
            pop     rbx
            pop     rsi
            pop     rdi
            ret
```

This has an unfortunate side effect - the use of a repeat section which repeats 15 times. This makes for a function of 1123 bytes. Perhaps it was worth it to execute the test in 2.52 seconds. The object file is only 240 bytes larger than the C code with unrolled loops.

17.3 Precomputing the number of bits in each byte

The next algorithmic improvement comes from recognizing that we can precompute the number of bits in each possible bit pattern for a byte and use an array of 256 bytes to store the number of bits in each possible byte. Then counting the number of bits in a quad-word consists of using the 8 bytes of the quad-word as indices into the array of bit counts and adding them up.

Here is the C function for adding the number of bits in the array without the initialization of the `count` array:

```
long popcnt_array ( long long *a, int size )
{
    int b;
    long n;
    int word;
```

```
        n = 0;
        for ( b = 0; b < size*8; b++ ) {
            word = ((unsigned char *)a)[b];
            n += count[word];
        }
        return n;
    }
```

This code took 0.24 seconds for the test, so we have a new winner. I tried hard to beat this algorithm using assembly language, but managed only a tie.

17.4 Using the popcnt instruction

A new instruction included in the Core i series processors is **popcnt** which gives the number of 1 bits in a 64 bit register. So on the right computers, we can employ the technique of using a specialized instruction:

```
        segment  .text
        global   popcnt_array
popcnt_array:
        push     r12
        push     r13
        push     r14
        push     r15
        xor      eax, eax
        xor      r8d, r8d
        xor      r9d, r9d
        xor      r14d, r14d
        xor      r15d, r15d
.count_more:
        popcnt   r10, [rcx+r9*8]
        add      rax, r10
        popcnt   r11, [rcx+r9*8+8]
        add      r8, r11
        popcnt   r12, [rcx+r9*8+16]
        add      r14, r12
        popcnt   r13, [rcx+r9*8+24]
        add      r15, r15
        add      r9, 4
        cmp      r9, rdx
        jl       .count_more
        add      rax, r8
        add      rax, r14
        add      rax, r15
```

```
        pop        r15
        pop        r14
        pop        r13
        pop        r12
        ret
```

We have a new winner on the Core i7 at 0.04 seconds which is 6 times faster than the nearest competitor.

Exercises

1. Write a function to convert an array of ASCII characters to EBCDIC and another to convert back to ASCII.

2. For 2 arrays of ASCII characters write a function to find the longest common substring.

Chapter 18
Sobel filter

The Sobel filter is an edge detection filter used in image processing. The operation of the filter is to process 3x3 windows of data by convolving each pixel by one 3x3 matrix to produce an edge measure in the x direction and another in the y direction. Here are the 2 matrices

$$S_x = \begin{bmatrix} -1 & 0 & 1 \\ -2 & 0 & 2 \\ -1 & 0 & 1 \end{bmatrix} \quad S_y = \begin{bmatrix} -1 & -2 & 1 \\ 0 & 0 & 0 \\ 1 & 2 & 1 \end{bmatrix}$$

For an individual pixel $I_{r,c}$ the x edge measure, G_x, is computed by

$$G_x = \sum_{i=-1}^{1} \sum_{j=-1}^{1} (S_{x,i,j} I_{r+i,c+j})$$

where we have conveniently numbered the rows and columns of S_x starting with -1. Similarly we compute G_y using

$$G_y = \sum_{i=-1}^{1} \sum_{j=-1}^{1} (S_{y,i,j} I_{r+i,c+j})$$

Next we compute the magnitude of the edge measure, G,

$$G = \sqrt{G_x^2 + G_y^2}$$

18.1 Sobel in C

Here is a C function which computes the Sobel edge magnitude for an image of arbitrary size:

```
#include <math.h>

#define I(a,b,c) a[(b)*(cols)+(c)]
```

```
void sobel ( unsigned char *data, float *out,
             long rows, long cols )
{
    int r, c;    int gx, gy;

    for ( r = 1; r < rows-1; r++ ) {
        for ( c = 1; c < cols-1; c++ ) {
            gx = -I(data,r-1,c-1) + I(data,r-1,c+1) +
                 -2*I(data,r,c-1) + 2*I(data,r,c+1) +
                 -I(data,r+1,c-1) + I(data,r+1,c+1);
            gy = -I(data,r-1,c-1) - 2*I(data,r-1,c) -
                  I(data,r-1,c+1) + I(data,r+1,c-1) +
                 2*I(data,r+1,c) + I(data,r+1,c+1);
            I(out,r,c) = sqrt((float)(gx)*(float)(gx)+
                              (float)(gy)*(float)(gy));
        }
    }
}
```

This code was compiled with -O3 optimization and full loop unrolling. Testing with 1024 × 1024 images showed that it computed 161.5 Sobel magnitude images per second. Testing with 1000 different images to cut down on the effect of cached images, this code produced 158 images per second. Clearly the code is dominated by mathematics rather than memory bandwidth.

18.2 Sobel computed using SSE instructions

Sobel was chosen as a good example of an algorithm which manipulates data of many types. First the image data is byte data. The **movdqu** instruction was used to transfer 16 adjacent pixels from one row of the image. These pixels were processed to produce the contribution of their central 14 pixels to G_x and G_y. Then 16 pixels were transferred from the image one row down from the first 16 pixels. These pixels were processed in the same way adding more to G_x and G_y. Finally 16 more pixels 2 rows down from the first 16 were transferred and their contributions to G_x and G_y were computed. Then these contributions were combined, squared, added together, converted to 32 bit floating point and square roots were computed for the 14 output pixels which were placed in the output array.

Tested on the same Core i7 computer, this code produced 1063 Sobel magnitude images per second. Testing with 1000 different images this code produced 980 images per second, which is about 6.2 times as fast as the C version.

Here are the new instructions used in this code:

pxor This instruction performs an exclusive or on a 128 XMM source register or memory and stores the result in the destination register.

movdqa This instruction moves 128 bits of aligned data from memory to a register, from a register to memory, or from a register to a register.

movdqu This instruction moves 128 bits of unaligned data from memory to a register, from a register to memory, or from a register to a register.

psrldq This instruction shifts the destination XMM register right the number of bytes specified in the second immediate operand.

punpcklbw This instruction unpacks the low 8 bytes of 2 XMM registers and intermingles them. I used this with the second register holding all 0 bytes to form 8 words in the destination.

punpckhbw This instruction unpacks the upper 8 bytes of 2 XMM registers and intermingles them.

paddw This instruction adds 8 16 bit integers from the second operand to the first operand. At least one of the operands must be an XMM register and one can be a memory field.

psubw This instruction divides the second set of 8 16 bit integers from the first set.

pmullw This instruction multiplies the first set of 8 16 bit integers times the second set and stores the low order 16 bits of the products in the first operand.

punpcklwd This instruction unpacks and interleaves words from the lower halves of 2 XMM registers into the destination register.

punpckhwd This instruction unpacks and interleaves words from the upper halves of 2 XMM registers into the destination register.

cvtdq2ps This instruction converts 4 double word integers into 4 double word floating point values.

Here is the assembly code:

```
%macro   multipush 1-*    ; I needed to push and pop all
    %rep   %0             ; callee save registers, so I
        push     %1       ; used macros from the nasm
        %rotate  1        ; documentation.
    %endrep
%endmacro

%macro   multipop 1-*
```

```
        %rep %0
            %rotate -1
            pop     %1
        %endrep
    %endmacro
;           sobel ( input, output, rows, cols );
;           char input[rows][cols]
;           float output[rows][cols]
;           border of the output array will be unfilled
;
            segment .text
            global  sobel, main
    sobel:
    .cols    equ    0
    .rows    equ    8
    .output  equ    16
    .input   equ    24
    .bpir    equ    32
    .bpor    equ    40
            multipush   rbx, rbp, r12, r13, r14, r15
            sub     rsp, 48
            cmp     r8, 3           ; need at least 3 rows
            jl      .noworktodo
            cmp     r8, 3           ; need at least 3
    columns
            jl      .noworktodo
            mov     [rsp+.input], rcx
            mov     [rsp+.output], rdx
            mov     [rsp+.rows], r8
            mov     [rsp+.cols], r9
            mov     [rsp+.bpir], r9  ; bytes per input row
            imul    r9, 4
            mov     [rsp+.bpor], r9  ; 4 bytes per output
    pixel

            mov     rax, [rsp+.rows] ; # rows to process
            mov     r11, [rsp+.cols]
            sub     rax, 2
            mov     r8, [rsp+.input]
            add     r8, r11
            mov     r9, r8           ; address of row
            mov     r10, r8
            sub     r8, r11          ; address of row-1
            add     r10, r11         ; address of row+1
            add     rdx, [rsp+.bpor] ; address of 1st
    output row
            pxor    xmm13, xmm13
            pxor    xmm14, xmm14
```

```
                pxor        xmm15, xmm15
.more_rows:
                mov         rbx, 1              ; first column
.more_cols:
                movdqu      xmm0, [r8+rbx-1]    ; data for 1st row
                movdqu      xmm1, xmm0
                movdqu      xmm2, xmm0
                pxor        xmm9, xmm9
                pxor        xmm10, xmm10
                pxor        xmm11, xmm11
                pxor        xmm12, xmm12
                psrldq      xmm1, 1             ; shift the pixels 1
                                                ; to the right
                psrldq      xmm2, 2             ; shift the pixels 2
                                                ; to the right

;       Now the lowest 14 values of xmm0, xmm1 and
;       xmm2 are lined up properly for applying the
;       top row of the 2 matrices.

                movdqa      xmm3, xmm0
                movdqa      xmm4, xmm1
                movdqa      xmm5, xmm2
                punpcklbw   xmm3, xmm13         ; The low 8 values
                                                ; are now words in
                punpcklbw   xmm4, xmm14         ; registers xmm3,
                                                ; xmm4, and xmm5
                punpcklbw   xmm5, xmm15         ; ready for math.
                psubw       xmm11, xmm3         ; xmm11 will hold
                                                ; 8 values of Gx
                psubw       xmm9, xmm3          ; xmm9 will hold
                                                ; 8 values of Gy
                paddw       xmm11, xmm5         ; Gx subtracts left
                                                ; adds right
                psubw       xmm9, xmm4          ; Gy subtracts
                                                ; 2 * middle pixel
                psubw       xmm9, xmm4
                psubw       xmm9, xmm5          ; Final Gy subtract
                punpckhbw   xmm0, xmm13         ; Convert top 8
                                                ; bytes to words
                punpckhbw   xmm1, xmm14
                punpckhbw   xmm2, xmm15
                psubw       xmm12, xmm0         ; Do the same math
                psubw       xmm10, xmm0         ; storing these 6
                paddw       xmm12, xmm2         ; values in xmm12
                psubw       xmm10, xmm1         ; and xmm10
                psubw       xmm10, xmm1
                psubw       xmm10, xmm2
```

```
            movdqu   xmm0, [r9+rbx-1]   ; data for 2nd row
            movdqu   xmm2, xmm0         ; repeat math from
            psrldq   xmm2, 2            ; 1st row with
            movdqa   xmm3, xmm0         ; nothing added to
            movdqa   xmm5, xmm2         ; Gy
            punpcklbw   xmm3, xmm13
            punpcklbw   xmm5, xmm15     ; 2nd row
            psubw    xmm11, xmm3
            psubw    xmm11, xmm3
            paddw    xmm11, xmm5
            paddw    xmm11, xmm5
            punpckhbw   xmm0, xmm13
            punpckhbw   xmm2, xmm15
            psubw    xmm12, xmm0
            psubw    xmm12, xmm0
            paddw    xmm12, xmm2
            paddw    xmm12, xmm2

            movdqu   xmm0, [r10+rbx-1]  ; data for 3rd row
            movdqu   xmm1, xmm0
            movdqu   xmm2, xmm0
            psrldq   xmm1, 1
            psrldq   xmm2, 2
            movdqa   xmm3, xmm0
            movdqa   xmm4, xmm1
            movdqa   xmm5, xmm2
            punpcklbw   xmm3, xmm13
            punpcklbw   xmm4, xmm14
            punpcklbw   xmm5, xmm15     ; 3rd row
            psubw    xmm11, xmm3
            paddw    xmm9, xmm3
            paddw    xmm11, xmm5
            paddw    xmm9, xmm4
            paddw    xmm9, xmm4
            paddw    xmm9, xmm5
            punpckhbw   xmm0, xmm13
            punpckhbw   xmm1, xmm14
            punpckhbw   xmm2, xmm15
            psubw    xmm12, xmm0
            paddw    xmm10, xmm0
            paddw    xmm12, xmm2
            paddw    xmm10, xmm1
            paddw    xmm10, xmm1
            paddw    xmm10, xmm2

            pmullw   xmm9, xmm9         ; square Gx and Gy
            pmullw   xmm10, xmm10
            pmullw   xmm11, xmm11
```

```
            pmullw    xmm12, xmm12
            paddw     xmm9, xmm11        ; sum of squares
            paddw     xmm10, xmm12
            movdqa    xmm1, xmm9
            movdqa    xmm3, xmm10
            punpcklwd xmm9, xmm13        ; Convert low 4
                                         ; words to dwords
            punpckhwd xmm1, xmm13        ; Convert high 4
                                         ; words to dwords
            punpcklwd xmm10, xmm13       ; Convert low 4
                                         ; words to dwords
            punpckhwd xmm3, xmm13        ; Convert high 4
                                         ; words to dwords
            cvtdq2ps  xmm0, xmm9         ; to floating point
            cvtdq2ps  xmm1, xmm1         ; to floating point
            cvtdq2ps  xmm2, xmm10        ; to floating point
            cvtdq2ps  xmm3, xmm3         ; to floating point
            sqrtps    xmm0, xmm0
            sqrtps    xmm1, xmm1
            sqrtps    xmm2, xmm2
            sqrtps    xmm3, xmm3
            movups    [rdx+rbx*4], xmm0
            movups    [rdx+rbx*4+16], xmm1
            movups    [rdx+rbx*4+32], xmm2
            movlps    [rdx+rbx*4+48], xmm3

            add       rbx, 14            ; process 14 Sobel values
            cmp       rbx, r11
            jl        .more_cols
            add       r8, r11
            add       r9, r11
            add       r10, r11
            add       rsi, [rsp+.bpor]
            sub       rax, 1             ; 1 fewer row
            cmp       rax, 0
            jg        .more_rows
    .noworktodo:
            add       rsp, 48
            multipop  rbx, rbp, r12, r13, r14, r15
            ret
```

Exercises

1. Convert the Sobel function into a function to perform an arbitrary convolution of an image with a 3 × 3 matrix

2. Write an assembly function to convert an image into a run-length encoded image.

3. Write a function to fill an array with pseudo-random numbers derived by using 4 separate interleaved sequences based on the formula
$$X_{n+1} = (aX_n + c) \bmod m$$
Use $m = 32$ for all 4 sequences. Use 1664525, 22695477, 1103515245 and 214013 for the values of a and 1013904223, 1, 12345 and 2531011 for the values of c.

Chapter 19
Computing Correlation

The final example of optimization is computing the correlation between two variables x and y given n sample values. One way to compute correlation is using

$$r_{xy} = \frac{\sum_{i=1}^{n}(x_i - \bar{x})(y_i - \bar{y})}{\sqrt{\sum_{i=1}^{n}(x_i - \bar{x})^2 \sum_{i=1}^{n}(y_i - \bar{y})^2}}$$

But this formula requires two passes through the data - one pass to compute averages and a second pass to complete the formula. There is a less intuitive formula which is more amenable to computation:

$$r_{xy} = \frac{n\sum_{i=1}^{n} x_i y_i - \sum_{i=1}^{n} x_i \sum_{i=1}^{n} y_i}{\sqrt{n\sum_{i=1}^{n} x_i^2 - (\sum_{i=1}^{n} x_i)^2} \sqrt{n\sum_{i=1}^{n} y_i^2 - (\sum_{i=1}^{n} y_i)^2}}$$

The computational formula requires computing 5 sums when you scan the data: the sum of x_i, the sum of y_i, the sum of x_i^2, the sum of y_i^2 and the sum of $x_i y_i$. After computing these 5 sums there is a small amount of time required for implementing the computational formula.

19.1 C implementation

The C computation is performed in the `corr` function given below:

```
#include <math.h>

double corr ( double x[], double y[], long n )
{
        double sum_x, sum_y, sum_xx, sum_yy, sum_xy;
        long i;
        sum_x = sum_y = sum_xx = sum_yy = sum_xy = 0.0;
        for ( i = 0; i < n; i++ ) {
            sum_x += x[i];
```

```
            sum_y  += y[i];
            sum_xx += x[i]*x[i];
            sum_yy += y[i]*y[i];
            sum_xy += x[i]*y[i];
    }
    return (n*sum_xy-sum_x*sum_y)/
           sqrt((n*sum_xx-sum_x*sum_x)*
                (n*sum_yy-sum_y*sum_y));
}
```

The gcc compiler generated assembly code which used all 16 of the XMM registers as it unrolled the loop to process 4 iterations of the **for** loop in the main loop. The compiler also correctly handled the extra data values when the array size was not a multiple of four. Performing 1 million calls to compute correlation on 2 arrays of size 10000 required 13.44 seconds for the C version. This is roughly 5.9 GFLOPs which is quite impressive for compiled code.

19.2 Implementation using SSE instructions

A version of the **corr** function was written using SSE instructions which will execute on many modern computers. Here is the SSE version:

```
            segment .text
            global corr
;
;           rcx:   x array
;           rdx:   y array
;           r10:   loop counter
;           r8:    n

;           xmm0:  2 parts of sum_x
;           xmm1:  2 parts of sum_y
;           xmm2:  2 parts of sum_xx
;           xmm3:  2 parts of sum_yy
;           xmm4:  2 parts of sum_xy
;           xmm5:  2 x values - later squared
;           xmm6:  2 y values - later squared
;           xmm7:  2 xy values

    corr:
            xor       r9d, r9d
            mov       r10, r8
            subpd     xmm0, xmm0
            movapd    xmm1, xmm0
```

```
        movapd    xmm2, xmm0
        movapd    xmm3, xmm0
        movapd    xmm4, xmm0
        movapd    xmm8, xmm0
        movapd    xmm9, xmm0
        movapd    xmm10, xmm0
        movapd    xmm11, xmm0
        movapd    xmm12, xmm0
.more:
        movapd    xmm5, [rcx+r9]      ; mov x
        movapd    xmm6, [rdx+r9]      ; mov y
        movapd    xmm7, xmm5          ; mov x
        mulpd     xmm7, xmm6          ; xy
        addpd     xmm0, xmm5          ; sum_x
        addpd     xmm1, xmm6          ; sum_y
        mulpd     xmm5, xmm5          ; xx
        mulpd     xmm6, xmm6          ; yy
        addpd     xmm2, xmm5          ; sum_xx
        addpd     xmm3, xmm6          ; sum_yy
        addpd     xmm4, xmm7          ; sum_xy
        movapd    xmm13, [rcx+r9+16]  ; mov x
        movapd    xmm14, [rdx+r9+16]  ; mov y
        movapd    xmm15, xmm13        ; mov x
        mulpd     xmm15, xmm14        ; xy
        addpd     xmm8, xmm13         ; sum_x
        addpd     xmm9, xmm14         ; sum_y
        mulpd     xmm13, xmm13        ; xx
        mulpd     xmm14, xmm14        ; yy
        addpd     xmm10, xmm13        ; sum_xx
        addpd     xmm11, xmm14        ; sum_yy
        addpd     xmm12, xmm15        ; sum_xy
        add       r9, 32
        sub       r10, 4
        jnz       .more
        addpd     xmm0, xmm8
        addpd     xmm1, xmm9
        addpd     xmm2, xmm10
        addpd     xmm3, xmm11
        addpd     xmm4, xmm12
        haddpd    xmm0, xmm0          ; sum_x
        haddpd    xmm1, xmm1          ; sum_y
        haddpd    xmm2, xmm2          ; sum_xx
        haddpd    xmm3, xmm3          ; sum_yy
        haddpd    xmm4, xmm4          ; sum_xy
        movsd     xmm6, xmm0          ; sum_x
        movsd     xmm7, xmm1          ; sum_y
        cvtsi2sd  xmm8, r8            ; n
        mulsd     xmm6, xmm6          ; sum_x*sum_x
```

```
mulsd    xmm7, xmm7    ; sum_y*sum_y
mulsd    xmm2, xmm8    ; n*sum_xx
mulsd    xmm3, xmm8    ; n*sum_yy
subsd    xmm2, xmm6    ; n*sum_xx-sum_x*sum_x
subsd    xmm3, xmm7    ; n*sum_yy-sum_y*sum_y
mulsd    xmm2, xmm3    ; denom*denom
sqrtsd   xmm2, xmm2    ; denom
mulsd    xmm4, xmm8    ; n*sum_xy
mulsd    xmm0, xmm1    ; sum_x*sum_y
subsd    xmm4, xmm0    ; n*sum_xy-sum_x*sum_y
divsd    xmm4, xmm2    ; correlation
movsd    xmm0, xmm4    ; need in xmm0
ret
```

In the main loop of this function the **movapd** instruction was used to load 2 double precision values from the **x** array and again the load 2 values from the **y** array. Then accumulation was performed in registers **xmm0** - **xmm4**. Each of these accumulation registers held 2 accumulated values - one for even indices and one for odd indices

After this collection of accumulations the **movapd** instruction was used again to load 2 more values for **x** and again to load 2 more values from **y**. These values were used to form accumulations into 5 more registers: **xmm8** - **xmm12**.

After completing the loop, it was time to add together the 4 parts of each required summation. The first step of this process was using **addpd** to add the registers **xmm8** - **xmm12** to registers **xmm0** - **xmm4**. Following this the "horizontal add packed double", **haddpd**, instruction was used to add the upper and lower halves of each of the summation registers to get the final sums. Then the code implemented the formula presented earlier.

When tested on 1 million correlations of size 10000, this program used 6.74 seconds which is approximately 11.8 GFLOPs. Now this is pretty impressive since the CPU operates at 3.4 GHz. It produced about 3.5 floating point results per cycle. This means that more than one of the SSE instructions was completing at once. The CPU is performing out-of-order execution and completing more than one SSE instruction per cycle.

19.3 Implementation using AVX instructions

The Core i7 CPU implements a new collection of instructions called "Advanced Vector Extensions" or AVX. For these instructions an extension of the XMM registers named **ymm0** through **ymm15** is provided along with some new instructions. The YMM registers are 256 bits each and can hold 4 double precision values in each one. This allowed a fairly easy adaptation of the SSE function to operate on 4 values at once.

In addition to providing the larger registers, the AVX instructions added versions of existing instructions which allowed using 3 operands: 2 source operands and a destination which did not participate as a source (unless you named the same register twice). The AVX versions of instructions are prefixed with the letter "v". Having 3 operand instructions reduces the register pressure and allows using two registers as sources in an instruction while preserving their values.

Here is the AVX version of the `corr` function:

```
        segment .text
        global corr
;
;       rcx:    x array
;       rdx:    y array
;       r10:    loop counter
;       r8:     n

;       ymm0:   4 parts of sum_x
;       ymm1:   4 parts of sum_y
;       ymm2:   4 parts of sum_xx
;       ymm3:   4 parts of sum_yy
;       ymm4:   4 parts of sum_xy
;       ymm5:   4 x values - later squared
;       ymm6:   4 y values - later squared
;       ymm7:   4 xy values

corr:
        xor     r9d, r9d
        mov     r1-, r8
        vzeroall
.more:
        vmovupd ymm5, [rcx+r9]          ; mov x
        vmovupd ymm6, [rdx+r9]          ; mov y
        vmulpd  ymm7, ymm5, ymm6        ; xy
        vaddpd  ymm0, ymm0, ymm5        ; sum_x
        vaddpd  ymm1, ymm1, ymm6        ; sum_y
        vmulpd  ymm5, ymm5, ymm5        ; xx
        vmulpd  ymm6, ymm6, ymm6        ; yy
        vaddpd  ymm2, ymm2, ymm5        ; sum_xx
        vaddpd  ymm3, ymm3, ymm6        ; sum_yy
        vaddpd  ymm4, ymm4, ymm7        ; sum_xy
        vmovupd ymm13, [rcx+r9+32]      ; mov x
        vmovupd ymm14, [rdx+r9+32]      ; mov y
        vmulpd  ymm15, ymm13, ymm14     ; xy
        vaddpd  ymm8, ymm8, ymm13       ; sum_x
```

```
        vaddpd    ymm9, ymm9, ymm14      ; sum_y
        vmulpd    ymm13, ymm13, ymm13    ; xx
        vmulpd    ymm14, ymm14, ymm14    ; yy
        vaddpd    ymm10, ymm10, ymm13    ; sum_xx
        vaddpd    ymm11, ymm11, ymm14    ; sum_yy
        vaddpd    ymm12, ymm12, ymm15    ; sum_xy
        add       r9, 64
        sub       r10, 8
        jnz       .more
        vaddpd    ymm0, ymm0, ymm8
        vaddpd    ymm1, ymm1, ymm9
        vaddpd    ymm2, ymm2, ymm10
        vaddpd    ymm3, ymm3, ymm11
        vaddpd    ymm4, ymm4, ymm12
        vhaddpd   ymm0, ymm0, ymm0       ; sum_x
        vhaddpd   ymm1, ymm1, ymm1       ; sum_y
        vhaddpd   ymm2, ymm2, ymm2       ; sum_xx
        vhaddpd   ymm3, ymm3, ymm3       ; sum_yy
        vhaddpd   ymm4, ymm4, ymm4       ; sum_xy
        vextractf128 xmm5, ymm0, 1
        vaddsd    xmm0, xmm0, xmm5
        vextractf128 xmm6, ymm1, 1
        vaddsd    xmm1, xmm1, xmm6
        vmulsd    xmm6, xmm0, xmm0       ; sum_x*sum_x
        vmulsd    xmm7, xmm1, xmm1       ; sum_y*sum_y
        vextractf128 xmm8, ymm2, 1
        vaddsd    xmm2, xmm2, xmm8
        vextractf128 xmm9, ymm3, 1
        vaddsd    xmm3, xmm3, xmm9
        cvtsi2sd  xmm8, r8               ; n
        vmulsd    xmm2, xmm2, xmm8       ; n*sum_xx
        vmulsd    xmm3, xmm3, xmm8       ; n*sum_yy
        vsubsd    xmm2, xmm2, xmm6       ; n*sum_xx -
                                         ; sum_x*sum_x
        vsubsd    xmm3, xmm3, xmm7       ; n*sum_yy -
                                         ; sum_y*sum_y
        vmulsd    xmm2, xmm2, xmm3       ; denom*denom
        vsqrtsd   xmm2, xmm2, xmm2       ; denom
        vextractf128 xmm6, ymm4, 1
        vaddsd    xmm4, xmm4, xmm6
        vmulsd    xmm4, xmm4, xmm8       ; n*sum_xy
        vmulsd    xmm0, xmm0, xmm1       ; sum_x*sum_y
        vsubsd    xmm4, xmm4, xmm0       ; n*sum_xy -
                                         ; sum_x*sum_y
        vdivsd    xmm0, xmm4, xmm2       ; correlation
        ret
```

Now the code is accumulating 8 partial sums for each required sum. The **vhaddpd** instruction unfortunately did not sum all 4 values in a register. Instead it summed the first 2 values and left that sum in the lower half of the register and summed the last 2 values and left that sum in the upper half of the register. It was necessary to use the "extract 128 bit field", **vextractf128**, instruction to move the top half of these sums into the lower half of a register to prepare for adding the 2 halves.

When tested with one million calls to compute correlation on 10000 pairs of values, the AVX version used 3.9 seconds which amounts to 20.5 GFLOPs. This is achieving an average of 6 floating point results in each clock cycle. The code had many instructions which did 4 operations and the CPU did an excellent job of out-of-order execution. The use of 2 sets of accumulation registers most likely reduced the inter-instruction dependency which helped the CPU perform more instructions in parallel.

Exercises

1. Write an SSE function to compute the mean and standard deviation of an array of doubles.

2. Write a function to perform a least squares fit for a polynomial function relating two sequences of doubles in 2 arrays.

Appendix A
Installing ebe

There are basically 2 choices for installing ebe: either install a precompiled binary package or install from source. Installing binary packages is the easy choice and requires downloading an installation exe file. It seems that the installation exe works for 64 bit Windows 7 and Windows 8. There may be problems with other versions of Windows. On the other hand installing from source requires setting up a development environment though the source code is quite portable between different versions of Windows.

Installing from binary packages

You can find Windows installation exe files at the qtebe sourceforge site: https://sourceforge.net/projects/qtebe/files/Windows. The Windows installation requires installing a tools package with a name like "`ebetools64-4.0.exe`" and the ebe package with a name like "`ebe64-3.0.9-setup.exe`". Simply download and execute these 2 programs. These are programs prepared using Inno Setup and will guide you through the installation process. The programs will install ebe, gcc, g++, gdb, astyle and nasm which are all that are needed to use ebe. The tools setup program installs the gcc compiler tools and the ebe setup program installs ebe, astyle and nasm.

Installing from source on Windows

Installing from source on Windows requires a little more effort, I suggest installing the Cygwin package to download the ebe source and Qt to build the ebe program.

Installing Cygwin

I have used Cygwin as a base for working with ebe. For the purpose of installing from source, it will provide the git program which is used to download the source code.

You can find the Cygwin setup program at http://cygwin.com. There is a 32 bit as well as a 64 bit Cygwin. I suggest using the 64 bit version, but either will do. Follow the instructions and select the git package while installing Cygwin.

Installing Qt

You start the Qt installation by clicking on the download link at http://www.qt.io. This initiates a sequence of questions related to whether you need to purchase a license or if you can use the non-commercial version. It will lead you to a page with a download link.

The downloaded file will be named something like "`qt-unified-windows-86-2.0.5-online.exe`". Execute this program to start the Qt installation.

You will need to have or create a Qt account as the first phase of installation. Then the program will download information about the available Qt versions. After selecting a directory for the installation you will be given choices of Qt versions to install. The default shows 3 different versions selected. I recommend selecting only the most recent one. Click on the ">" symbol to the left of this version and it will give you a list of different compiler choices. I recommend selecting MinGW 5.3.0 32 bit (or perhaps a later version).

Back to the main list you will see the Tools item which needs to be selected. I recommend selecting MinGW 5.3.0 again here. This is asking the installer to install the compiler. The previous MinGW selection was asking for the Qt libraries built for that compiler.

After selecting the Qt version and compiler, click on the Next button to complete the installation. It will download the libraries and tools you need and install them.

Downloading the source code

From a Cygwin windows you can use git to copy the source code from sourceforge using

```
git clone git://git.code.sf.net/p/qtebe/code ebe
```

This will create a directory named ebe which contains all the source code. Git is a source code management system which makes it possible to update the source code using "`git pull`" from the ebe directory in the future. It will download only the changes.

Compiling ebe and installing

There is a bash script named "qrc" which needs to be executed in a Cygwin terminal window in order to convert text messages in ebe into the various languages it supports. Use this command after installing the Qt tools

```
cd ebe
./qrc
```

After running the qrc script, you can do the rest in the Qt Creator program. Open the ebe.pro project file with the Creator and it will open up an IDE where you can edit and debug Qt programs. I suggest using the Build menu choice to run qmake once. Then you can use the Build menu Build project "ebe" choice to build ebe. When successful it will place ebe.exe in ebe\release.

Appendix B
Using ebe

This book has introduced ebe a little at a time, as needed, to help students progress through increasing assembly mastery. Most of the discussion of ebe so far has been about debugging. Here we discuss editing, projects, debugging and more.

Major features

Beyond the basic issues of successfully starting and ending ebe, it is important to learn how to find help within the program. The first learning tool is a set of tooltips. Next is the help system accessible from the menu. The third learning tool is the set of keystrokes visible within the menu system. However possibly the greatest aid to learning is curiosity.

Tooltips

Move the mouse over the various subwindows and items within the subwindows and wait about a half second and ebe will popup tooltips. The tooltips are pretty persistent. If you are editing use the mouse to set the editing cursor and move the mouse cursor to the open space in a title bar to make the tooltip disappear. Tooltips will help as you get used to the program, but they will become an annoyance after you've memorized what they say. You can turn off the tooltips in the menu by unchecking the "Tooltips" option in the "View" menu.

Help

The help system operates by clicking "Help" in the main menu and then clicking on one of the help options. Each help file is displayed in a different window and can be dismissed in the normal manner for windows on your computer.

Menu

The menu system contains nearly everything which can be done in the program. Nearly all the menu options have keyboard shortcuts. Use the menu to figure out what all can be done and learn some keyboard tricks as you progress. A few things like using control with the arrow keys, home and end are not in the menu, so experiment.

Movable toolbars

There are a collection of 4 toolbars in ebe: the file toolbar, the edit tool bar, the debug toolbar and the template toolbar. Each of these has icons to perform common actions and each has a "grab point" on the left or top which can be used with a left click to move the toolbar. You can move a toolbar out of the program to make it a separate window. You can also right click on the grab point to select which toolbars are visible. Below the debug toolbar is shown as it appears as a separate window.

Ebe remembers the configuration of the ebe main window, the toolbars and its subwindows using the file ".ebe.ini", so you can relocate the toolbars as you wish to make using ebe more convenient. There is a separate ".ebe.ini" in each directory where you use ebe, so you can customize the appearance for different languages or projects.

Movable subwindows

In addition to have movable toolbars ebe has a collection of movable or dockable subwindows: data, register, floating point register, terminal, project, toy box, bit bucket, backtrace and console windows. Ebe keeps track of the visibility and location of these subwindows in ".ebe.ini" to make it easy to customize. Below we see ebe with a few of the windows in their "docked" location.

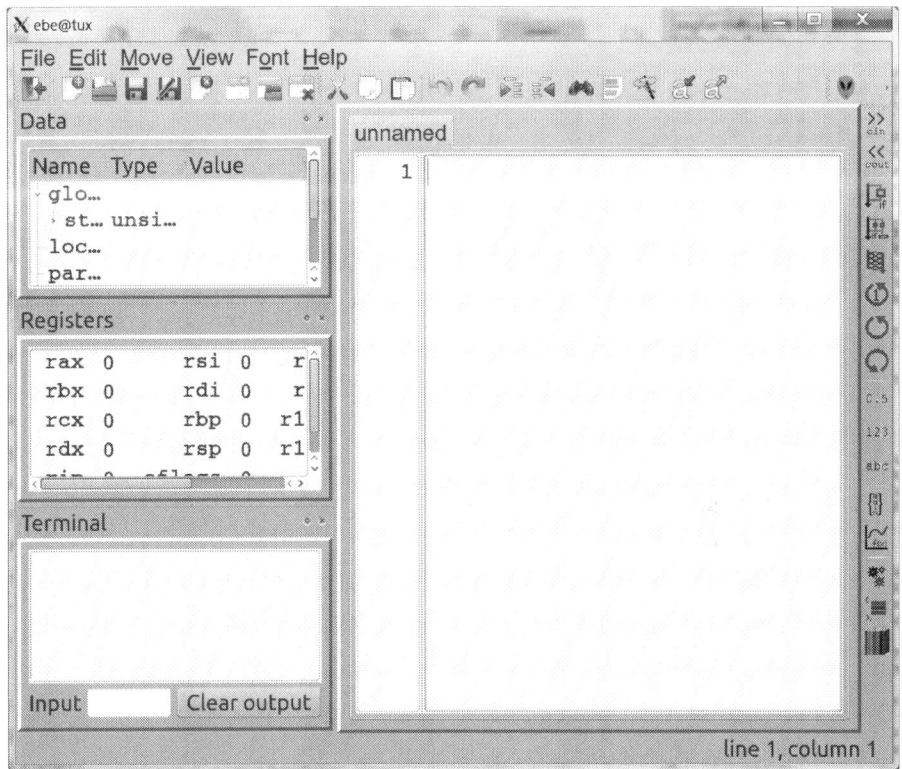

Between each of the docked windows is a "resize bar" which can be used with a left click to adjust the division of space allotted to the docked windows. There is also a resize bar between the docked windows and the source window which can be used to adjust the width of the docked windows.

Each docked window has a "title bar" at the top. There are 2 tiny icons on the right of each title bar which can be used to make the window stand-alone or to make the window disappear. You can also use a right click on a title bar to pop up a menu allowing you to select with dock windows and toolbars are visible. Visibility can also be controlled using the View menu.

You can use a left click on a dock window title bar to drag it around. You can drag it out of ebe to make it stand-alone or to a different vertical position in the dock area. You will notice a gray area in the dock area where the window will drop when you release the left button. You can even drag a dock window to the right of the ebe window or the bottom to use 2 different dock areas. Finally you can drag a dock window on top of another one to create a collection of tabbed dock windows. Perhaps you would like to be able to switch easily between the data, register and floating point register windows. Below we see a dock window with 3 tabs at the bottom for these 3 windows and the terminal window below.

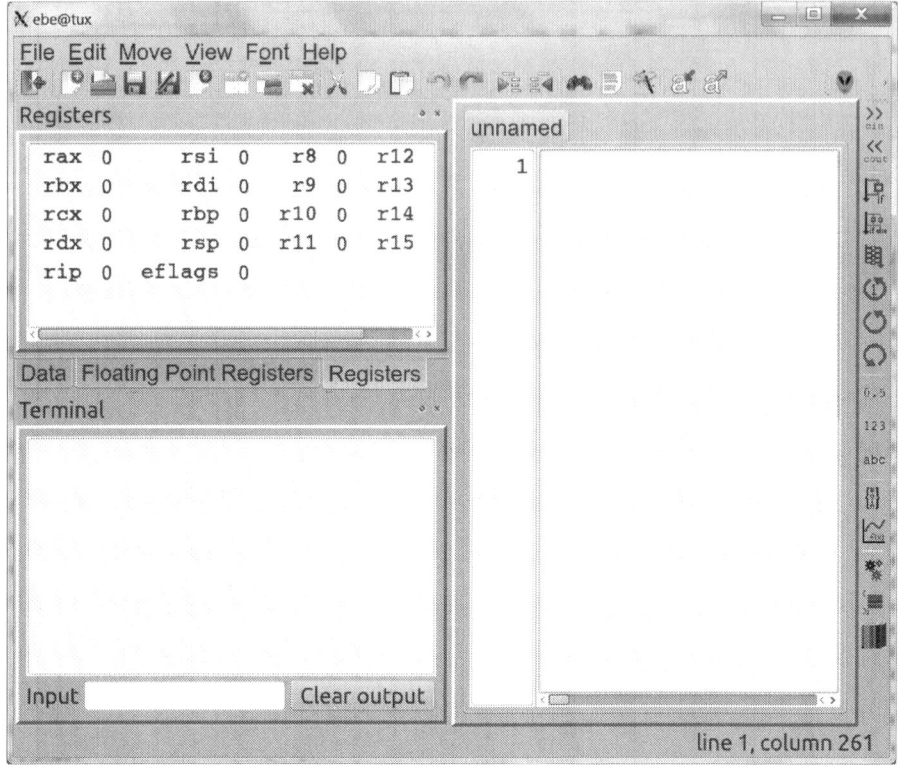

Editing

Editing in ebe uses the mouse and keyboard in mostly normal ways for editors. Special keys like Delete and Enter work as expected. For many of these normal keys an additional action is invoked using the Control key and the normal key. Most editing actions are available in the menu system which will also show the shortcut keys for the actions.

For simplicity the discussion of editing in ebe refers to using the Control key to invoke shortcuts. On OS X this is usually done using the Apple key. Fortunately the menu system displays the proper shortcuts. In addition the shortcuts are based on normal editing shortcuts obtained from Wikipedia:

http://en.wikipedia.org/wiki/Table_of_keyboard_shortcuts
.

Navigation

Scrollbars There are vertical and horizontal scrollbars which can scroll through the file. Scrolling can also be done using the mouse wheel.

Arrow keys Moving 1 character at a time is done using the left and right arrow keys on the keyboard. Up and down arrows move up or down one line at a time.

Control + Arrow keys Control-Right moves 1 word to the right. Control-Left moves 1 word to the left.

Home/End Home moves to column 1 on the current line. End moves to the end of the current line.

Control + Home/End Control-Home moves to column 1 of line 1. Control-End moves to the end of the file.

PageUp/PageDown These keys move up/down one screenful at a time.

Control-T/Control-B Control-T (top) moves to column 1 of the top line currently on the screen. Control-B (bottom) moves to column 1 of the last line currently on the screen.

Control-M Control-M scrolls the screen until the current line is at the middle of the screen.

Control-L Control-L will pop up a dialog where you can enter a line number to go to.

Cut, copy and paste

The first step in cutting or copying is to select the text to copy or cut.

Left mouse Dragging with the left mouse button held down can be used to mark a section of text. Double clicking with the left mouse button will select a word of text.

Select all You can select all of the text using Control-A or the Edit menu option.

Select none You can cancel any select using Control-0 (zero) or the Edit menu option.

Selected text can be cut, copied and pasted using either options in the Edit menu or the normal shortcuts: Control-X for cut, Control-C for copy, or Control-V for paste. The edit toolbar also has buttons for cut, copy and paste.

Undo/redo

Control-Z will undo an edit operation. Insertions will be undone basically one line at a time. Shift-Control-Z will redo an edit operation. You can also do undo/redo using the menu system or the edit toolbar. The editor keeps track of a large number of editing steps which allows undoing a lot of changes.

Find and replace

Use Control-F to pop up the Find/Replace dialog. There is a text entry box there for entering a string to find. The focus is ready for you to type the search string when the dialog starts. If you simply want to find, then enter either Enter, Control-F or the Find button as many times as you wish. If you wish to change the string, then use Tab to move to the text entry box for the replacement field and enter a string. To replace the string, use Control-R or the Replace button. You can end the Find/Replace dialog using the Cancel button.

Deleting text

Backspace will delete the character to the left of the cursor while Delete will delete the character to the right of the cursor. Control-Backspace will delete the word to the left of the cursor and Control-Delete will delete the word to the right of the cursor.

Using tabs

Entering a tab character will enter enough spaces to move to the next tab stop. Tabs are at columns 5, 9, 13, ... - indenting 4 characters for each tab. Control-Tab will delete space characters to the left of the cursor to position to the previous tab column. The tab spacing value can be changed by editing ".`ebe.ini`" or by using "Edit settings" from the Edit menu.

Auto-indent

The editor will automatically enter spaces so that a new line will be indented just the same as the previous line. Ebe will indent the next line after a line ending in "{". Likewise it will unindent when a line begins with "}". Adjusting indentation for a new line can be done using Tab or Control-Tab.

Prettify

Ebe will call the external program astyle to format C and C++ programs if you use the "Prettify" option under the Edit menu or the "magic wand" icon on the edit toolbar. You can change the options used for astyle or even replace the program with another by editing ".ebe.ini" or using the "Edit settings" option under the Edit menu.

Indent/unindent

After marking a group of lines you can indent it one tab stop at a time using Control-> which resembles the C right shift operator (>>). You can shift the text left (unindent) using Control-<. There are also menu options for indent/unident and edit toolbar icons.

Comment/uncomment

Control-K will comment out the current line or a range of lines if some text is selected. Control-U will uncomment either the current line or a range of lines. Ebe will use comment syntax for the appropriate language.

Word/number completion

Ebe keeps track of words and numbers to simplify entering/re-entering longer words. It starts with the a collection of keywords and adds words and numbers as you edit. When you enter some text ebe will pop up a list of words to the right of where you are editing. Simply select the desired word (or number) and press "Enter" to accept the suggested completion or enter additional characters to narrow down the choices.

Editing multiple files

It is possible to maintain several open files in ebe. You can open multiple times using the File menu or possibly you could use a project which consists of multiple files. The various files will be accessible as tabbed windows in the source subwindow of ebe.

If you are not using a project ebe will compile or assemble only the currently selected file from those opened. This might be useful if you are working on a few similar programs or if you want to prepare a data file for your program to access. If you are using a project, then ebe will build the program using the source files in the project. Once again it is possible to have a data file as part of a project.

Debugging

The debug toolbar is shown below. There are 4 icons or buttons which are used to control debugging. Each time you click on the Run button the program saves your source code, runs the compiler and/or assembler and then starts running your program in the debugger. Most likely you will want to set a breakpoint before clicking Run. Do this by clicking to the left of a source code line where you would like to have the program stop and inspect things. Then you can click Run and Next/Step to step through your program 1 line at a time. Use Next to stay within the same function or subroutine. Use Step if you wish to debug inside a function or subroutine. You can skip past a bunch of statements using Continue which will execute until it reaches the next breakpoint. The Stop button will end the debugging process.

Breakpoints

A breakpoint is a point in your source code which will cause the debugger to stop executing your program when it runs your program. If you set a breakpoint on line 10 of your code, the debugger will execute all lines up to line 10 when you click the Run button. Line 10 will not be run until you take another action like using one of the Next, Step or Continue buttons.

Every line of source code has a line number in the line numbers column to the left of the source code. A breakpoint is visually identified in the source code window by using a red background for the line number for the line with a breakpoint.

You set or clear a breakpoint using a left click on a line number. The first click with set the breakpoint and the second will clear it. A right click will pop up a menu allowing management of breakpoints inclucing an option to delete them all.

Running a program

The first step is to set a breakpoint on the line where you want your program to stop. Left click on the line number and you will see the line number for the line change to a bright red background. Click again if this is the wrong line.

After setting one or more breakpoints, you need to click on the Run button. This button will save your source code file, run the proper compiler for your code and then start the gdb debugger on the compiled program. When the program reaches a line with a breakpoint, it will stop and ebe will highlight the line using a pastel blue-green background. The highlighted line will be the next line to execute.

Terminal window

The terminal window is one of the dock windows which supports terminal input and output. It does not include a real terminal emulator. Instead all input is done using a text input box and the text displayed is all printed by the program plus the input echoed to make it all look more normal. The picture below shows the terminal window in a program being tested.

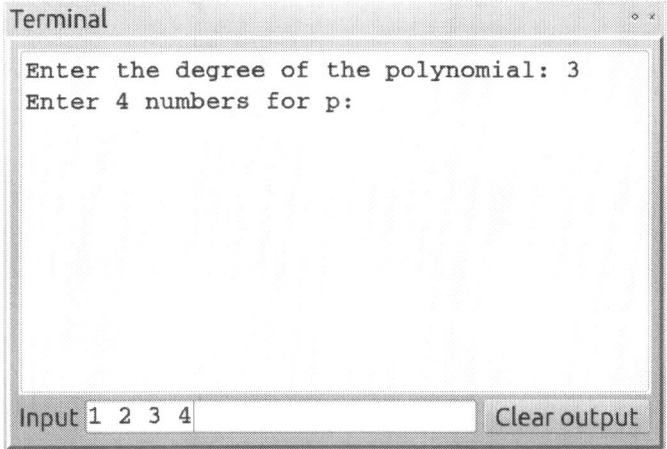

In the previous session one input operation has been done and one is in progress. The first input, 3, was typed into the Input box and after pressing Enter 3 was echoed in the terminal window. The next input is in progress. Four numbers have been typed into the Input box, but Enter has not been pressed which would complete the input.

It is possible to use Control-D or Control-Z in the Input box to send an end of file indication into the program. However this only works if the EOF is signaled before the input operation is performed. This is abnormal, but it works fine if you are single-stepping. Then you enter Control-D prior to executing the **scanf** call (or another form of read).

Next and step

Both the Next and Step buttons will step through your code, line by line. The difference is that Next will stay in the current function or subroutine, while Step will step into a function if one is called on the highlighted line. You generally only want to use the Step button to step into a function in the same source file or another file in the project.

Continue

The Continue button will resume normal execution of the program and it will only stop if it encounters a breakpoint. You probably would use this to rapidly step past some debugged code to reach a breakpoint in some code which currently has an error.

Assembly Data window

The assembly data window displays variables in your program. There is a separate data window for C/C++. The display of variables in .data and .bss is automatic. The program depends upon running the ebedecl program to determine the lengths of variables and initial format. For variables in the data segment the data definition is used as a guide for the format. For bss variables, ebe will display the data as 1 byte hexadecimal variables.

You can right click on variables to change their format. You can choose from 1, 2, 4, and 8 byte integers in decimal or hexadecimal. You can choose a variety of formats for floating point values (floats and doubles). These floating point formats include normal decimal notation, binary floating point and as a collection of fields which includes sign, exponent field and fraction field.

Register window

The register window provides a live display of the 16 general purpose registers, the instruction pointer and the CPU flags. Here is a sample

```
Registers
  rax  480                      rsi  0x7fffffffeb38    r8   0x400cca
  rbx  0x0                      rdi  0x1               r9   0x0
  rcx  0xffffffffffffffff       rbp  0x7fffffffea50    r10  0x1
  rdx  0x7fffffffeb48           rsp  0x7fffffffea40    r11  0x246
  rip  0x400c33               eflags IF
```

Registers `r12`-`r15` have been left out so that the rest of the registers could be displayed using larger characters. You can change the format of a register (other than `rip`) by right clicking on its name. This will pop up a form allowing you to choose decimal or hexadecimal for that register or for all the registers. The flags which are currently set are displayed. In the sample the interrupt flag is set. Some interrupts can be ignored if `IF` is set while there are other non-maskable interrupts which are beyond software control.

Floating point register window

The floating point registers are displayed in a separate dockable window. Here is an example

Floating Point Registers			
xmm0	3.25	xmm8	0
xmm1	10.53	xmm9	0
xmm2	13.78	xmm10	0
xmm3	0	xmm11	0
xmm4	2.34181e-38	xmm12	0
xmm5	0	xmm13	0
xmm6	0	xmm14	0
xmm7	0	xmm15	0

The floating point registers can be used to hold floats, doubles, packed floats, packed doubles and a variety of packed integers of various sizes. Using AVX instructions doubles the number of packed floats or doubles in each register. This makes it important to be able to select the format for the floating point registers. Right clicking on a register or its content will pop up a menu for selecting formatting one register or all. Then you get to select from all the possible interpretations of the registers.

Projects

A program in ebe is generally managed using a project file to keep track of the source code files in the program. The name of a project is the name of the program with ".ebe" appended to the name. Thus to build a program named "hello", you would use a project file named "hello.ebe".

It is not necessary to use a project file with programs consisting of a single source code file. Ebe starts execution with no known project name (if not given on the command line). As long as there is no known project name, it is assumed that there is only 1 source file. Creating a project or opening a project will change the state so that ebe will be aware of having a project file. After that point ebe will keep track of the files using the project file.

Viewing the project window

You may need to check the Project checkbox in the View menu in order to display the project window. The project window is one of several optional windows which are intitially placed to the left of the source window. You can see an empty project window below. You can move the window to be a "floating" window by left clicking in the title bar of the project window and dragging it until it is outside of the main window of ebe.

For the project window right clicking will allow you to add or delete files from the project.

Creating a new project

You can create a new project using the "New project" option under the File menu. This option will allow you to navigate to a new directory and specify the name of the new project file. After creating the project file, any open source files will be closed and the project will be empty. Any changes to the project will be written automatically so there is no need to save a project file.

Opening a project

You can open an existing project using the "Open project" option under the File menu. This option will allow you to navigate to a new directory and open a file with the ".ebe" extension. After opening the project file, any open source files will be closed and the first file in the project will be opened in the editor.

Adding files to a project

A right click in the project window will pop up a menu which will allow you to remove the selected file from the project, open the selected file in the ebe editor, or add a file to the project. A project is simply a file with a collection of file names – one per line, so it is also possible to edit a project file with a text editor.

Closing a project

If you close the active project ebe will return to the default mode of not using a project. It will close all open files.

Toy box

The ebe toy box is a dockable subwindow which allows experimentation with expressions in C/C++ or Fortran. The basic idea is to place variable definitions in one table and expressions in expressions in a second table. A variable definition includes a name, a type and a value. The types are selected from a list of simple types in the language. The names and values must be entered.

The second table has expressions in the first column. After you enter an expression you click on the "do it" button to the right and ebe generates a program in the selected language, compiles it and executes it. From the program's output it determines the type of the expression and its value which are added to the table. Then you can choose a variety of formats depending on the type. For the integer types you can choose decimal, hexadecimal or binary. For the floating point types you can choose decimal, hexadecimal, binary, binary floating point, or fields. In the toy box window below I have included several expressions which help in understanding floating point to integer conversion and floating point format.

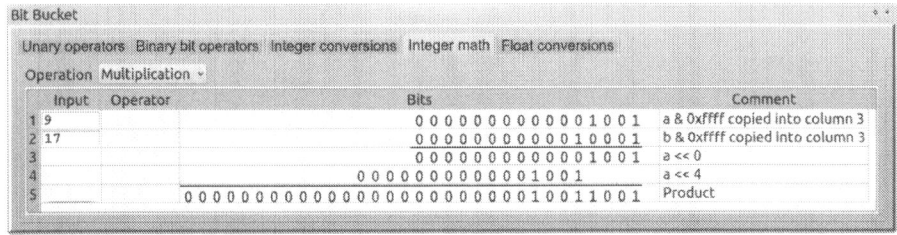

Bit bucket

The ebe bit bucket is a lower level educational tool. It is targeted primarily at assembly language students. It allows you to experiment with a variety of computer operations. It allows you to observe how binary operations like and, or, exlusive or, addition and multiplication work. It shows the steps in converting a decimal number to binary or hexadecimal. It illustrates how to convert a floating point number like 1.625 into its internal representation as a float. Here is an example illustrating multiplication.

You can see that there are 5 tabs in the bit bucket. I have selected "Integer math". After that I used the pull down list to the right of "Operation" to select "Multiplication". Initially there were 2 "Input" boxes to enter 2 numbers and a "*" in the "Operator" column on row 3. After the first clicking of "*" it converted the 2 numbers to binary in column 3. Then I clicked the "*" again and it filled in row 3 and moved the "*" to row 4. After a couple more steps the product was presented on row 5.

The 5 tabs include a large number of illustrations. An assembly language student should find the bit bucket a great tool for learning how a computer works.

Backtrace window

The backtrace window displays the information gleaned from stepping backward through the stack and examining the stack frames for each function invoked. The gdb command for this is "**backtrace**" or simply "**bt**". In the picture below we see that the function in the top stack frame is **time** and the program is stopped at line 18 of "**testcopy.c**". Next we see that **time** was called from the **test** function at line 26. The values of the parameters to **test** are displayed as well. Last we see that **test** was called from **main** at line 47.

```
Back Trace
#0  time () at /home/seyfarth/asm/testcopy.c:18
#1  0x0000000000400dea in test (name=0x401197 "rep movsb",
    copy=0x400f80 <copy_repb>, a=0x2aaaab8b6010 "", b=0x2aaaac240010 "",
    count=10) at /home/seyfarth/asm/testcopy.c:26
#2  0x0000000000400f10 in main (argc=1, argv=0x7fffffffeb38)
    at /home/seyfarth/asm/testcopy.c:47
```

Console

The ebe console provides a way to access gdb directly while debugging. In its text window it displays all the communication with gdb. There is also a command entry box where you can issue a gdb command. After you press "Enter" it executes the command and the results are visible in the text window. I executed "p $rip" to print the instruction pointer register. The next instruction to execute is at **0x400ed1** which is located in **main**.

```
Console
0x7fffffffeb38: 140737488350534
(gdb)
0x7fffffffed46: "/home/seyfarth/asm/testcopy"
(gdb)
0x7fffffffeb40: 0
(gdb)
$34 = (void (*)(void)) 0x400ed1 <main+50>
(gdb)

gdb command  p $rip
```

Ebe settings

Using the "Edit settings" under the Edit menu will pop up a form with a lot of adjustable features about ebe. Here is how it looks when set for a gray color scheme.

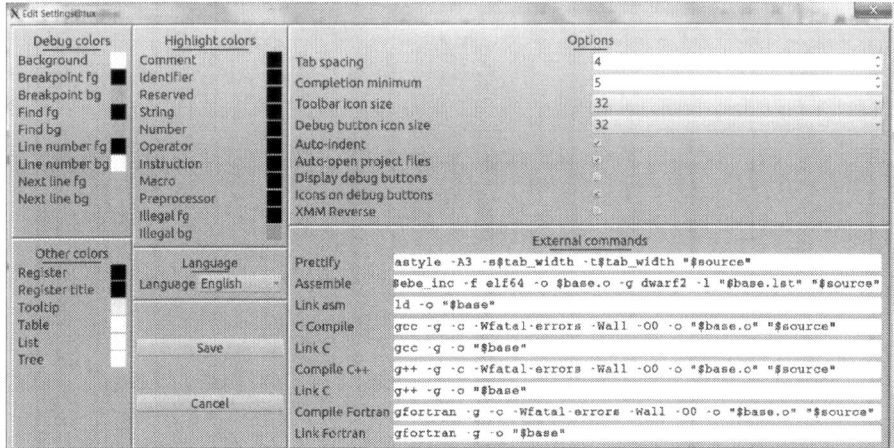

All these settings are stored in ".ebe.ini" in a very simple format, so it is possible to edit the file successfully. However the settings dialog is easier to manage.

Note that there is a "Language" option which is set to "English". Ebe can also operate in Arabic, Chinese, Danish, French, German, Hindi, Indonesian, Japanese, Portuguese, Russian, Spanish and Swedish. I have had excellent assistance for a few languages, but some of these are the direct result of using Google Translate. Some of the translations might be comical. I hope that none are offensive.

Ebe Register Alias Macros

Ebe has several macros which you can use to provide new names for the integer registers and the floating point registers. These can be useful with complex code to give meaningful names to registers. In addition the register window and the floating point register window will display the aliased registers with their new names.

alias

The alias macro provides an alias for one of the integer registers. You can use it like this

    alias   rbx, Count

The effect of this is to allow you to use **qCount**, **dCount**, **wCount**, **bCount** and **hCount** to reference **rbx**, **rbx**, **bx**, **bl** and **bh** in your code. I suggest beginning the alias with an uppercase name to end up using Camel-case. It works will all the integer registers except **rsp**.

To remove the effect of an alias use unalias as below:

    unalias Count

This will remove all 5 aliases you previously defined.

fpalias

The fpalias macro works with the XMM and YMM registers. You would use it as

    fpalias   1, Sum

This provides 2 aliases: **xSum** and **ySum** which give new names to **XMM1** and **YMM1**.

To remove a floating point alias use **fpunalias** as below:

    fpunalias Sum

Appendix C
Using **scanf** and **printf**

The simplest method for input and output is using the C library's **scanf** and **printf** functions. These functions can handle virtually all forms of text input and output converting to/from integer and floating point format.

It may be that modern programmers are familiar with C++ I/O and not with C. It would not be simple to call C++ I/O facilities, while it is simple to call C functions. So there is probably a need for a slight introduction to the 2 basic workhorses of C I/O: **scanf** and **printf**. These are sufficient for the I/O needs for learning assembly language. Practical uses of assembly language will likely be writing computational or bit manipulating functions with no requirement for I/O. Therefore this appendix will stick to the basics to facilitate writing complete programs while learning assembly programming.

scanf

The simplest way of explaining how to use **scanf** is to show C calls, followed by assembly equivalents. **scanf** is called with a format string as its first parameter. Depending on the format string there can be an arbitrary number of additional parameters. Within the format string are a series of conversion specifiers. Each specifier is a percent character followed by one of more letters defining the type of data to convert. Here are the basic format specifiers:

format	data type
%d	4 byte integer (int)
%hd	2 byte integer (short)
%ld	4 byte integer (long)
%I64d	8 byte integer (long long)
%f	4 byte floating point (float)
%lf	8 byte floating point (double)
%s	character array (C string)

So if we wish to read a double followed by a character string we could use the format string "%lf %s".

Each additional parameter for scanf is an address of the data location to receive the data read and converted by scanf. Here is a sample C call:

```
double x;
char s[100];
n = scanf ( "%lf %s", &x, s );
```

scanf will return the number of items converted. In the call above it will return 2 if a number and a string are successfully entered. The string will be placed in the array s with a 0 at the end of the string.

Here is how to do the same thing in assembly:

```
        segment .data
x       dq      0.0
n       dd      0
s       times   100 db 0
fmt     db      "%lf %s",0
        segment .text
        lea     rcx, [fmt]
        lea     rdx, [x]
        lea     r8, [s]
        call    scanf
        mov     [n], eax
```

There are a couple of pitfalls possible. First the format string needs a 0 at the end and it can't be enclosed in the double quotes. Second there are no floating point parameters - &x is a address parameter and it is stored in rsi so rax must be set to 0 before the call.

printf

printf allows printing in a wide variety of formats. Like scanf its first parameter is a format string. The format string contains characters to print along with conversion specifiers like `scanf`. Data printed with `printf` is likely to be stored in a buffer until a new-line character is printed. In C, the new-line character can be represented as \n at the end of the format string. Nasm does not support C escape characters in strings, so it is necessary to explicitly add new-line (0x0a) and 0 bytes.

Here is a C printf call

```c
char name[64];
int value;
printf ( "The value of %s is %dn", name, value );
```

Here is the same `printf` call in assembly

```
        segment .data
value   dd      0
name    times   64 db 0
fmt     db      "The value of %s is %d",0x0a,0
        segment .text
        lea     rcx, [fmt]
        lea     rdx, [name]
        mov     r8d, [value]
        call    printf
```

When you print a floating point value the XMM register's value must be copied without conversion into the corresponding general purpose register. This is most easily done using the instruction "`movq`" which moves a value from an XMM register to a general purpose register or the reverse pattern. Here is some code printing 2 doubles stored in memory locations.

```
;       printf ( "sqrt(%lf) = %lf\n", a, b );
        segment .data
fmt     db      "sqrt(%lf) = %lf", 0x0a, 0
        segment .text
        lea     rcx, [fmt]
        movsd   xmm1, [a]       ; second parameter
        movq    rdx, xmm1       ; also in rdx
        movsd   xmm2, [b]       ; third parameter
        movq    r8, xmm2        ; copied into r8
        call    printf
```

Appendix D
Using macros in nasm

Nasm provides both single line macros and multi-line macros. Both of these can be used to provide abbreviations with meaningful names for commonly used instructions. While these might obscure the mechanisms of assembly language while learning the language they can be of significant utility in practical situations.

Single line macros

A single line macro uses the **%define** preprocessor command. Let's suppose you are tired of seeing **0x0a** for the new-line character. You could define a macro for this as

```
%define newline 0x0a
```

From that point forward you could simply use **newline** and get **0x0a** inserted in replacement for the macro.

Single line macros can have parameters. Let's suppose you wanted to define a while loop macro. You might wish to compare a value in a register against a value and if a condition is satisfied jump to the top of the loop. Here is a possible **while** macro:

```
%define while(cc,label) jmp%+cc label
```

The **%+** allows concatenation of tokens. After this definition we could use code like

```
        cmp rax, 20
        while(l,.more)
```

Multi-line macros

Using a multi-line macro can simply our **while** macro to include the required **cmp** instruction:

```
%macro  while 4
        cmp %1, %3
        j%2 %4
%endmacro
```

The number 4 on the **%macro** line suggests that 4 parameters are expected. You can access each parameter as **%1**, **%2**, etc. You can also access the number of parameters as **%0**.

Now this definition leaves the fairly pleasant feel of creating an instruction, since the macro invocation does not use parentheses:

```
while rax, l, 20, .more
```

Admittedly this creates an instruction with 4 parameters which must be learned, but it simplifies things a little bit.

How about the standard production of a stack frame:

```
%macro function 2
        global  %1
    %1: push    rbp
        mov     rbp, rsp
        sub     rsp, %2
%endmacro
```

We might as well simplify the ending of a function:

```
%macro return 1
        mov     rax, %1
        leave
        ret
%endmacro
```

Now we can write a simple program using these macros:

```
        function main, 32
        xor eax, eax
.loop   inc rax
        while rax, 1, 10, .loop
        return 0
```

A fairly useful pair of macros from the nasm manual are **multipush** and **multipop**. These were used earlier in the Sobel example. It makes sense to have a pair of macros to push and pop all callee-save registers for use in register intensive functions.

```
%macro pushsaved
        push rbp
        push rbx
        push r12
        push r13
        push r14
        push r15
%endmacro

%macro popsaved
        pop r15
        pop r14
        pop r13
        pop r12
        pop rbx
        pop rbp
%endmacro
```

Now these by themselves don't preserve 16 byte stack alignment, so perhaps a better choice would be needed for some functions. Maybe you could combine the creation of a stack frame with pushing the rest of the registers and subtracting from the stack pointer to achieve alignment and room for local variables.

Preprocessor variables

Nasm allows defining preprocessor variables which can be used in macros using %assign. You could assign a variable i in one spot and modify it later:

```
%assign i 1
. . .
%assign i i+1
```

For more information about nasm macros visit the nasm web site at http://www.nasm.us/doc which discusses topics like looping and string length.

Appendix E
Sources for more information

nasm user manual

Look at `http://www.nasm.us/doc/` for the nasm user manual. This is the assembler used in **ebe**.

Stephen Morse's 8086/8088 primer

Stephen P. Morse is the architect of the 8086 Intel microprocessor. He has a primer on the 8086/8088 at

`http://www.stevemorse.org/8086/index.html`.

Dr. Paul Carter's free assembly book

Dr. Carter has prepared an excellent book on 32 bit x86 programming which can be downloaded at `http://www.drpaulcarter.com/pcasm/`.

64 bit machine level programming

Drs. Bryant and O'Hallaron of Carnegie Mellon have provided an excellent treatise dissecting how gcc takes advantage of the x86-64 architecture in a document located at

`www.cs.cmu.edu/~{}fp/courses/15213-s07/misc/asm64-handout.pdf`

GDB manual

You may find a need to learn more about gdb. Send your browser to http://www.gnu.org/software/gdb/documentation.

Intel documentation

Intel provides excellent documentation about their processors at http://www.intel.com/products/processor/manuals/.

You should probably review the architecture in "*Intel 64 and IA-32 Architectures Software Developer's Manual, Volume 1: Basic Architectures*".

The instructions are described in great detail in "*Volume 2A: Instruction Set Reference, A-M*" and "*Volume 2B: Instruction Set Reference, N-Z*". These manuals are quite helpful, but some categorization of instructions would help. There are a bewildering number of instructions and looking through the alphabetized list can be overwhelming.

Index

%macro, 224
  multipop, 224
  multipush, 224
%rep, 216
80386, 45
8086, 45
add, 50, 52, 56
addition
  binary, 18
addpd, 144
addps, 144
address, 4, 28
  logical, 28
  physical, 28, 39
  virtual, 38, 39
addsd, 144
addss, 144
ahr, 84
alias, 257
align, 143
alignb, 172, 174
aligned data, 143
and, 71, 72, 74, 84
argc, 136
argv, 136
array, 126
  index, 126
Atlas, 3
AVX, 1, 113, 130, 141, 143, 206, 213, 233, 234, 236
binary, 12
  to decimal, 12
binary addition, 18
binary constant, 13
binary multiplication, 19
binary number, 4, 12

binary tree, 199
  find, 200
  insert, 201
  new_tree, 200
  node struct, 199
  print, 202
  root struct, 199
  traversal, 202
bit, 3, 12, 70, 71
  flipper, 73
  numbering, 12
  setter, 72
bit bucket, 25
bit field, 74, 80, 84
  extraction, 74
  insertion, 75
bit field selector, 71
bit fields, 70
bit operations, 70
bit test. *See* bt
bit test and reset. *See* btr
bit test and set. *See* bts
break, 93
breakpoint, 33
bss segment, 30, 32
bt, 83
btr, 80
bts, 80, 81, 84, 85
buffered I/O, 177
byte, 4
C stream I/O, 177
C wrapper function, 164
cache, 44, 205
  matrix multiply, 206
call, 106
carry, 18

CF, 62, 80, 83
cl, 83
cld, 101, 102
close, 168
CloseHandle, 159
cmovl, 134
cmp, 90, 94, 95, 98, 101
cmpsb, 102
command line parameters, 105, 134, 136
comment, 6
common subexpression elimination, 207
continue, 93
correlation, 230
   AVX, 233
   C, 230
   SSE, 231
counting bits, 94, 215
   assembly shift/and, 216
   byte at a time, 218
   C, 215
   popcnt instruction, 219
counting lo, 98
counting loop. *See* for loop
CR3, 38
CreateFile, 156
cvtdq2ps, 224
cvtpd2ps, 146
cvtps2pd, 146
cvtsd2si, 147
cvtsd2ss, 146
cvtsi2sd, 147
cvtsi2ss, 147
cvtss2sd, 146
cvtss2si, 147
cvttsd2si, 147
cvttss2si, 147
data segment, 30, *see* segment...data
db, 20
dd, 20
dec, 58, 85
decimal
   to binary, 13
   to hexadecimal, 14
DF, 100

direction flag, 100
distance in 3D, 150
div, 65
dl, 83
dot product, 150
double word, 20
doubly-linked list, 189
   deque, 189
   insert, 191
   newlist, 190
   node struct, 190
   print, 191
   queue, 189
   stack, 189
   traversal, 191
do-while, 93
do-while loop, 96, 97
dq, 20
dw, 20
ebe, 8, 46, 58
   breakpoint, 33, 52
   data window, 51
   next, 47, 111
   register window, 46
   run, 9, 33, 47
   source window, 51
   step, 47, 111
   terminal window, 137
echo, 11
eflags, 46, 81, 90
eliminate stack frames, 212
environment, 105
EOF, 179
equ, 119, 122, 165
errno, 167
exit, 165
exponent, 20, 21, 23, 24
exponent bias, 20
exponent field, 20, 21, 23, 24
extern, 119, 165
fclose, 183
fgetc, 179, 180
fgets, 180
FILE, 168, 178, 179
file name patterns, 136
float, 20, 23
floating point

addition, 23
exponent, 20
fraction, 20
to decimal, 23
floating point comparison, 147
floating point conversion, 146
floating point multiplication, 24
floating point number, 19
fopen, 178
   mode, 178
for loop, 98
fpalias, 257
fprintf, 179
fputc, 179, 180
fputs, 180
fraction field, 20, 21, 23, 24
fread, 181
free, 130
fscanf, 179
fseek, 182
ftell, 182
function, 105, 106, 112
   parameters, 112, 113, 121
   return value, 112
   variable number of parameters, 114
fwrite, 181
gcc, 7, 8
   function prefix, 7
   generate assembly, 95
   stack size, 37
   unroll loops, 96
gdb
   backtrace, 115
getchar, 177
global, 7
HANDLE, 156
hash function, 193
   integer, 193
   string, 194
hash table, 192
   find, 195
   insert, 195
   node struct, 194
   print, 196
   traversal, 196
heap, 30

heap segment, 30
hexadecimal, 5, 14, 21, 23
   to binary, 15
Horner's rule, 151
huge page, 41
idiv, 65
   to shift, 72
IEEE 754, 20
IEEE 754 format, 19
if, 91
IF, 46
if/else, 91
if/else-if/else, 92
immediate, 47
imul, 60
   1 operand, 60
   2 operands, 62
   3 operands, 62
inc, 56, 98
index, 82
infinity, 20
inline functions, 212
instruction, 5, 7
integer, 55
   maximum, 16
   minimum, 16
   signed, 16, 17
   unsigned, 16
interchange loops, 210
interrupt enable flag. *See* IF
istruc, 172
ja, 148
jae, 90, 148
jb, 90, 148
jbe, 148
jc, 90
je, 90, 98, 101
jg, 90
jge, 90, 91, 95
jl, 90
jle, 90
jmp, 88, 89, 98
   rip relative, 88
jnae, 90
jnb, 90
jnc, 90
jne, 90

jng, 90
jnge, 90
jnl, 90, 91, 94, 95
jnle, 90
jnz, 90, 99, 101
jump. *See* jmp
  conditional, 90
jz, 90, 102
kernel mode, 155
label, 7
large page, 41
ld, 119
lea, 114
leaf function, 115, 134
least significant bit, 12
least significant byte first, 21
leave, 56, 116
linked list, 185
  insert, 186
  newlist, 186
  node struct, 186
  print, 187
  traversal, 187
Linux, 1, 2, 7, 8, 28, 29, 30, 39, 49, 112, 113, 155, 166
local label, 132
local labels, 89
local variable, 121, 132
lodsb, 101
logical address, 28
loop, 99
  branch at bottom, 208
loop invariant, 211
lseek, 167, 168
machine language, 5
main, 7
malloc, 30, 130, 131, 132, 185, 200
mapping registers, 29
mask, 71, 72, 73, 75, 84
mathematical functions, 148
maxpd, 149
maxps, 149
maxsd, 149
maxss, 149
memcmp, 102
memory

address, 28
page, 28
protection, 29
memory latency, 44
memory reference, 127
merge loops, 210
minpd, 149
minps, 149
minsd, 149
minss, 149
most significant bit, 12
mov, 46, 47, 48, 51
  from memory, 49
  immediate, 47
  register to register, 52
  sign extend. *See* movsx
  to memory, 51
  zero extend. *See* movzx
movapd, 143
movaps, 143
movdqa, 224
movdqu, 224
movsb, 100
movsd, 143
movss, 143
movsx, 50
movsxd, 51
movupd, 143
movups, 143
movzx, 50, 102
multiplication
  binary, 19
nasm, iv, 8, 13, 14, 21, 32, 49, 60, 95, 119, 131, 159, 166, 170, 171, 172, 174, 260, 261, 262, 263, 264
  equ, 165
  listing, 21
  struc, 186, 190
neg, 55
negative, 21
negative infinity, 20
new, 30
nibble, 5, 15, 23
not, 70, 71
NULL, 180, 185
OF, 56, 58, 62

open, 165, 166
or, 72, 85
OS X, 1, 2, 7, 8, 28, 39, 49, 113
overflow flag. *See* OF
packed data, 143
paddw, 224
page
  fault, 29
  huge, 41
  kernel, 28
  large, 41
  user, 28
page table, 41
page directory pointer table, 40
page directory table, 40
page table, 40
palindrome, 104
parity flag. *See* PF
perror, 167
PF, 46
physical address, 28, 39, 41
pipelining, 44
PML4, 38, 39
pmullw, 224
polynomial evaluation, 151
pop, 106
popcnt, 219
positive infinity, 20
printf, 105, 114, 119, 133
pseudo-op, 7
psrldq, 224
psubw, 224
punpckhbw, 224
punpckhwd, 224
punpcklbw, 224
punpcklwd, 224
push, 105
pxor, 224
pythagorean triple, 62
Pythagorean triple, 104
QNaN, 147
quad-word, 20
quotient, 65
random, 131
read, 167, 177
ReadFile, 160
recursion, 122

register, 4, 44, 45
ah, 45
al, 45, 48, 50, 100, 101
ax, 45, 46, 50, 100
bh, 45
bl, 45
bp, 45
bx, 45
ch, 45
cl, 45, 74
cx, 45
dh, 45
di, 45
dl, 45
eax, 45, 47, 48, 50, 100
ebp, 45
ebx, 45
ecx, 45
edi, 45
edx, 45
eflags, 46, 52
esi, 45
esp, 45
preserved, 119
r12-r15, 119
r8, 113
r8-r15, 45
r9, 113
rax, 45, 47, 48, 49, 50, 52, 100, 113, 114
rbp, 4, 45, 115, 119
rbx, 45, 52, 119
rcx, 45, 99, 100, 101, 102, 113
rdi, 45, 100, 101, 102, 113, 119
rdx, 45, 113
rdx:rax, 60, 65
rflags, 45, 46, 56
rip, 45, 49, 108, 111, 112
rsi, 45, 100, 101, 102, 113, 119
rsp, 45, 105, 106, 115
sp, 45
ST0, ST1, 141
xmm0, 113
xmm0-xmm15, 141
ymm0-ymm15, 142
register window, 46
remainder, 65

rep, 99, 100
repe, 102
repne, 101
resb, 32
resd, 32
ret, 110, 116
return address, 106
rip, 46
rip relative, 49
rol, 78
ror, 78, 85
rotate left. *See* rol
rotate right. *See* ror
rounding, 149
rounding mode, 149
roundps, 149
roundsd, 149
rsp, 7
sal, 74
sar, 74
scanf, 105, 114
scasb, 101
section. *see* segment
sector, 177
segment, 7
  .bss, 30, 32
  .data, 30
  .text, 29
  data, 20
  text, 7
segmentation fault, 29
set, 71, 80, 81
  complement, 71
  difference, 72
  intersection, 72
setc, 81, 83
SF, 52, 55, 56, 58, 67
shift, 74
  left, 74
  right, 74
shift arithmetic left. *See* sal
shift arithmetic right. *See* sar
shift left. *See* shl
shift right. *See* shr
shl, 74, 85
shr, 74, 85
sign bit, 16, 21, 23, 74

sign flag. *See* SF
signed, 16
signed integer, 16, 17
SIMD, 1, 141
SNaN, 147
Sobel, 222
  C, 222
  SSE, 223
specialized instructions, 212
split loops, 210
sqrtpd, 150
sqrtps, 150
sqrtsd, 150
sqrtss, 150
sscanf, 180
SSE, 1, 141
stack, 112
  alignment, 113, 115, 196, 263
stack frame, 115
stack segment, 30
stack size, 37
stack size option, 37
status, 11
std, 102
stdin, 105
stosb, 100, 101
stosd, 100
strcmp, 102
strength reduction, 207
strlen, 101
struc, 171
  alignment, 172
struct, 170, 171
  array, 174
sub, 52, 58
subpd, 145
subps, 145
subsd, 144
subss, 144
switch
  using jmp, 89
syscall, 164
system call, 155
System V ABI, 112
text segment, 29
TLB, 41, 42
translation lookaside buffer, 41

two's complement, 16, 17
ucomisd, 148
ucomiss, 148
ungetc, 179
unrolling loops, 208
unsigned, 16
unsigned integer, 16
vaddpd, 144
vaddps, 144
virtual address, 39
VMMap, 30
vmoupd, 144
vmovups, 144
vsubpd, 145
vsubps, 145
while, 93, 98
while loop, 94, 95
win32n.inc, 157
Windows, 2, 42, 112, 113, 119
Windows API, 156
word, 20
write, 164, 165, 167
WriteFile, 157
x86-64, 45
xor, 58, 73
zero flag. *See* ZF
ZF, 46, 55, 56, 58, 65, 67

Made in the USA
Middletown, DE
02 March 2018